THE RENASCENCE

OF THE

ENGLISH DRAMA

THE RENASCENCE

OF THE

ENGLISH DRAMA

ESSAYS, LECTURES, AND FRAGMENTS

RELATING TO THE MODERN ENGLISH STAGE, WRITTEN
AND DELIVERED IN THE YEARS 1883-94

BY

HENRY ARTHUR JONES

AUTHOR OF 'THE TEMPTER,' 'THE CRUSADERS,' 'JUDAH,' 'THE DANCING GIRL,'
'THE MASQUERADERS,' 'THE CASE OF REBELLIOUS SUSAN,'
'THE MIDDLEMAN,' ETC.

London

MACMILLAN AND CO.

AND NEW YORK

1895

PREFACE

I CAN well understand and sympathise with the feelings of impatience and resentment which these essays and lectures have aroused in many quarters during the last ten years, and I have always known that there was much worldly wisdom in the advice of the many friends who have so constantly urged me to hold my tongue upon the subject of the drama. It is a shrewd instinct in the public mind which prompts it to suspect that in matters of art the same great law prevails which it so constantly finds true in matters of morals—namely, that talking and doing are in inverse proportion to each other. And no one is more firmly convinced than I of the stupendous uselessness and impertinence of all preaching and criticism that does not fall in with the growing tendencies of thought around it.

Ten or fifteen years ago it seemed almost hopeless to look for any such change in the public taste as would allow the sincere treatment and representation of life upon our stage, or the success of any play that was not frankly theatrical, superficial, and addressed to a Cockney crowd seeking amusement on the lowest and easiest terms. But I perceived, or thought I perceived, amongst playgoers a growing dissatisfaction with the old stale devices of the theatre and a growing disposition to welcome a less childish and trivial form of English drama. Under these circumstances it seemed permissible to speak of the difficulties that lay in the dramatist's way, and to point out in what direction and along what lines an advance could be made. Had the playgoing public of 1882 been the playgoing public of 1894, that is, if there had been in 1882 a body of cultivated playgoers sufficiently numerous to understand and welcome such plays as have recently been successful in some of our West-End theatres, not a single word of the following papers would have been written or spoken.

But when one recalls the names of those giants in the drama, in literature, in poetry, in music, and in painting who have written of their art and explained its principles—names such as Molière, Ben Jonson, Goethe, Milton, Shelley, Wordsworth, Swinburne, Arnold, Wagner, Sir Joshua Reynolds—one is not inclined to offer much apology for following a practice honoured by such examples.

With the gradual change, however, that has lately taken place, both in the constitution of our audiences and in their way of regarding a play, the necessity of any further exposition of the principles upon which a school of modern English drama must be founded has to a great extent passed away. And so I have bound together these essays and lectures in the hope and intention of pleasing those numerous friends and well-wishers of mine who have so long desired me to keep silence on these matters. I can truly say that to nobody have these addresses and papers been a source of such endless vexation, irritation, and weariness as to myself, whom they have continually plagued and interrupted in the most delightful task of writing plays.

Three things I have fought for during the last ten years, as will be gathered from the following pages. Or perhaps it would be more correct to say that time has been fighting for them, and I have been merely hacking in his rear and slaying his slain.

1st. I have fought for a recognition of the distinction between the art of the drama on the one hand and popular amusement on the other, and of the greater pleasure to be derived from the art of the drama. I have been constantly misrepresented as seeking to deprive theatre-goers of their enjoyment; yet all my aim has been to show them how they may increase it. There is not a lecture or paper in this book that does not contain a statement explicit or implicit, repeated and re-repeated *ad nauseam*, that the theatre exists for the one end of giving pleasure, that it can instruct and educate only as the other fine arts do; that is, incidentally and indirectly, never with any set purpose. And there is scarcely a paper that does not also acknowledge the high value to our public of all sorts of amusement and entertainment that are good of their kind. Yet I find myself constantly accused of sour-mindedness, churlishness, and illiberality towards other forms of entertainment. I have never been illiberal or sour or churlish to anything except vulgarity, imbecility, insincerity, and putridity. To these I have indeed been venomous, but never to mere fun and nonsense.

But I do affirm that popular amusement is one thing and the art of the drama another. That time is fighting to separate them may be seen from a glance at the history of the stage during the last thirty years. A generation ago women of the town used to assemble in certain recognised partitions of many of our theatres, in the same way that they now assemble at many music-halls. A clean sweep has been made of this species of popular amusement from all recognised theatres devoted to comedy and drama, and there is no doubt that to-day our best West-End houses are as free from suspicion in this respect as our churches and chapels. Mr. Irving tells of a play-bill where Macready, our recognised foremost tragedian, was announced to appear with the elephant Rajah, and with songs between the acts. Everything marks the progressive differentiation of the art of the drama from popular amusement.

2nd. I have fought for the entire freedom of

the modern dramatist, for his right to portray all aspects of human life, all passions, all opinions ; for the freedom of search, the freedom of phrase, the freedom of treatment that are allowed to the Bible and to Shakespeare, that must necessarily be allowed to every writer and to every artist that sees humanity as a whole.

3rd. I have fought for sanity and wholesomeness, for largeness and breadth of view. I have fought against the cramping and deadening influences of modern pessimistic realism, its littleness, its ugliness, its narrowness, its parochial aims. Here again I am surely fighting on the side of time. As in philosophy the pendulum, which after the disturbances caused by the discovery of the law of evolution, swung for more than a generation towards materialism and towards a materialistic interpretation of life, is returning now towards spiritualism and towards a spiritualistic interpretation of life, so the stage, which has falteringly and fitfully begun to follow the main forces and currents of national thought — the stage is, I think, as I write returning towards a representation of the more imaginative and mysterious aspects of human life. And realism is quite powerless to deal with these.

On the *destructive* side it may be gratefully acknowledged that the modern dramatic criticism which has asserted realistic principles has been of great service to the recent development of the

English drama.   Much of this modern criticism has been very fearless, very sincere, very poignant.   If it has not shaken down the great pasteboard strongholds of bunkum and theatricality, it has made many a rent in their walls, and it has indirectly strengthened the hands of those who were trying to rear other and more enduring edifices.

On the *constructive* side, however, the dramatic critics who have advocated realistic principles have often, by their admiration of mean, perverse things, been antagonistic to the permanent advance of the English drama.   The four chief qualities that any work of art can possess, be it play, picture, poem, or statue, are beauty, mystery, passion, imagination.   It is the possession of some or all of these qualities that proclaims the masterpieces of art. These are the great things.   These are the eternal things.   These are the things that remain and perpetually draw the praise and love of mankind.

Now the modern realistic drama not only lacks these great qualities, beauty, mystery, passion, imagination, but it sets itself to deride them, and brags that it does not possess them.   The one virtue of realism is its sincerity and truthfulness.   And it is perhaps fortunate in some respects that a powerful destructive influence, a powerful corrosive, has been applied to the English drama during the last few years.   But this influence has been operative on the destructive side only.

To sum up in one sentence the results of modern realistic criticism upon the English drama, we may say — "It tried to seduce us from our smug suburban villas into all sorts of gruesome kitchen-middens." Now it really does not matter what happens in kitchen-middens. The dark places of the earth are full of cruelties and abominations. So are the dark places of the soul. We know that well enough. But the epitaph — it is already written—on all this realistic business will be—" It does not matter what happens in kitchen-middens."

A word on the arrangement of these papers. They have been addressed to widely different audiences and classes. I have therefore collected those which appeared in the monthly reviews, and have placed them first, acknowledging the source from which each article has been taken, and the permission of the editor to use it in this form. Next to these I have placed the lectures which have been generally given to more popular audiences and are therefore couched in a more popular style. Then follow one or two prefaces which I have thought worth while to include as containing principles of general interest. And I have ended with fragments and extracts from those articles and lectures that did not seem to be worth printing *in extenso*, or that contained repetitions of things already said. A few thoughts and jottings from my memorandum book seemed also to be worth a fugitive glance.   Where there are apparent contradictions it will, I think, be found on examination that they are different and mutually reconciling aspects of the same truths.   Where there is repetition, it is of something that seemed to need a continued enforcement and reinforcement.

I have been accused of discontent with my actors, my managers, my audiences, and my critics, and of rebellion against them.   There is a great difference between discontent with the position of one's art and discontent with one's own personal status in it.   So far as this latter is concerned I can only say that if during the last fifteen years the English drama had held the position I desire for it, both in national and universal esteem, I fear I should not have received the consideration, the praise, and the rewards of all kinds that have been so generously showered upon me.

3rd November 1894.

CONTENTS

I

THE THEATRE AND THE MOB

(Reprinted from the *Nineteenth Century Review* for September 1883
by the kind permission of Mr. James Knowles)

A CLEVER and thoughtful dramatist has lately com-
plained that playgoers of to-day will not accept
literature and poetry from modern authors. The
question thus raised is too wide and complex to be
settled by a definite "Yes" or "No." Among the
many hopeful signs of a real and permanent dramatic
revival in England there are only too many assur-
ances that, while on the whole playgoers may be
said to desire literature and poetry, the great body
of them also much more desire many much less
worthy things—sensation, realism, noise, tricks of
surprise, huge scenic effects, tawdry dresses, foolish
songs—anything but the quiet, steady, faithful portraiture of character in natural, fitting language. On
the one side we have Shakespeare glorified, and a
manager telling us that he seeks to raise the drama
and make his theatre the worthy home of intellectual
plays ; on the other side we have Shakespeare decried
as a bungling, tedious, impracticable impostor, who
did not know how to write a play, and we have a

manager telling us that he considers himself a shopkeeper, and, rightly interpreting his duty as a shopkeeper in a nation of shopkeepers, is of course bound
to supply the public with whatever compound, dele-
terious or otherwise, it may have a passing fancy for.
And in the meantime many new plays of all kinds
are produced, much fuss is raised over them, but
they all " grow up and perish as the summer fly " ;
they have no permanent value or influence ; crowds
go to see them, and come away, like a man behold-
ing his natural face in a glass, straightway forgetting
what they have seen ; and, on the whole, the modern
English drama remains, in its literary aspect, as far
as ever from attaining the dignity of a great national,
self-respecting art.

Compare the drama with her sister arts—poetry,
music, painting. Each year sees the production of
some permanently valuable work in each of these
spheres. No year is absolutely barren, while looking
back on the nineteenth century as a whole we see
that it is rich almost to plethora in all these arts.
But of all our modern plays, and their name is
legion, can one be pointed out that has roused or
penetrated the mind of the nation, shaken its conscience, bitten a hold upon any serious problem of
life, or come to us with any authentic tidings of the
destiny of

> Man who passeth by,
> So like a God, so like the brutes that die?

While, coming to those plays that pretend to
deal seriously with lofty and vital concerns, does not
Urania meet their contrivers " with darkened brow,"
as Hecate met the witches, and ask of them how

they dare, saucy and overbold, to traffic in the mysteries of life and death without her aid ? And of all the plays that have been recently successful, is there one that will have any value or interest in fifty years' time, beyond perhaps raising some curious sociological question as to what kind of old shoe-leather broth English playgoers thankfully swallowed as good dramatic victual in such or such a year ?

It would be therefore rash to affirm in a round, unqualified way that the British public want literature and poetry on their stage, for it is quite clear that to a great part of the theatrical entertainments nightly taking place in London, literature and poetry are not merely indifferent, but directly antagonistic. And yet all these widely different kinds of entertainment are to a great extent patronised by the same body of habitual playgoers, and many units of the same crowd that to-night are making the success of a Shakespearean revival, will to-morrow night be making the success of an empty burlesque.

Looking closely into the matter and trying to discern which way we are drifting, it is essential to notice two opposing sets of facts and tendencies.

1st. The great majority of playgoers never have come to the theatre, and in no period of time that can be safely reckoned upon are they likely to come to the theatre, for literature and poetry, for any kind of moral, artistic, or intellectual stimulus, or for any other purpose than mere amusement and pastime. Putting aside the specially selected audience of a first night, the great bulk of every audience of every theatre, even where an artistic and intellectual

programme is provided, look upon an evening at
the play as an alternative to going to see a new
giantess, a new conjuring trick, a new feat of horse-
manship, or a new murderer at Madame Tussaud's.
They come jaded from the impure air of shops,
factories, and offices, from the hard stress of business,
professional, or domestic duties, and they are in-
capable or impatient of the intellectual exertion
and prolonged attention necessary to judge a serious
work of art.

A poem may be written for the few, a picture
may be painted for the few, and the poet and painter
may wait with contemptuous patience for the verdict of the centuries. But a play must be successful
at once ; it must catch the crowd on its first week,
or the manager cannot afford to keep it on his bills,
and it is withdrawn with the stigma of failure fixed
to it for ever. Milton's noble wish, " Fit audience
let me find though few," must always be held in
scornful reprobation by theatrical managers and
dramatic authors. Under this hard condition, therefore, of immediate recognition, immediate approval
by the multitude,—that multitude, as Ruskin says,
" always awake to the lowest pleasures art can bestow
and blunt to the highest,"—under this hard condition
every play is produced. One may get some notion
of what a blighting effect this must have had, and
may continue to have, upon our drama, by imagining
the present condition of English literature if no
works had survived except those stamped by the
immediate acceptance of the mob.

Putting aside modern burlesque as a product
which neither art nor common-sense need be very

much concerned with, it has followed from this condition of immediate popular acceptance that, in the lighter drama and comedy, only those plays have succeeded that have ministered to the smug self-complacence and avoided shocking the petty conventional morality of British philistinism. And accordingly, in one popular piece, amongst much real fun and kindly humour and genuine and true touches of character, we find the main drift is to show that butter-men on the whole are pleasanter, franker, more jovial, and more genuine than baronets. And as so many more of us belong to the butter-man class than to the baronetage, we all feel highly flattered and reassured when it is proved to us that, after all, our own snobbishness and vulgarity are much to be preferred to the snobbishness and vulgarity of the upper classes.

Passing from the middle classes, we may see where the verdict of an *upper*-class mob leads us in another popular piece, where, smeared afresh with the agony and bloody sweat of Inkermann, with its wounds yet festering, and its noble dead scarcely buried all around us, we are asked by those who carry on the serious interest of the play to dwell upon nothing but the important fact that Miss Featherstonhaugh, who always used to wear " pink," wears " green " now; and by those who carry on the comic interest to join in some quite infantile gambols over an unloaded gun and a roly - poly pudding. Leaving the comic business to be justified, if it may, by a reference to that strange incessant interply of comedy and tragedy which is the surest fact in human life, and the unerring grip of which is the final test of the master-humorist, leaving the comic business, what can be said, what can be thought of a heroine meeting her lover in such a time and such a place and having nothing to say but " Miss Feather-stonhaugh has left off dressing in pink and wears green now." To which the hero replies, " Good gracious ! " which is followed by other items of conversation of the same stamp. And if it is urged that this is just what *may* have been said under the circumstances, one can only reply, " So much the worse for the facts ; the drama should paint the *truth* of human life, and not the *facts*."

And by way of antidote let us call up for a moment the soldier-dramatist who " chased the Medes at Marathon," and let him show how the toils and glories of a soldier's life should be painted ; and him, too, the reconqueror and renowner of Agincourt, and let us ask him how a soldier should meet his mistress. From all his swarming examples let us take two : that one on the strand of Cyprus—

> *Othello*.   O my soul's joy !
> If after every tempest come such calms,
> May the winds blow till they have waken'd death !
> And let the labouring bark climb hills of seas
> Olympus-high, and duck again as low
> As hell's from heaven ! If it were now to die,
> 'Twere now to be most happy ; for, I fear,
> My soul hath her content so absolute
> That not another comfort like to this
> Succeeds in unknown fate.

And that other one, more glorious still, under the walls of Alexandria, last flickering triumph of a falling demigod—

Antony.   O thou day o' the world !
Chain mine arm'd neck ; leap thou, attire and all,
Through proof of harness to my heart, and there
Ride on the pants triumphing !
    Cleopatra.   Lord of lords !
O infinite virtue ! Com'st thou smiling from
The world's great snare uncaught ?
    Antony.   My nightingale !
We have beat them to their beds.   What, girl ! though gray
Do something mingle with our younger brown,
Yet ha' we a brain that nourishes our nerves
And can get goal for goal of youth.

On comparing these scenes with that ot the
modern dramatist, we find that, though Shakespeare
has not been careless of actual facts and words, he
has made it his first business to render the truth and
spirit of the scene ; the modern dramatist has seized,
certainly not the truth and spirit, and probably not
even the bare, mean, ignoble facts.   And allowing, of
course, a world of advantage to Shakespeare in the
vehicle that he used, the blank-verse form, we shall
on careful examination find that the vital intrinsic
difference between the scenes, both professing to deal
with the same ever-recurring incidents of human life,
arises from the fact that, while Shakespeare was
possessed of his theme and thought about nothing
except how he could glorify it and picture to the
world for ever that meeting between Antony and
Cleopatra, the modern dramatist was thinking of
his public and not of his theme, and was therefore
most likely occupied in devising the best method of
bringing down the immortal heroism of Inkermann to
the level of a quantity of barren spectators in the
Tottenham Court Road, and setting them on to

brainless giggling upon a subject which they had neither the feeling nor the wisdom to demand should be treated in a higher manner. If it be thought absurd that Shakespeare and a modern dramatist should be compared, may it not rather be asked how much more absurd it is to let our great national models lie rusting and unused, or used only to miss the spirit and slavishly imitate the form, that blank verse form, which in the hands of the nineteenth-century dramatists has hitherto only served to stamp their plays as lifeless, stilted, and unreal. And in this connection may it not also be worth while to ask why it is that the English stage has of late years been dependent upon French sources for almost every play of strong interest and passion. Is it because we have no national drama of our own, rich in passion, in feeling, in healthy portraiture of healthy human life and splendid choice and treatment of splendid themes, in perpetual harbourage and out-pouring of all the sources of our national character and national greatness, rich in every equipment for an English dramatist of to-day except those techni-calities and tricks (must one call them?) of the stage which can only be learned by a long hard apprentice-ship before and behind the curtain? Does not the spirit of that Elizabethan age, wild, glowing, majestic, uncouth, elate, meet our modern managers and adaptors on their way to Paris to snuff up stale fumes in the precincts of the Palais Royal—does it not meet them as the fiery Tishbite met the envoys of Ahaziah, and ask, " Is it not because there is not a God in Israel that ye go to inquire of Baal-zebub, the god of Ekron? " And does not the spirit of that age also assure our hybrid, fantastic, French-English, English-French, neither-English-nor-French drama, that from the bed to which it is now gone up it shall not come down, but, impotent, outworn, and bed-ridden, there it shall surely die?

Returning to discuss the influence of verdict by the mob on the present state of our English drama, we come to inquire how it has affected the stronger class of plays—those which may be classed under the head of melodrama. Plays of this kind, though appealing in some measure to all classes of society (as, indeed, all plays must do, to succeed), are yet more generally designed to catch the lower-middle and working classes. In melodrama we find that those plays have been most successful that have contained the most prodigious excitement, the most appalling catastrophes, the most harrowing situations, and this without much reference to probability of story or consistency of character. The more a play has resembled a medley of those incidents and accidents which collect a crowd in the streets, the more successful it has been. On the whole, a melodrama has succeeded much in proportion as the general impression left by it is the same as the general impression left by the front page of the *Illustrated Police News;* and our most popular melodramas have borne about the same relation to dramatic art as an engraving in the *Police News* bears to an etching by Rembrandt.

Carlyle says that the strong man is not he who gets into a fit and takes ten men to hold him down; the strong man is he who can longest carry the

heaviest weight.   So the strong play is not the play
that goes into fits of horror and antics of sensation,
and rushes through a whirlwind of terrifying and
bewildering incidents, defying common-sense to re-
strain it; the strong play is the one that bears to
the end, patiently and easily and unobtrusively, its
great burden of thought and motive and character
and passion.

So we find that this condition under which every
play is produced of immediately striking the fancy
and satisfying the appetite of the populace, has
tended to lower the standard of dramatic work, and
that though it may be affirmed (as in an almost
complete dearth of good plays it may) that no good
play has failed, yet it must be allowed that many
bad ones have succeeded, and many very middling
ones have been enormously successful.   The amount
of success has been out of proportion to the merit of
the pieces ; and if it is said that this is the same
in all arts, it may be fairly replied that it is not so
in the same degree.   Open to question and necessarily faulty in many instances as is the annual
selection of pictures by the hanging committee of
the Royal Academy, it is doubtful if the arrangement would be bettered by leaving the choice in the
hands of the first two thousand persons of all sorts
and conditions who could be picked up haphazard
out of the London streets.   Even then, out of the
thousand or so of pictures selected, there could not
fail to be some good ones.   But suppose instead of
there being room for a thousand pictures there was
room only for the same number as we have theatres
—say twenty-five.   Suppose also that each of these

pictures had to be chosen at a set time and place by the verdict of the mob, and that all other pictures were condemned to rot unseen like unacted plays, so that the year's art comprised only these twenty-five pictures, and suppose further that such a principle of selection had been carried on year after year with no standard outside and above the public taste, what would be the state of English painting as an art?

Thus, on inquiring why we have no national drama at all worthy of the name, we are met first of all by the fact that the drama is not merely an *art* but a *popular amusement*, in a different sense from that in which poetry, music, and painting are popular amusements. The drama is an art, but it is also a competitor of music-halls, circuses, Madame Tussaud's, the Westminster Aquarium, and the Argyll Rooms. It is a hybrid, an unwieldy Siamese Twin, with two bodies, two heads, two minds, two dispositions, all of them, for the present, vitally connected. And one of these two bodies, dramatic art, is lean and pinched and starving, and has to drag about with it, wherever it goes, its fat, puffy, unwholesome, dropsical brother, popular amusement. And neither of them goes its own proper way in the world to its own proper end, but they twain waddle on in a path that leads nowhere in particular, the resultant of their several luggings and tuggings at each other.

The next discouraging fact that strikes us is that managers and authors have no better beacon to guide them than the restless doubtful flickerings of popular fancy. So that, instead of advancing in a straightforward course, they have constantly to tack about and trim their sails in obedience to every shifting impulse it may take. And we see that in the meantime the middle classes have chiefly chosen plays that confirm and flatter them in their own self-content and genial, ignorant self-worship ; and the upper classes have chiefly chosen plays that studiously reject everything heroic, and studiously insist on mean and commonplace details about aristocratic persons like Miss Featherstonhaugh ; and the lower classes have chiefly chosen plays that, like the rank raw spirit they drink, have no nourishment, but give a rousing hot sensation while they are being swallowed.

And also we find flourishing in a brazen, unchecked way the detestable doctrine that a manager is obliged to choke the public with whatever garbage it relishes for the moment, and managers are encouraged to consider themselves as cheesemongers, bound, it appears, by every established maxim of British commerce, to corrode the palates and poison the stomachs of their customers—if it pays. This hateful doctrine of managerial shopkeeping, so full of hideous, ruinous degradation to dramatic art, has lately been preached with such loudness and impudence that it has obtained a general acceptance in the dramatic profession, and all the more readily because it contains sufficient truth to coat over its monstrous falseness. For though it is true that there is a continual demand on the part of the public for frivolity, nonsense, and corruption, yet this demand in respect of any particular kind of frivolity, nonsense, or corruption, brisk and eager as it may be for a short season, is yet transitory, fitful, uncertain, and eternally barren. But the demand for truth, for reality, for thought, for poetry, for all kinds of high and inspiring examples, difficult as it may be to rear at the first, is yet perennial, constant, assured, and eternally fruitful. However far we may get from truth, from reality, from nature, we shall always find ourselves beckoned or led or whipped back to them at last. Every position of honour, every position really worth coveting in the dramatic world to-day, whether of manager, or actor, or author, has been gained not by the base idea of catering for every passing appetite of the multitude, but by unflagging appeals to the better judgments of the few, by coaxing, by watching, by alluring, by guiding, and not by pandering to the public. Every manager, every actor, every author who has made himself secure in an honourable position, has done so by creating and educating his own audience, by imposing his own will, his own tastes, and his own personality on them. And though it is comparatively easy to educate an audience in folly and absurdity, yet a position so gained can never be safe or honourable or lasting ; " that two-handed engine at the door " stands always ready to smite its holder once and no more into contempt and oblivion.

One would imagine that any man placed in a post of such influence and responsibility as is implied in the management of a London theatre, if he did not seek to dignify and glorify his office, would at least have the decent hypocrisy to refrain from openly proclaiming it sordid and contemptible.

Finally, the one main reason why we have no

great national modern drama, the reason from which all other reasons shoot and branch, is deeply rooted in the present social condition of the English people at large.   It has been finely and truly indicated by him who most of all our teachers of this age has "seen life steadily and seen it whole," and who, looking upon all the vast maze of our complex religious, political, and artistic life, has read each wound and each weakness clearly, and, striking his finger upon the place, has said, "*Thou ailest here and here.*"   Mr. Matthew Arnold, in the *Nineteenth Century Review* for August 1879, amongst many other wise words which everybody interested in dramatic art would do well to lay heed to, says—" In England we have no modern drama at all.   Our vast society is not homogeneous enough, not sufficiently united, even any large portion of it, in a common view of life, a common ideal capable of serving as basis for a modern English drama."   Yes, there is the main deep-seated reason of our troubles.   A nation's life, a nation's heart, is the quarry from whence the dramatist must hew his temple.   Just as some Gothic church is hewn from out its own wooded hillside, and then stands for ever afterwards with its delicate pinnacles and airy proportions to point the eternal contrast between the straight, determinate lines, the aspiring *intention* of man's workmanship, and Nature's lovely *carelessness*, so a nation's art is hewn from out the negligent, shapeless, indeterminate block of a nation's life, is indeed part and parcel of that life as the church is part and parcel of the hillside, and then stands for ever afterwards on the summit of that life to embody a definite purpose and draw the eye away from the surrounding negligence and irregularity from which itself arose, upwards to the infinite heavens beyond. But if the stone in the hillside be nothing better than rubble and crumbling conglomerate, how withal shall the fair temple arise for the heart of man to take shelter in? What can the builder do? Better indeed to hold his hand than willingly to build with hay and stubble that he well knows will not stand the fire.

The dramatist of Elizabeth's time, looking about for ideals, for men representing the leading current of the nation's life, found himself cheek by jowl with Raleigh and Sidney. But the poor modern vamper-up of plays, searching for a general definite heroic idea and heroic persons to embody it, finds himself able to seize nothing better than a steady, persistent glorification of money-making and industrious, respectable business life, and in place of Raleigh and Sidney is met by the eminent head of some great city firm. And as the Elizabethan drama reeks of the spirit of Raleigh and Sidney and is relative to the age of the Spanish Armada, so the Victorian drama reeks of the spirit of successful tradesmen and is relative to the age of Clapham Junction. It is impossible to make laws or plays very much ahead of the general moral or artistic instincts of the people. From this consideration it is plain there can be no sudden dramatic, as there can be no sudden political, millennium. Such good as may be brought about must be painfully and laboriously worked for, mostly by means of agencies already in operation. And it is certain that for a long time to come those who desire such a millennium can do

little more than hail it from very far off, and, like
the pilot of some small night-foundered skiff, wait
patiently and hope while night invests the sea and
the wished morn delays.

2nd. Turning from the barren contemplation of
obstacles and delays to ask what chances there are
of the furtherance and accomplishment of dramatic
reform, we encounter a crowd of hopeful signs.
There is a general awakening of art-feeling and art-
curiosity in the country.   The incessant trumpets of
our great critics are shaking the citadel and beginning to pierce the ears of the philistine where he
lies snoring and sprawling with his senses sealed ;
he is awaking, not as Eve awoke to behold herself
lovely in the midst of God's created loveliness, but
to find himself hideous in the midst of hideousness
of his own miscreation.   This art-quickening has
been longer to reach the stage than the other arts,
but it has reached it and is beginning to leaven the
whole lump.   The touch of truth has been the touch
of life.   We find everywhere a growing interest in
the drama as an art, in opposition to the drama as a
popular amusement of the circus or music-hall type.
Not that dramatic art seeks to deprive the masses of
their amusement, not that it demands that they
shall be dull, but that they shall laugh with the
beneficent, side-shaking, heart-easing mirth of wise
men, instead of with the heart-withering, heart-
hardening laughter of fools.   It insists that if the
Siamese-Twin connection with popular amusement
is to be preserved, its unwholesome brother shall
get himself purged and shrived, and render him-

self amenable to discipline ; it insists on dragging
popular amusement up to its level, and it refuses to
be dragged down to the level of popular amusement.
And the end is not to rob the people of their
pleasure, but to increase and rationalise and purify
it.   Only it also insists that the people shall take
the pains to understand what is put before them for
their amusement ; that, in the words of Sainte-
Beuve, they shall not be merely amused, excited,
carried away with enthusiasm, but that they shall
know whether they were right to be so amused,
excited, and carried away.   It needs some little
energy of attention, some little observation and
study of human nature to enjoy thoroughly the
comic characters of Shakespeare, whereas most of
our modern comic characters are purposely void of
every trait that demands thoughtfulness to comprehend them, so that the silliest person in the audience
can immediately fathom them, and cackle loudly
over their emptiness.   But surely, if one would take
a little pains to understand these things, there is
more life-giving joyousness and merriment in one
twinkle of Falstaff's eye than in all the bodies rolled in
one, of all the comic stage personages of this century.

We find that the audiences of certain theatres,
where this increased energy of attention has been in
some measure demanded, are more and more ready
to concede it, and correlatively to exact more and
more depth and sincerity of character - drawing.
Obviously these demands on the one side for increased
energy of attention, and on the other for increased
truth and meaning in what is represented, will
continue to grow together and to react upon and

C

re-encourage each other, and may be fostered to an incalculable extent. As the flower has nourished and developed the insect, the insect has fertilised and developed the flower.

Then of late years the space accorded in the daily papers to notices of theatrical performances has been much enlarged. It is true that a greedy lover of the theatre may think that the production of a new play is of much more public importance than many events and speeches which have yet more space and prominence allotted to them ; but this is a matter that rests chiefly with the public, and when editors and newspaper proprietors discover, as they are doing, that there is a growing demand for early and exhaustive theatrical intelligence, they will naturally take means to supply it. What is of more importance to note, is, that the higher literary criticism has again begun to occupy itself with the drama, and there is everything to be hoped from its appearance. To this removed standard, to this higher criticism, the modern drama must repair again and again, and ask for no favour but to be judged by its strictest rules. For surely the adoption of the severest and most searching standard of criticism is what all must welcome and none can fear, except those who have seized and hedged round for themselves a comfortable freehold in the contented ignorance of the populace.

Further, we have on our first nights, interspersed with perhaps a few ticklish but easily quieted elements of mischief, that serried pack of bright, earnest, intelligent faces in the first row of the pit, lovers of the drama for the drama's sake, whose

self-appointed duty it is to give a loud and un-
mistakable verdict of approval or condemnation.
In reply to the charges of ill-conduct and rowdyism
brought against this body it may be mentioned that,
though many bad plays have been rightly and
necessarily condemned by them, yet so far as the
memory of an old first-nighter may serve, no play
within this generation has been damned on its first
act, however bad.   There is always a wish to see
a play retrieve itself; there is always a wish at
starting to make a play a big success if it deserves
it ; while the amount of enthusiasm run to waste on
some plays that one remembers, were enough, one
would think, to nurture a breed of Shakespeares.
It is only when a play has failed to satisfy this
enthusiasm, when it has baulked and irritated it,
that it turns and rends authors, actors, anything
that comes in the path of its derision.

Indeed, to sum up, one might in a sanguine
moment be inclined to say that we have ready to
our hands in abundance every element of a great
dramatic renascence—except good plays.   So far
from the English people resenting literature and
poetry on the stage, it would be truer to say that
they rarely get a chance of encouraging them.
This has partly arisen from some vagueness in the
managerial mind as to what literature and poetry
are, and to the inability of authors to blend them in
an actable and tractable play.   Every now and then
we are treated to some five-act, unactable, intractable
tragedy, with phantoms for characters and spouting,
lifeless, blank-verse lines for dialogue.   It fails, and a
loud cry arises that the public will not have poetry on

the stage. But the truth is, that what they will
not have is unreality. They want reality, and if
they cannot get it, they will have realism rather than
unreality. A real cab-horse on the stage is after all
less offensive than an imitation man. So even in
their demand for realism the public must not be too
much condemned. But how far can poetry and
literature be given them in a modern play? It is
always impossible to predict what way or how far
a people ripe for guidance may be led by the
coercion of an extraordinary mind and will bending
all its energies to one end. And one would be loath
to predict that from the nation which our sacred
Milton saw, in his great livid heat of prophecy,
mewing her mighty youth and amazing the peoples,
and whose resplendent destiny thus forecast every
son born of her may fire himself with an exulting
pride to claim that she has fulfilled—one would be
loath to predict that from our England shall never
again arise as loud and sweet and strong a chorus of
dramatic song as suddenly burst from her when
that jolly brood of celestial singing-birds made their
nests on the English stage three hundred years ago,
and from thence let loose the riot of their passion
and music. Ay, even to-day, in the arid heart of
this nineteenth century, amidst all its dry dust of
faithlessness and frivolity, its grime of money-making,
its unholy merchandise of body-and-soul-corrupting
toil, its horrid reek of complaining millions, even
amidst all this, one would be loath to lay it down as
impossible that somehow, by the all-compulsive stress
of genius, such a note of dramatic song could be
wrung from our nation. One would not confine

the imagination or the ambition in setting such a
goal before it.   Though silk purses are not made
out of sows' ears, Burns has shown us that real
heroines can be made out of servant-maids.   It all
lies with the poet.   If the English stage does not
swarm with heroes and heroines, we may take it that
the fault rests rather with the English playwrights
than with the English people.   It is not so much that
the lives of men and women are unworthy of representation on the stage, as that we who undertake
to interpret them stand bleared and gibbering and
daunted before this great pageant of human existence, and cannot tell what to make of it.

But, apart from the advent of a heaven-sent
genius, which it would be unwise to reckon upon, it
is unlikely that the present generation will take any
interest in modern verse-plays.   The tide is not
setting that way.   That is no reason why we should
not have a modern national drama.   It may perhaps
for many years be quite a second-best kind of thing,
and on a lower platform altogether than our Elizabethan drama.   If we cannot raise Gothic cathedrals,
we may, however, build pleasant, healthy cottages,
taking care our materials and workmanship are
sound.   For there is a heart and core of soundness
in the English people, and there is always being
lived somewhere amongst us a balance of healthy
existence which is worth being portrayed if one will
but take the trouble to find it.   As in the Black
Country, where man has blasted and scarified the
earth, so soon as he withdraws the scourge of his
footsteps Nature hastes to spread her living greenery
over the spot, and smothers his departing heel-marks

with flowers, as quickly destroying his ravages as he destroyed her loveliness, so in the garden of human life wherever foul and dismal lives are lived Nature is always waiting to root them out and swill the void places with her perpetual beauty and strength and virtue. And to her nothing is ever dead or corrupt or useless or old, but all things are ever living and clean and vigorous and new; and she is as busy with forethought and potency of beauty in the noisome places of the cities where decrepit bestial figures stagger and moulder up dark alleys, as amongst the dog-rosed hedges and the garlanded meadows and the fern valleys and the poppies and the corn. Our corruption is the weft of her loveliest gown, and our soundness its warp; our rags are her viands; our dust and ashes are her jewels; our waxing and our waning, our health and our disease, our life and our death are alike but the shakings to us of the superflux of her immortal vigour. It is the business of the dramatist to persuade himself of this perpetual healthfulness and renewal in Nature and flowing from Nature to her pensioner, man. The vitality of the nation and not its disease is the measure of the possibility of any art-manifestation. Leaving all foul and devil-possessed things to take their leisurely or headlong course to destruction, it is the business of the play-writer to search out the sources and currents of the nation's healthy life, and to attach and let his work run parallel thereto, so that all that he does may have a lifeful and not a deathful savour.

For nothing is typical of life but what is pre-servative. That quality of a thing which destroys

it can never be typical or essential. And in this
respect art will strictly follow Nature, for as Nature
out of a thousand seeds brings only one to bear, so
art carries the process of selection but one step
further, and chooses but one out of the thousand
that Nature chose from a million.

So from all that has been said it is clear that if
we are to have a modern national drama it must be
put in connection with all that is vital and preserva-
tive and honourable in English life. And round
such a drama all the best elements of society, all
that is soundest and most characteristic and of
national importance, may be invited and may be
trusted to assemble. It is not without reason that
until lately some of the soundest and best elements
of English life have been severed from the theatre
for these two hundred years past. But all classes
are coming back, and the drama has a transcendent
chance of establishing itself as a great national art
and influence. It can only become this if and in so
far as it really ministers to the nation's welfare and
intelligence. Now is the time for its representatives
to choose whether it shall lapse into the nation's
bauble and toy, as was prophesied in the *Westminster
Review* a few years since, or whether it shall assert
itself and claim its right to embody and repicture to
us our best selves and the best possibilities of our
present life. If such a view of the drama were to be
upheld by its representatives, it is certain that the
arts of painting and music would soon fall into their
rightly secondary places, for neither music nor painting has intrinsically and of natural birthright such
scope and influence as the drama. Whatever changes

may come about in religion and in society, whatever creeds may be upheld or upheaved, the heart and soul of man will always remain the things of greatest price in the universe, and these to their utmost bounds will always be the entailed inheritance and inalienable domain of the drama.

The chief obstacles and delays and the chief incitements and helps to a dramatic renascence have now been recounted, and we have seen what reasons there are for believing that we are on the threshold, not merely of an era of magnificent spectacular and archæological revivals, but of a living, breathing, modern drama—a drama that shall not fear to lay bold and reverent hands on the deepest things of the human life of to-day and freely expose them, and shall attempt to deal with the everlasting mysteries of human life as they appear to nineteenth-century eyes. Nothing has been said of technical qualifications, for stage-technique is a thing that must be learned by a long and patient routine. It is far harder to write a play than to build a house—nobody starts building a house without a course of previous training, yet hundreds of people start to write plays with no better acquaintance with the details of play-construction than a man might gain of house-construction in a few casual glances at the outside of one.

What has been written, has been written in no assumption of guidance or control or authority, but has been thrown out as gropings and feelings after the right path, if haply it might be found.

And if we need to lift some banner to rally the

lovers of dramatic art to-day, what better words could be inscribed on it than the words of the great Greek seer as transcribed by our great English seer who is yet amongst us ? Consider for a moment what a change would soon be brought about in our drama if from this time forward every piece at our theatres were to be conceived, worked out, acted and judged in the spirit of these words :—

Must it be then only with our poets that we insist they shall either create for us the image of a noble morality, or among us create none ? Or shall we not also keep guard over all other workers for the people (including our playwrights, and managers and actors), and forbid them to make what is ill-customed, and unrestrained, and ungentle, and without order or shape, either in likeness of living things or in buildings, or in any other thing whatsoever that is made for the people. And shall we not rather seek for workers who can track the inner nature of all that may be sweetly schemed ; so that the young men as living in a wholesome place may be profited by everything that in work fairly wrought may touch them through hearing or sight, as if it were a breeze bringing health to them from places strong with life.

RELIGION AND THE STAGE

(Reprinted from the *Nineteenth Century Review* for January 1885
by the kind permission of Mr. James Knowles)

*Je sais bien que, pour réponse, ces messieurs tâchent d'insinuer que
ce n'est point au théâtre à parler de ces matières; mais je leur demande,
avec leur permission, sur quoi ils fondent cette belle maxime.*—MOLIÈRE,
Preface to the *Tartuffe*.

A RECENT production at a London theatre has
obtained a greater success perhaps than it merits
because it has incidentally raised the question of
how far it is lawful or expedient for a modern playwright to touch religious questions and to put
modern English religious life upon the stage.

Upon any question of dramatic craftsmanship,
literary skill, or originality of plot, a playwright will
do well to abide by the wholesome rule that forbids
an artist to speak of his own work or to question
any verdict that may be passed upon it. It is true
that this rule at times presses somewhat severely
upon a dramatic author, inasmuch as, while all other
artists are judged by their own performances, a playwright is judged partly by the performances of others,
and is praised or blamed not merely for what he
has done or misdone for himself, but for what the
management, the actors, the scene-painters, and the
carpenters have done or misdone for him. Thus

Shakespeare himself would hardly escape severe
condemnation as a sorry bungler in stagecraft, were
he an unknown playwright and his masterpieces had
now to be submitted to the public for the first time
at an afternoon performance with stock scenery and
slovenly stage-management.

The curiously divergent values and meanings
which a public representation may attach to a play
or to certain portions of a play from what the
author attaches to them, or that different audiences
may attach to the same play, or that the same
spectator may attach to the same play seen under
fresh conditions and with new actors,—these are
among the hundred risks inseparable from the
playwright's calling. And it is useless—especially
would it ill become one who has been unusually
fortunate in the interpretation and discussion of his
work—to cavil at those conditions and limitations of
his art which are at present unavoidable and irre-
mediable. All success or failure that may be due
to adequate and skilful, or inadequate and unskilful
production and interpretation, all curious variances
of critical and public judgment upon technical
questions, are best met with the discreet silence of
a quiet smile, and may be allowed to pass on without comment to play their little momentary part in
the stupendous comedy of human affairs, thence to
be dismissed into forgetfulness. And when one
remembers how little difference there is between
what the public acclaims as a good play and condemns as a bad one—when one considers how comparatively little harm would be done to English
literature and art if every acting play since Sheridan

and Goldsmith were irrecoverably lost to-morrow, one may well hesitate to vex the public ear with the discussion of any matter appertaining to modern dramatic work.

But when a playwright is challenged by a part of a first-night audience as to his right to depict any section of the community, or rather as to his right to depict them truthfully and make them use the language that is natural to them ; when he is counselled and countercounselled upon the expediency of altering what is distinctive and what he conceives to be faithful and lifelike in his portraiture—in such a case he may perhaps be permitted a word of apology and explanation upon the ground that, small and unimportant as the individual case may be, and not in itself worth a moment's consideration, yet, seeing that the meanest matters may contain the widest issues, the entire question of the future development of the English drama and its right to press on and possess itself of the whole of human life is more or less raised when any veto is placed, or sought to be placed, upon the dramatist's perfect freedom of choice of subject, persons, place, and mode of treatment. The only restriction that should be placed upon him is that he shall not offend against the recognised code of social decency, and here we have a sufficient safeguard in the censorship and the " common-sense of most."

The question has an aspect of expediency that it may be well to deal with first. Obviously, as a matter of expediency and worldly prudence, a dramatist will do wisely to avoid giving offence to the prejudices and susceptibilities of any great portion of his possible audiences. Indeed, so perfectly has this rule been understood upon the recent English stage, so eager have we been to exclude everything that might be offensive or tedious or incomprehensible to any possible spectator, that by a process of continual exhaustion and humble deference to everybody's prejudices we have banished from the stage all treatment of grave subjects but what is commonplace and cursory and conventional. The course of the drama has been diverted and hopelessly cut off from the main current of modern intellectual life. While the companion arts—painting, poetry, and music—are allowed to present every aspect of human life, on the stage only the narrow, ordinary, convenient, respectable, superficial contemplation and presentation of human affairs is allowed. Though off the stage the gravest matters have been in heated hourly prominence, on the stage nothing of much greater importance has been bruited than how a tradesman's family may prepare itself for alliance with the aristocracy. And such tradesmen ! And such aristocrats !

Nothing could better show the impotence and poverty of the modern English drama than the account it has rendered of modern English business life ; nothing could better show how strangely far we are from sincerity and faithful insight in character-drawing, how fond the public is of what is superficial and conventional, than the type of business man that has been most popular on the stage in recent years. It will be allowed that if Englishmen have been in earnest about anything the last fifty years, they have been in earnest about money-making and commerce. Of gods and saints, of heroes and martyrs and kings, modern English life has not been quite so prolific as an eager playwright might wish, and in their rarity or absence from his daily sphere he may be forgiven if he fails when he tries his unaccustomed hand upon their portraiture. But there has been no dearth of business men in England this generation. No playwright can excuse himself on the plea of want of models to study and paint from. Surely if sincerity and truth may be reasonably demanded from the drama in any one particular, it is in the handling of modern business life. Yet upon turning to the stage what do we find? Of course there is no lack of business men in our modern plays; rather, of one certain type of business man, hereafter to be examined, there is an inordinate profusion. Indeed, this particular individual, under various aliases and constantly changing his trade, may be said in one sense to have been the great prop and mainstay of English comedy for some twenty years past. He is simply a peg to hang jokes upon. He invariably drops his H's and puts in superfluous aspirates. He is everlastingly making blunders upon his introduction into what passes upon the stage for *polite* society. And these blunders are so dwelt upon and exaggerated that any pit or gallery spectator can instantly detect them and pride himself upon his superior breeding to the person who makes them, who is yet assumed to be moving in a better position, and to have better opportunities for learning good manners, than the pit or gallery spectator. And when the good-hearted tradesman makes these

blunders, the aristocratic people on the stage at
once call attention to them, and correct them with
an utter absence not merely of the spirit but of the
forms of good-breeding. And this type of business
man has made the fortune of many modern comedies.
Now it is not to be denied that many retired tradesmen do drop their H's and commit social blunders;
and these apparently are the especial traits of character that are most acceptable to an English audience
and most easily make it laugh. But the want of all
sincerity and searchingness in the portrait must be
apparent to any intelligent person who will take the
trouble to read a modern comedy where an English
tradesman is depicted, and then compare it with the
average English tradesman who can be met with
behind any counter in town or country. And a
playwright sitting down to write the part of an
English man of business does not first consider how
he can faithfully portray such and such an individual,
and through him the heart and meaning of English
commercial life, but how he can most readily make
an average audience laugh at outrageous verbal dis-
tortions or pronounced social blunders. The same
want of truthfulness will be found upon comparing
that curiously unreal nondescript, the rustic of the
London stage, with any living English peasant.

Now, while the stage remains so swaddled in
pettiness and superficiality, the playwright who
wishes to be successful will indulge the public and
continue to manufacture for them their pet conventional stage-types. Out of the thousand spectators
that nightly watch a play it may be safely assumed
that nine hundred will be struck by some outward,

obvious peculiarity of speech or manner rather than
by any inward, significant truth or suggestion of
character. And the whole scheme and aim of
dramatic art in this country being to attract the
multitude, and no existence being possible to it
except upon this footing, every play is framed upon
the principle of immediately flattering and satisfying,
not the one student of character and lover of literature, but the ninety-and-nine pleasure-seekers and
sight-seers. And these pleasure-seekers have also a
few tough British prejudices which the judicious
playwright must beware of offending. The two
chief subjects which are by common consent supposed to be most difficult of stage treatment are
religion and politics, because these are the subjects
upon which counter opinions are most rife and
popular feelings most easily raised.

As regards politics, they scarcely touch the moral
or emotional nature of man at all. Surely the
present disposition of political parties in this country,
and the present aims of statesmanship on either side,
do not invite any attention from a serious dramatist.
They would make a very worthless theme for any
dramatic work except a farce. And the modern
playwright need not give himself a moment's uneasiness because he finds himself debarred from
treating English political life except in the spirit
of farce, or in that bland and sugary way which,
complimenting both sides upon being alike right,
equally conveys that there is no question of human
interest in the struggle between them. But suppose
it were found that upon any matter of deep moral
or emotional concern the two parties were divided,

then who could deny the dramatist the right of en-
forcing so much upon the stage? With religion the
case is far different from politics, though the same
motives of expediency have banished from the
modern stage all treatment of it that is not purely
conventional and superficial.[1]

The present attitude of religious persons towards
the stage is a somewhat curious one. For some
two hundred years religious opinion in England has
been more or less antagonistic to the theatre. But
gradually the far-seeing and more liberal-minded
teachers in the different sects have become alive to
the fact that the theatre is immensely popular, and
must be tolerated and reckoned with. It threatens to
become a powerful influence in the moral life of the
nation. And religious persons are also fast discovering
that, in the huge sempiternal dulness and mechanical
routine of English life, theatre-going is not an un-
pleasant way of spending the evening. Like Dame
Purecraft in the matter of eating pig, they wish to
have it made as lawful as possible. So they come
timorously, with the old notion still clinging to them
that they are in "the tents of the wicked." How
welcome to weak consciences have been the various
entertainments that, under some convenient name or
cloak, have afforded to religious persons a satisfaction
of the ineradicable dramatic instinct, and saved them
from the sin of going to a theatre! How ludicrous

[1] I should like to enlarge this paragraph, and so far change its drift as
to claim for the stage the same right to deal searchingly and truthfully
with politics as with religion. To-day our modern drama should lay bold
hands upon every province of human life and thought, and be satisfied
with nothing less than sovereign sway and masterdom over the whole
realm.—*25th April* 1891.

is the spectacle of religion shivering on the brink of
Shakespeare at the Lyceum, and turning away to
regale itself at the Christy Minstrels or the Chamber
of Horrors! What a blank and stupefying denial
of all the genial humane qualities of our nature is
implied in the recent wholesale condemnation of
the theatre by the great Boanerges of the Baptists!
But the truth is that religious persons, after having
vilified the theatre for two centuries, are fast coming
back to it. Not all Mr. Spurgeon's shouting to his
flock to stay and batten in his sheep-pens on the
barren, dismal moor of hyper-Calvinism will long keep
them from straggling down to the green pastures
and broad waters of the nation's intellectual life.

There is, then, in every audience at all our
leading theatres, except perhaps those that are
devoted to broad farcical comedy and burlesque, a
certain proportion of religious persons, who come
timidly to the theatre with a vague sense of wrong-
doing, and are shocked if there is any mention of
religious subjects. Their views of life are such, that
there is no general reconciliation possible between
the two ideas of religion and the theatre, and so they
wish to keep them utterly apart, in the same way
that many worthy people find it convenient to keep
their science in a separate mental compartment from
their religion, from an uncomfortable feeling that if
once they get face to face one of them will destroy
the other.

In every audience there is a much larger proportion of simply indifferent persons, who would be
the first to disclaim any particular reverence for any
doctrine or precept of religion whatsoever, yet who

pay the ordinary Englishman's ear and lip reverence to the current creed. And these also feel uneasy if religion is broached on the stage, because, having conveniently dispensed with it to a great extent in regulating their everyday lives, they think it may be very well allowed to remain in its present condition of honoured and respectable superannuation, as an affair of Sundays, and parsons, and churches, and chapels.

Strange Englishmen! so cunning in the art of self-deception! Has, then, this religion of yours grown so valetudinarian that it can no longer take the robust exercise of out-of-door life? that you must shelter it from the keen, life-giving winds of science, and the daily uphill trudge of business, and the glow and bustle of healthy amusement? that you must deny it all the vigour and movement of everyday life, and only take it out for a little very gentle exercise once or twice on Sundays? Well, wrap it up then, keep it warm! It's in a "parlous state" truly; and when the worst happens, Heaven send us a good, serviceable, sound-winded, work-a-day religion to take its place.

Speaking generally, we may say that from old-accustomed prejudice, whose grounds they have never taken the trouble to examine, ordinary playgoers have a haunting feeling of the impropriety of the theatre as a place for even hinting that there is in the English nation to-day any such thing as religion at all. The idea of human life as being about six-sevenths secular and one-seventh sacred keeps possession of them, and they do not wish to have this convenient fiction disturbed or examined. Then, too, the dramatic faculty is so little developed in a general audience, there is so little knowledge and appreciation of character, that they cannot discriminate between an author speaking *in propriâ personâ* and his allowing his personages to speak whatever is natural and becoming to them. How little essential reverence of heart is at the bottom of the average playgoer's dislike of the mention of religion upon the stage may be gathered from the fact that plays that are implicitly choke-full of the deathfullest sort of Atheism, the denial of all divinity to man, are allowed to pass without protest, and run their hundreds of nights.

As a matter of expediency, then, it may be freely conceded that the playwright is wise in his day and generation not to meddle with religious matters, but to accept the arbitrary and conventional division of human nature into secular and sacred, and to ply his trade wholly in the secular domain, in apparent ignorance of whether there is anything sacred or no in man's nature, and whether Englishmen have a religion to-day, and whether it has any influence upon their character. Nor must the sadly comic spectacle of our two hundred sects — all of them right and all of them wrong—tempt him to a smile or a sigh, though one would fancy that the wasteful joke of starting two hundred agencies to the same end, the existence of each one implying the uselessness of the other one hundred and ninety-nine, must at last become apparent to the perpetrators of it. It is quite certain, however, that the existence of such a restriction upon the dramatist forbids the hope that the English drama will ever reach forward to be a great art, and condemns it to remain as it is, the plaything of the populace, a thing of convention and pettiness and compromise. It is useless to upbraid modern playwrights for not producing great plays when, in so small a matter as putting upon the stage such a common type of modern English life as a middle-class tradesman, one is not allowed to paint him thoroughly, according to one's poor judgment, in a faithful, searching way, and to give, so far as the exigencies of dramatic art allow, a truthful picture of the man and his environment, and of the man moulded or modified by his environment. If a dramatist may not faithfully paint his brother British shopkeeper whom he has seen, how shall he be trusted to faithfully paint heroes and saints and demigods and other " tremendous personages " whom he has not seen ? The drama claims for its province the whole heart and nature and soul and passions of man ; and so far as religion has to do with these, so far is the dramatist within his right in noting the scope and influence of religion upon the character he has to portray. The whole teaching of modern psychology, the conception of human character as a natural production arising from the action of the various surrounding agencies upon the individual man and his ancestors through countless ages, and the reactions resulting therefrom : this doctrine forbids the dramatist to accept any reservation of a certain plot or parcel of a man's nature which must be screened off and veiled and assumed to be non-existent before the analysis of the character can be made. Every character is woven all of a piece ; if some threads are taken out, the garment is mutilated and falls to bits. The whole of the nature of man

is sacred to the dramatist, as the whole of the body
of man is sacred to the physician. One part is not
more sacred than another. The folly, and hate, and
meanness, and envy, and greed, and lust of human-
kind are just as sacred in this sense as the higher
and nobler qualities, and are treasured with the same
care. One might as well dictate to a surgeon that
in his survey of the human body he must omit to
take note of the presence of such and such an organ
and its influence upon the rest of the body—say the
heart—because of some sacred mystery attaching to
it, as dictate to a dramatist that he shall not be
allowed in his study of a certain character to mark,
if necessary, the shaping and leavening of the whole
of that character by the religious *milieu* in which
it has been produced. Those who would deny
to the dramatist the right to depict religious life
upon the stage should show, either that religion has
become a quite unessential and useless portion of
human life, and is effete and defunct, and has no
bearing upon character in England to-day, in which
case the playwright can afford to treat it as a
naturalist does an organ that has lapsed into a
rudimentary state ; or they should show why religion
should not occupy the same part in the dramatist's
scheme and view of human life that it is supposed
to occupy in the outer world around him—shall we
say a seventh ?

So far as the matter is part of the general compromise and toleration upon religious matters without which social life would be rendered grievously
uncomfortable, it would doubtless be unwise to try
to disturb the present equanimity and to arouse bitter

passions that are now disarmed or slumbering. And also one would not willingly offend the sincere feeling of any worshipper, were it even of the most degraded and brutal fetich. There is a small enough stock of reverence in England to-day; one may well be content to endure a little of it directed wrongly and towards unworthy things.

But the matter is also part of the question whether our drama shall ever rise to the dignity of its calling and exercise its right to portray, and interpret, and faithfully reflect the main and vital features of our national life; and upon this point the humblest writer for the stage has a right to be jealous and alert, and to see that his art is not rendered weak and lifeless, and its sustenance given to feed the beggarly array of decrepit prejudices that totter about this breathing world and suck into their numb and withered anatomies the nourishment that should go to build up a healthy body of public opinion.

Inasmuch as religion is a matter of controversy and doctrine, the dramatist may be content to leave it in the clouds where the arguments and sophistries of divines have floated it. In this respect the relation of art towards religion is fixed in Tennyson's memorable lines—

> I take possession of man's mind and deed,
>   I care not what the sects may brawl;
> I sit as God, holding no form of creed,
>   But contemplating all.

In no case could it be profitable for the stage to become the backer or antagonist of any doctrine or creed. But inasmuch as religion is also a matter of conduct and practice and character, the drama has every right to take it for part of its subject-matter.

And before quite resigning ourselves to the dominion of the popular prejudice, which holds that the dramatist should blink the question of man's spiritual nature and beliefs, it may be as well to glance at the accepted relations of religion and the drama during the times of the greatest dramatic activity and creation. The Greek tragedians made unsparing use of their country's religion, and wove it into their plays. In masterful and unquestioned sway over the destiny of man they reigned coequal with the gods, and usurped omnipotence in their dealings with the creatures of their hands. Again, all through our own Elizabethan writers there is the freest handling of religious matters whenever these come within the sweep of their pen. One has only to imagine the whole batch of dramatists of that era set to write a play that should be successful upon our modern English stage if produced for the first time to-day, to learn how much the temper and state of preparation of the audience, and the knowledge of the dramatist that what he writes will be accepted seriously and in good faith, have to do with the production of great plays. We will take the three greatest and most representative names of that age, Marlowe, Shakespeare, and Ben Jonson, and ask how they dealt with religious matters. The comparison is very interesting, as it also incidentally discovers the different bent of each genius and the different texture of his mind. The essential reverence of these three writers will scarcely be questioned if reverence is to be reckoned by the wholesomeness of the feelings rather than by the squeamishness of the ears. Though even in the matter of words it may be asked whether the clean and healthy outspokenness of some of the Elizabethan writers is not more reverent of everything worth reverence than the putrid leer and imbecile suggestiveness of some music-hall songs that have been imported into the modern theatre.

To begin with Christopher Marlowe, " Son first-born of the morning, sovereign star ! " In Marlowe there is none of the familiar playful quotation of Scripture so frequent in Shakespeare, or the broadly comic portraiture of religious hypocrisy unctuously mouthing Holy Writ to its own ends that Ben Jonson delights in. Marlowe's fiery genius sets directly about its main ends, and in *Doctor Faustus* seizes the heart and core of the Christian doctrine, and appropriates as much as is necessary for the scheme of his play. There is no hesitation, no question in Marlowe's mind as to the perfect right of his art to enter this region and take full possession of it. Fragments of Christian dogma are tossed hither and thither in the burning whirlpool with waifs and strays of heathen history and mythology, while the livid heat of the poet's imagination binds and mats all the strange ingredients into one liquid flame of terror, and the spectator watches, with harrowing suspense, and breathless inescapable impression of reality, the damnation of a soul. Omitting the wretched buffoonery of the comic scenes as possible interpolations or concessions to the groundlings, there is no room left for any thought of reverence or irreverence. The question of the comparative truth of the Greek mythology and the creed of Christendom sinks into a matter of "words, words, words" as we contemplate the awful picture of the death-agony of Faustus.   Marlowe compels our acquiescence that *that* at least is real, is true.   It would be impertinent to defend the *Faustus* against any possible charge of irreverence which the rancid, bilious temperament of superfinical godliness might bring against it.   No poet ever reaches such inaccessible heights of inspiration without remaining quite impervious to, and out of the reach of, harm by any assault from that quarter.   It could only be in an outburst of bewildered indignation or riotous satire that one could put the question, whether in the matter of reverence of man's spiritual nature the age that produced Marlowe's *Faustus* has any need to feel ashamed of itself when brought to the bar of the age that demanded a version of the same legend brought down to the intelligence of a modern burlesque audience.

Upon turning from Marlowe to Shakespeare, we find a difference in the treatment of sacred subjects and the poet's attitude towards religion such as corresponds with the difference in the genius and temper of the two men.   In none of his four great tragedies is Shakespeare employed upon so vast and tremendous a theme as Marlowe had to work upon in *Faustus*.   Neither *Hamlet, Macbeth, Lear,* nor *Othello* has the same inherent supernatural grandeur, though all of them are far more human and domestic. It is useless, though it is most interesting, to speculate, supposing that the ground had not been already occupied by Marlowe, what Shakespeare might have given us if he had treated the legend of Faustus in the meridian of his powers, in the *Hamlet* and *Macbeth* period.

In no respect is the varied, universal play of Shakespeare's genius, and his royal dominion over all things human and divine, more fully shown than in the use he makes of the Bible. He treats the Scriptures as if they belonged to him. Bishop Wordsworth, in his *Shakespeare and the Bible*, finds in the poet more than 550 Biblical quotations, allusions, references, and sentiments. *Hamlet* alone contains about eighty, *Richard the Third* nearly fifty, *Henry the Fifth* and *Richard the Second* about forty each. Shakespeare quotes from fifty-four of the Biblical books, and not one of the thirty-seven plays that appear under his name is without a Scriptural reference. Genesis furnishes the poet with thirty-one quotations or allusions, the Psalms with fifty-nine, Proverbs with thirty-five, Isaiah with twenty-one, Matthew with sixty, Luke with thirty-three, and Romans with twenty-three. Shakespeare does not take religious dogma for the foundation of any play, as Marlowe did in *Faustus*, nor does he search into the private life of religious persons, as Ben Jonson and Molière did. All the bishops, friars, and legates who figure in his plays do so in their official capacity. How significant is the wide difference of Shakespeare's portraiture of hypocrisy in the " prenzie Angelo " from Ben Jonson's and Molière's portraiture of the same vice in the Banbury Puritan and the *Tartuffe!*

What most strikes us in considering Shakespeare's attitude towards religion is the thorough saturation of his plays in the spirit and sentiment and phraseology of the moral rather than the doctrinal portion of Scripture. Though doctrinal allusions are far from scanty in his works, yet they are so little pronounced, so vaguely or discreetly worded, or belong so clearly to the official position of the speaker rather than to the conviction of the author, or are so common to all the sects, or if pertaining to one of them are cancelled by allusions to other doctrines sanctioned by other sects—in a word, so little sectarian bias peeps out in Shakespeare that Catholics and Anglicans and Congregationalists have alike claimed him as belonging to their communion.

Shakespeare may or may not have been a believer in baptismal grace. It is, however, refreshing in the present dearth upon our stage of original English comedy to find so lively a compensation for its absence from our theatres, and so illustrious a proof of its present and perennial vitality in English life, as is afforded by the spectacle of a bishop laying the flattering unction to his soul that Shakespeare was a devout believer in this same doctrine of baptismal grace, because of two rather meagre and casual allusions to it which Shakespeare has placed in the mouths of two such widely diverse and problematic subjects for the operation of the sacrament as Henry the Fifth and Iago. Our sense of obligation to the good bishop is further deepened by his skilful complication of the situation in the introduction upon the scene of Mr. Bowdler. Mr. Bowdler, it appears, in his *Family Shakespeare*, has, with an access of cautious reverence which the bishop feels must cause the judicious reader surprise and regret—Mr. Bowdler has seen reason to put half-asunder such an evidently unsuitable pair of yoke-fellows as Iago and baptismal grace, which Shakespeare had joined together.   Mr. Bowdler has omitted the latter of Iago's lines :—

> To win the Moor—were 't to renounce his baptism,
> All seals and symbols of redeemèd sin.

Could ingenuity of mortal man devise a more exquisitely humorous situation than is here, without any connivance of our own, forced upon us? What aspect of the imbroglio to glance at first or last, what logical way out of the manifold perplexity, whom to sympathise with first or most, Bishop Wordsworth, or Mr. Bowdler, or Shakespeare handcuffed between them, one knows not, so thickly the higgledy - piggledy crowd of incongruities comes tumbling upon us!   Poor, timid Bowdler, very anxious to preserve Shakespeare for our families if one could do it without offence to decency and religion, still more anxious to preserve our families pious and respectable from contamination by Shakespeare's irreverence and loose talk, must at least stop Iago's mouth from blabbing of matters that Iago has no business to know anything about.   The good bishop must have our Shakespeare for a devout Anglican, and lo! here is baptismal grace in our Shakespeare's soul, apparently tottering upon the rickety foundation of two incidental quotations in the lips of two such dubious connoisseurs of spiritual matters as Harry of England and Iago ; while our poet's confirmed, desperate, ineradicable, irreclaimable, irrefragable paganism stands sure and " foursquare to all the winds that blow," based upon no less than one hundred and twenty-nine adjurations

and appeals to heathen Jove and Jupiter, to say
nothing of the rest of the Pantheon. The good
bishop will, however, at all costs have our Shakespeare for a sound Churchman; will, in the present
predicament, hazard the matter and baptize him
will-he nill-he, were it but for the sake of so illustrious an example to his countrymen in a schismatic
nineteenth century. And now up comes the wretched
Bowdler with his whitewashing apparatus, and, applying the proverbial zealous ignorance of indiscriminate " Church restoration " to Shakespeare, is actually
shaking down one of the two slender props of grace
in our poet's soul; has actually taken away from us
the welcome evidence of the irreproachable Iago—
we must hasten and bolster up the frail tenement
with our own episcopal shoulders and administer a
gentle episcopal chastisement to Bowdler, the well-
meaning, mischief-doing little man!

Shade of that immortal genius, with what a smile
of kindly pity dost thou elude all our attempts to
cabin, crib, and confine in the fetters and tatters of
our particular sect thy spirit, whose creed was broad
and general as the casing air, as wide and universal
as the beneficent heaven whose arch rests impenetrably bright or impenetrably dark over every soul
of man! How small a concern Shakespeare had
for creeds and doctrines may best be gathered from
the absence of any marked influence upon his plays
of the religious struggle which England had passed
through in the previous generation. And yet he is
steeped in the language and spirit of the Bible.
And it is just this attitude of his towards the
English Scriptures that fits him to be the repre-

sentative poet of England. With more care for dogma he might have sunk into the mere poetical figurehead of a sect or a creed ; with less care for morality his work would have lacked the deep and permanent foundation that all great art instinctively chooses, of resting upon wide-reaching principles of justice and truth that all human hearts as instinctively recognise and accept. The hateful, foolish, convenient maxim so often dinned into our ears of late that the English modern drama should teach nothing and believe in nothing, receives no countenance from the greatest dramatists of the past, least of all from Shakespeare. The greatest art is as instinctively, as relentlessly, *though as unobtrusively*, moral as Nature herself. One cannot always perceive it, but there is no escaping it. Dante inflicting damnation upon myriads of innocent babes is as relentless as Nature in England to-day sentencing myriads of English babes to the deep damnation of the lifelong inheritance and propagation of their fathers' and forefathers' vices and diseases and crimes. Nature can do that ; so can Dante, and Calvinists may take heart of grace from contemplating the fact.

It will not be necessary to dwell upon the didactic side and purpose of Shakespeare's constant employment of Scriptural phrases, precepts, and aspirations. Many of his best known and most frequently quoted passages are parallelisms or paraphrases of Scripture morality, or of some part of that large body of moral axioms and worldly wisdom and justice which belongs alike to the Bible and to other systems of religion and philosophy. Instances are so numerous and well known that they will occur to every one.

It is generally and carelessly assumed that these didactic passages convey the nature and extent of Shakespeare's relations and obligations to the Bible. But this is far from being the fact. His didactic use of Scripture history and morality, though it is the noblest and most valuable, is by no means the only result, nor is it the personal and distinguishing mark, of Shakespeare's close acquaintance with the Bible. Many other poets have freely employed Scripture for serious and didactic ends, from Milton down to Montgomery. What distinguishes Shakespeare is the perfectly free and playful and everyday use he makes of Scripture by putting it into the mouths of all sorts and conditions of people on all sorts of occasions. Surely those keen huntsmen of " lewd and pernicious enormity" in innocent places, those playgoers who strain at the gnat of a solitary Scriptural allusion in a modern play, can have no notion what herds of camels they swallow every time they witness a play of Shakespeare's in its integrity.

How utterly subservient Shakespeare deems the treatment of religion upon the stage to the preservation of dramatic truth and reality may be seen in *Richard the Third*, where religion and morality become the flimsiest child's baubles in the merciless intellectual grasp of the tyrant.

Iago, besides being an authority on the efficacy of baptismal grace, is " full of most blessed condition" in his reference to Holy Writ and his constant display of wise and moral maxims. Poor Bowdler cannot understand it, and smells irreverence.

Richard the Second so far allows his sense of human injury to get the better of his sense of religious propriety that he institutes a comparison, in the matter of treachery, between himself and Christ ; and earlier in the play he cries out upon Bagot, Bushy, and Green as " three Judases, each one thrice worse than Judas ! " Poor Bowdler can do nothing but hold up his hands in horror and excise the passage, and Bishop Wordsworth smilingly pats his approval. No possible testimony to the efficacy of baptismal grace to be squeezed out of such a line ! Away with it !

Shylock has several allusions to Old Testament personages and facts, whose use is not very apparent to the dim, bewildered, tender-conscienced, narrow-visioned Bowdler. While what can family respectability and piety make of such a speech as, " Yes, to smell pork ; to eat of the habitation which your prophet the Nazarite conjured the devil into " ?—a speech in which the heights of dramatic propriety and religious impropriety are simultaneously reached at one bound. Bowdlerism can only sorrowfully shake its poor bewildered head at the dramatist's readiness to outrage its pet prejudices, and, at all costs, to give the full and exact truth of Shylock's manner of speech.

There are a large number of Scriptural allusions in Shakespeare which apparently have neither any moral to enforce, nor any special dramatic fitness to the speaker or the occasion. Of such is Antony's—

> Oh, that I were
> Upon the Hill of Basan to outroar
> The horned herd !

E

which shows Shakespeare's, rather than Antony's, diligent study of the Old Testament, and which indiscriminate and unnecessary employment of Scripture language again shocks and grieves our poor sensitive Bowdler, and fills the soul of Samuel Johnson with "pity and indignation." Leaving Bowdlerism to digest or reject as it may this frequent indiscriminate and casual employment of Scripture by somewhat unqualified persons, we pass on to notice what is more shocking and irreverent still, the extensive acquaintance with sacred terms and topics shown by Shakespeare's clowns and common personages.

Hamlet and *Richard the Third* may justly have some concern with the affairs of conscience, but what moral necessity, except perhaps the sufficiently obvious and imperative one of shocking all the tribe of Bowdlers, can there be to give Launcelot Gobbo a long soliloquy about conscience and the devil? What is there to be said for Cassio's broaching the awful tenets of Calvinism in a state of drivelling drunkenness? How are we to view the utter disregard of all poor Bowdler's sense of moral fitness, the reckless, callous, ingrained want of all consideration and fellow-feeling for jaundiced, green-sick, sour-milk, retchy, maudlin, sniffing, nibbling, dyspeptic, venomous, blear-eyed, addle-headed, spasm-bitten, puffy, flatulent, east-wind-swollen, nineteenth-century religiosity, which Shakespeare discovers in his unscrupulous relish for putting, on comic occasions, Scriptural allusions and terms and scraps into the mouths of such personages as Sir Toby Belch, Feste, Moth, Armado, Jaques, Celia, Touchstone, Mrs.

Quickly, Justice Shallow, Prince Henry, Pinch the schoolmaster, Dromio of Syracuse, Mrs. Page, the gravedigger, the clown in *All's Well*, and the porter in *Macbeth*? "Most unkindest cut of all," and double - superlative topsy-turvy perversion of all reverence, morality, and religion as Bowdler understands them, the arch-quoter and arch-purloiner of odds and ends from Holy Writ in all Shakespeare is none other than—whom could one guess?—Sir John Falstaff. Sir John—Heaven forbid one should fail of all due honour and respect to him when he comes so pat to support one's theory!—Sir John never loses an opportunity of patching up his old body for heaven by seasoning his conversation with godly saws and ancient instances. He is a perfect mine of Scriptural illustration, and seems to have had every qualification for editing a Reference Bible. "I am as poor as Job, my lord, but not as patient." "In the state of innocency Adam fell, and what should poor Jack Falstaff do in the days of villainy?" "Oh, if men were to be saved by merit, what hole in hell were hot enough for him?" "A whoreson Achitophel." "I never see thy face but I think on hell-fire and Dives that lived in purple, for there he is in his robes, burning, burning, burning." "Slaves as ragged as Lazarus in the painted cloth, where the glutton's dogs licked his sores." "In the shape of man, Master Brooke, I fear not Goliath with a weaver's beam, because I know also life is a shuttle," —two allusions in one sentence. "If to be fat is to be hated, then Pharaoh's lean kine are to be loved." "If then the tree may be known by the fruit." "And for thy walls a pretty slight drollery, or the story of the prodigal." " His face is Lucifer's kitchen, where he doth nothing but roast malt-worms." " I think the devil will not have me damned lest the oil that is in me should set hell on fire." No abuse, good Mr. Bowdler, no abuse in the world ! Falstaff does but dispraise reverence before the wicked, that the wicked may not fall in love with it. " God be thanked for these Scriptural quotations ; they offend none but the virtuous."

Bowdlerism stands aghast, shuddering, wofully " tickled in its catastrophe " ; cannot for its life understand how this reckless want of reverence for all its consecrated baggage and pedlar's pack of shibboleths and symbols and phrases is yet twinned with the deepest heart-reverence for virtue, and truth, and justice, and faith, and honesty, and beauty, and righteousness.

But, O Bowdlerism, think it over, what if Shakespeare's main idea about religion was even briefly this, the very same as another Teacher's idea about the Sabbath which also poor British Bowdlerism can never bring itself to accept—namely, that religion was made for man, and not man for religion.

On leaving Shakespeare and turning to Ben Jonson we are again met with a characteristic change in the poet's attitude towards Scriptural things. " Broad-based, broad-fronted, bounteous, multiform " Ben is more akin to Molière than to Shakespeare in his treatment of religious affairs and persons. Though Ben has no religious figure of such grave and terrible importance and tragic significance as Tartuffe, he has drawn the hypocrites of his time with a fierce and unsparing hand. There is a riotous

glee and overflowing merriment of satire in his
delineations of Puritan hypocrisy in *Bartholomew
Fair* and the *Alchemist.* The full-length portrait of
Zeal-of-the-land Busy is without parallel and beyond
all chance of competition in its immitigable force of
broad, truthful humour and merciless exposure of
that constant type in English life, the religious professor who has but one object in life, the promotion
of the self-same and identical interests of the glory
of God and his own stomach. The scene in the
fair in which, after having gorged himself with
Bartholomew pig as a protest against Judaism, he
upsets Joan Trash's basket of gingerbread images
as a protest against Popery, is one of the finest and
richest pieces of comedy in our literature. A noticeable feature of Ben Jonson's religious professors is
their inveterate habit of quoting Bible phrases.
His deacons quote Scripture by the yard. Tribula-
tion Wholesome, Ananias, the Banbury man, and
Dame Purecraft are incurably afflicted with this
loquacity of Scriptural quotation. One meets with
as many as sixteen Scriptural allusions and phrases
in about as many speeches. Ben Jonson seems to
have been troubled with no qualms about the propriety of making his religious persons speak their
natural, everyday language. To what a small extent
this perfectly free treatment of Scriptural matters in
Marlowe, Shakespeare, and Jonson is part of the
general coarseness and freedom of speech in that
time, is seen by the impossibility of tearing out and
wrenching away these several portions of their works
without great damage and injury to the remainder,
and leaving the writer's mind and spirit misrepre-

sented and mutilated ; while almost every coarse and indecent expression in these writers may be readily stripped and detached from the setting in which it is found.

The mere mention of *Tartuffe* and its acknowledged position as one of the glories and masterpieces of universal dramatic literature, is a sufficient reply, one would think, to all who urge that it is not lawful to treat religion upon the stage. The play and Molière's preface to it remain as a triumphant assertion for all time of the sovereignty of the drama in its own domain. And that domain is the whole of the nature, and heart, and passions, and conduct of men.

There is an old proverb which will of course be flung at any modern playwright who mentions such names as Shakespeare, Marlowe, Molière, and Ben Jonson. He will be reminded that fools rush in where angels fear to tread. But by your leave, good folks, the boot is fast stuck on the other leg this time. There is no maxim that forbids even fools to tread where angels have rushed in, and it is for you to prove how and why a modern playwright does wrong in treading after those whose shoe-latchets he is unworthy to loose. The quotation upon our stage by any character of any portion of the noblest example of our noble literature could never have sounded strange in modern ears until the debts of our language to those writings had been forgotten and annulled, and until their influence had decayed and become a dying fragrance in the land.

The success or failure of any individual play is of the merest momentary consequence, and need not here be brought into our thoughts. But the matter of a free atmosphere for dramatists to work in, the matter of some sort of an appeal or tribunal beyond the heated, changeful prejudices and caprices of the populace, is of the greatest importance to the future of the drama.

The question of the right of dramatists to faithfully depict modern religious life is only part of the much wider and more general question of their right and duty and ability to deal faithfully with whatsoever aspect of the huge, unwieldy mass of modern human life engages their attention. That larger right and duty indubitably contains the smaller, and cannot in any way be detached from it.

O human life ! so varied, so vast, so complex, so rich and subtle in tremulous, deep organ-tones, and soft proclaim of silver flutes, so utterly beyond our spell and insight, who of us can govern the thunder and whirlwind of thy ventages to any utterance of harmony, or pluck out the heart of thy eternal mystery ?

III

THE FIRST-NIGHT JUDGMENT OF PLAYS

(Reprinted from the *Nineteenth Century Review* for July 1889
by the kind permission of Mr. James Knowles)

A MINOR philosopher who recently crossed the
Atlantic, tired of watching the everlasting stretch
of waters, to relieve his weariness dropped a
plummet into that other and vaster ocean—boundless, unfathomable, innavigable—the ocean of human
credulity and fatuity. At the hour before dinner,
when it is customary for passengers to take their
constitutional on deck, he sauntered up to one of
the air - funnels on the *Etruria* and putting his
arm down it, he kept it there for some ninety
seconds, and then withdrawing it with an expression
of pain, he asked the guileless passers-by how it was
that by putting one's arm down that particular
funnel one received, after a minute or so, a severe
electric shock at the elbow. About a hundred
passengers were induced to try the experiment.
With this curious result. Some forty of them
received slight electric shocks, some ten or a dozen
received violent shocks, and four or five of them
entered into elaborately scientific, but mutually de-

structive, explanations of an occurrence that had never taken place.

If of a hundred people taken from the class who occupy the saloon of a Cunard steamer, and who may be supposed to be considerably above the average in education, intelligence, scientific knowledge, and general balance of mental power—if of this hundred, fifty can, by the merest suggestion, be persuaded that they experience an acute bodily sensation, when in fact they experience nothing, how many of the ordinary mass of theatre-goers, taken haphazard from all ranks of society and intelligence, can be persuaded, or may persuade themselves, that they have seen a good play when they have seen a bad one, or that they have seen a bad play when they have seen a good one? If the average man cannot be trusted in a thing so simple and direct as knowing whether he feels an electric shock or not, how can he be trusted in a mental operation so subtle, so complex, so indefinite, so elusive of demonstration as the formation of an opinion on a work of art? And yet everybody who is present at a theatre on a first night immediately passes the glibbest and surest judgment on a new play.

The implied suggestion that a modern play may be considered as a work of art will be received with a smile and a sneer. It will draw a smile from those who remember that the English drama is still supposed to be a branch of English literature, that any enduring renown it may win must be not merely theatrical but literary as well, that the one great flowering time of our national drama was the very midsummer of our national literature. It will raise a sneer and a shout of contempt from all the throng whose busy interest it is to spread the hateful maxim that the theatre is nothing but a shop to purvey any empty amusement that the public may clamour for, and that therefore any mention of art in connection with the stage must come from the lips of an impostor or a fanatic. And doubtless these two classes of objectors, from very opposite reasons, will resent the suggestion that the judgment pronounced upon a modern play has any farther-reaching consequence or influence than the varying amount of cash it may transfer from the pockets of the public to the pockets of the manager, or that it can be worth while to examine the methods whereby a play becomes popular, any more than it can be worth while to enter into an exhaustive discussion of the methods whereby the public is taught to appreciate what is called high-art furniture in the Tottenham Court Road.

Indeed, one is forced to take an apologetic tone when one speaks of our modern drama, and the time seems to be a long way off when it will be permitted for any one with a sense of proportion or a memory of the wise Arnoldian precept about "seeing things as they are," to boast of our having a living English drama at all commensurate with and responsive to the national life, and flashing back upon a theatre-loving and theatre-going community the faithful image of themselves. In no sense can the Victorian drama be said to bear any such relation to the Victorian literature and the Victorian age, as the Elizabethan drama bears to the Elizabethan literature and the Elizabethan age. We have a great Victorian literature, we have plenty of stagecraft,

but when the great masters of our modern literature
have written plays they have only shown that they
do not know the stage. There is no reason in the
nature of things why we should not again have a
literary drama if we only set about it the right way.
And in a confused and bewildered way we do seem
to be struggling towards some sincere form of
national drama, and there does seem to be springing
up a growing discontent with the puerilities and
transparent unrealities that have so long held sway
on the English stage. But even the most earnest
well-wishers to the theatre, those who are most
anxious that it should cease to be the people's
bauble, and become a real power in our intellectual
and artistic life — even these do not quite seem
to know what they want of it, or how they would
have it set about its new career.

It is the object of this paper to examine the
machinery in present use for the formation and
direction of public opinion in the judgment of plays,
and to inquire whether it is defective at any point
and how far it can be mended in the interests of the
drama. And if it be retorted that the machinery is
perfect and cannot be mended and must not be
tampered with, one can only ask, " Then how is it
we have no modern English drama to-day at all
worthy of the dignity and opulence of our nation ? "
If it be contended that we have such a modern
drama, that our stage is in an entirely satisfactory
condition, that it handles our complex modern life
in a large and masterly way, and has seized upon
the spirit of the age with a sovereign grasp of vitality
and truth, and is rendering it in works that will

possess a permanent attraction for those who may
chance to see or read them in a future generation—
if this is contended, one can only remember Mr.
Micawber's alternative, and "sardonically smile."   I
will give one instance, and one only, of the modern
drama's failure, not merely to assign its due prominence to what is perhaps the chief factor of our
modern life, and to render it with any pretensions to
likeness, or to truth, or to penetration, but even to
recognise that there is anything to be dealt with,
that there is such a shaper and transformer of conduct and character and life in our midst.

When the dust that we have raised round ourselves has cleared away, and this age and its works
can be dispassionately viewed and weighed, who can
doubt that its prime achievements, its crowning
glories, its great prizes will be adjudged to science?
Calm, invincible, celestial ministrant, whose still,
small voice is beginning to be heard above the
ravings of our two hundred sects, whose healing
secrets are for all ears, how sure is thy future rule
over all the turbulent, disordered human race !

But on the stage on such rare occasions as the
man of science is introduced, it is always, even in a
serious play, in a farcical or burlesque spirit, as a
weak-minded, insincere, comic old fool, or a weak-
minded, insincere, comic young fool, with an entirely
false, ridiculous jargon, and generally with a very
strong dash of the impostor. And this is not
because the majority of the audience recognise the
portrait as in any sense true, even in a burlesque or
farcical sense, but because searchingness and sincerity
are not demanded on the stage.   There is no appeal

made by the author to the sense of truthfulness in his audience, and indeed the audience do not expect it. Parallel cases might be instanced in other character-types on the stage, but would take us too far from our present subject.

Returning to the question of the apparatus for the judgment of plays, it is necessary first of all to lay down the two main rules which, sooner or later, every modern playwright has to bend to and steer his course by :—

1. The public is the judge.
2. The public must not be bored.

1st. The public is the judge. Resist, rebel, revile as we may, accuse the public of caprice, of ignorance, of neglect, of fatuity, of frivolity, of want of taste, the public remains our master.

" Nonsense, sir ! Allow *me* to be the best judge of whether I'm cutting your nose or no ! " says the barber in the farce to his protesting victim.

But it is not the author-barber, nor the bystander, who has to decide whether the public's nose has been cut, but the public, the victim himself. And it is curious that when the victim in any particular case has been emphatically assured by the bystander that his nose has not been cut, and has yet felt from his own sensations that he has been bled— it is curious to remark that when the victim says to the bystander, " Sir, would you please look again ? Are you sure there isn't a slight scratch on my nose ? " the reply generally is, " A scratch ? A fearful gash, sir ! "

Yes, the public is our master, and in the theatrical as well as the political world the only practical thing is to make haste and recognise it. But is not this a frank acknowledgment of the irresistible force of the shopkeeping dictum that the author and manager are bound to provide the public with the exact kind of nonsense or folly it has a relish for? Not at all. The public taste is modifiable within very wide limits. The public may be led almost anywhere, easily but temporarily to any kind of new sensation or falsity, strenuously but permanently to the appreciation of what is of lasting worth. One hears constantly an outcry against the absurdity of trying to educate the public in matters of amusement, but all the while a very real education is going on amongst us. Consider the intolerable course of preliminary education a candidate for one of the stalls at some of our burlesque theatres must undergo before he can get the full flavour of the entertainment upon his palate! How rigorously he must deny himself the contemplation of all heroic actions and personages in history, in fiction, and in surrounding modern life! How severely he must abstain from all acquaintance with the graces of English literature, the beauties of his mother-tongue! What entire surrender he must make of all his pleasant leisure, that he may cultivate the society of the debased persons who haunt our public bar-rooms! How constantly alert he must be to catch all the *nuances* of their peculiar slang, and to enter into their subtlest perversions of our language! How willing he must be to sacrifice, not merely his superfluous faculties, such as his reverence for women and his ear for poetry, but such coarser possessions as logic

and common-sense! How patiently he must discipline himself towards the barmaid's ideal of life!
And then, after a number of years, if he has dili-
gently employed his time, he will at last be able to
enter with frantic raptures, such as never Garrick,
Kean, or Irving inspired, into the inner meaning
and occult appreciation of some travesty, scrofulous
with slang and fetid with diseased cockneyisms, of
one of

> those wise and lovely songs
> Of Fate, and Chance, and God, and Chaos old—
> And Love ;

some burlesque that burlesques nothing, but only
beslimes with the cheapest and filthiest modern
cynicism some old-world legend such as that which
tells of the deathless passion that snatched Eurydice
for a moment to its embrace, or the deathless con-
stancy that welcomed the loved Ulysses after his
wanderings.

The public cannot be educated, we are told.
But it *is* being educated, and rapidly, and in some
quarters to a strange end. And if it can be trained
to delight in nonsense, in imbecility, in bunkum, in
clap-trap, in sensation, in all sorts of passing extravagance and emptiness, shall we say that it cannot be
trained to delight in the wise picturing of what is
real, essential, enduring, and of perennial influence
and far-reaching result in our national life? The
public cannot be educated? Let the theatrical
bear-wards of our gilded youth respond! I think
the cubs can be taught to dance, and to a pretty
tune. In the fact that the public taste can be
trained and diverted in almost any direction lie

our best hopes for the future of the drama. The public, then, is the judge. But this rule is tempered by the consideration that the public is pliable, volatile, flexible, ignorant to an incalculable degree.

2nd. The public must not be bored. The Olympian gods laughed consumedly at Vulcan because he was lame. A scarcely less august assemblage— the English upper classes at a fashionable club— shouted with delight at " Two Lovely Black Eyes." One may be permitted to keep an unmoved countenance in presence of these supreme manifestations of humour without quite forfeiting one's reputation for the perception of comedy, or without incurring a charge of disrespect towards the dread audiences whose pleasure it was to be thus tickled.

It is illustrative of the curiously complex growth of modern humour that an eager participator in the great, perpetual mundane comedy is now so often compelled to satisfy his appetite for the ludicrous, not in what his fellows laugh at, but in the fact that they laugh at all. The minor philosopher before mentioned saw a crammed theatre shaking with laughter at the most dreary, witless piece of cockney inanity. The whole point of this involved, elaborate jest lay, not in the fact that the people on the stage had come there to amuse the audience, but that the entire audience had come there to amuse him, the minor philosopher—had cheerfully deserted their occupations, had given up the golden leisure that they might have spent so much more profitably in twiddling their thumbs, and the shillings that they might have spent so much more profitably by throwing them in the gutter, had done all this with, of course, the co-operation of the whole body of people on the stage, to please a single spectator, the lucky, but scarcely deserving, minor philosopher. It struck him as a costly and wasteful joke, but he laughed. It isn't everybody who can have a performance all to himself like the late King of Bavaria. So he laughed. And perhaps it was a member of that same audience who had his revenge a few days later upon our small philosopher when the latter was evidently enjoying with all his heart a performance of Shakespeare. "I don't see anything in Shakespeare myself," said to him a young man of the day. "It is quite optional," was the cheerful reply; and there the discussion ended. But doubtless the young man inwardly chuckled, and knew himself to be superior to a person who could enjoy such stuff.

It is all optional; it is all relative; and when one reflects upon the huge sempiternal dulness that pervades two-thirds of English life, of the evident determination of the English people to turn the whole country into one big railway suburb of smoky yellow brick, so that the ideal England of the future may be a sort of Clapham Junction and its immediate neighbourhood "writ large," one is puzzled to know what a people domiciled under such conditions may or may not find humorous or dull, what indeed they could possibly find that was not dull, and whether in some rare moment of inspiration it might not occur to them that the whole of their existence, their amusements included, was not one great sacrifice upon the altar of dulness.

F

But the people must not be bored at the theatre, that's flat. This may lead to some astonishing results. A few years ago Mr. William Archer printed at length the most popular and laughter-producing scene from the most popular and laughter-producing comedy of our times. It was a cruel exposure. But modern comedies are not meant to be read. Why not, pray? it is exactly those qualities that make *The School for Scandal* a readable play that have preserved it on the stage for a hundred years, and will preserve it for a hundred years more. The cleverness of its great situation alone would not have saved it. But the public don't want to read plays, and the public must not be bored. It is true that this may disthrone all the great humorists of the past, and seat in their honoured place some pert cockney monstrosity of the music-halls. But the public must not be bored. This may tend to banish from our stage every species of wit that requires an intellectual energy of attention to understand, and that can be dwelt upon afterwards and re-enjoyed upon reflection. But the public must not be bored. This may degrade the stage from being in any sense an exhibitor and preceptor of manners and life, and conclusively prove its true function to be that of a dictionary for the dissemination of eccentric forms of slang and *double-entendre*. Yet the public shall not be bored.

This is the second rule a playwright has to bear in his mind and submit to, whether he likes it or not. A play must not bore the public. This rule is tempered by the fact that different classes of the public are bored by and take delight in totally opposite things. It was necessary to state at some length the conditions under which a playwright works, and to test the exact value of the two rules he is so constantly reminded of, lest it should be said that this inquiry was started in rebellion against, or in ignorance of, what are supposed to be permanent and fundamental limitations of stage-work. These limitations being stated and frankly accepted for whatever they may be worth, we may go on to the main inquiry, bearing them in our mind.

If there is one form of art that from the nature of things might demand a special tenderness and carefulness in its judges, it is surely a stage-play. " As good almost kill a man as kill a good book," said Milton, when it was a question of applying to literature a summary process of stamping out, akin to that which plays sometimes undergo. If a picture is condemned it may yet find one appreciative buyer to reward the artist's trouble. And it stays perfect on the canvas to justify or refute the criticism. If a book is condemned it is yet in print and is obtainable ; it can be read by anybody who cares to test the judgment pronounced upon it. Neither picture nor book is snuffed out. What would English literature be if every book that did not immediately obtain the suffrages of the public was burnt to the last copy by the hangman, and the author put in the pillory ? What would have survived during the last few years, except *Called Back* and a few things on that level ? While almost everything of higher and more lasting reference and import would have perished.

But an unsuccessful play, and especially a play of serious intention, very rarely recovers from the hisses and jeers of a first night.   It is always crippled and deprived of its immediate influence. One is frequently challenged to quote a good play that has failed, but the very fact that it has failed is the test to most of us that it was not a good play. And it is generally a right test.   But it may be also noticed that some plays which have been saved by the skin of their teeth are now pronounced good that would surely have been remembered only with condemnation if by some accident they had not managed to survive.   Therefore the judgment of a play would seem to demand very unusual qualities of balance, calmness, penetration, expertness, and leniency.   And in addition to these, in all cases except those of the most transparent insincerity or incompetence, one might plead for a very large measure of suspension of judgment.   Now, there is no doubt that these qualities do exist to some extent in a first-night audience and are frequently exercised.   And it would be churlish and perverse for one who has received very distinguished marks of sympathy and approval from first-night audiences to quibble over any minor inequalities of praise or blame, or to raise any question of the justice of any particular verdict, upon merely personal grounds. Where a large debt of gratitude has to be freely acknowledged on a run of dealings, it is not worth while to dispute about the odd halfpence in any single transaction.

Very frequently the state of mind of first-night audiences is rather more akin to that of an excited political meeting than to that of any committee of judges upon a work of art.   There is a vast amount of excitement, a vast amount of genuine enthusiasm, trained, half trained, and almost wholly untrained. This enthusiasm is really anxious at the outset for a great success, but, being balked, it turns as easily as the Roman citizens did at the words of Antony, and seems to become quite as anxious for a great failure. There is also in a first-night audience a considerable amount of cynicism and boredom, though less perhaps than might be expected as the natural results of a long course of modern play-seeing. And there is also, as might be anticipated when the prizes of the stage are so much coveted, a certain amount of envy in those who have failed as authors and actors, or who are impatient to succeed. These latter feelings, which are latent and kept in check while the play is going well, make themselves very potent when things are going wrong. And when once things have gone wrong, or apparently have gone wrong, and hissing has set in, all judgment becomes impossible to the majority of the audience. A short time ago at a first night, during an important scene the electric light began to play pranks and jump up and down. The effect was instantly visible in the distraction of the audience, and in their inability to follow what was taking place on the stage. The actors, too, became frightened and lost their self-control. Happily the light behaved itself in time before the thread of interest had completely snapped. But for practical purposes and so far as the power of judgment is concerned, the effects of hissing and of violent eccentricity on the part of the electric light are very much about the same.

But it will be asked, Do you wish to abolish the right of hissing in theatres? By no means. Hissing is perhaps only enthusiasm turned wrong side out. We cannot afford to part with the enthusiasm. Besides, for all worthless work the swiftest and sternest condemnation is the kindest and the most economic. But let us be quite sure that it is worthless. Except in the very worst cases of insincerity and ineptitude, I think hissing is a whip that should be held in strict reserve. There should always be very great hesitation in using it, except for downright obscenity and profanity. And even here, the evident sense of the majority who do not hiss is quite as effective as the more pronounced condemnation of those who do. That the things which commonly provoke hostile demonstrations on the first night are not as a rule offensive to the ordinary playgoer, and would not disturb him or move his anger, is proved by the fact that it would be difficult to point to a case of hissing after the first night. There is generally a ghastly apathy, a terrible gloom and downheartedness, about audience and actors on the second night of a failure. And this may be even worse than the hissing. But there is no hissing. And if it be urged that also, even in the case of a success, there is no such enthusiasm and applause as is shown on a first night, it must be replied that very often the enthusiasm of a first night is as ill judged and as uncalled for as the hissing. We cannot afford to lose the least spark of trained, well-grounded enthusiasm, but the mere noise that mechanically cannons and thunders over the safe advent of some outrageous masterpiece of bunkum is far

more noxious than any amount of hissing, and
could surely be grateful to no ear that had once
caught the faintest whisper of that "strain of higher
mood":

> Fame is no plant that grows on mortal soil,
> Nor in the glistering foil
> Set off to the world, nor in broad rumour lies ;
> But lives and spreads aloft by those pure eyes
> And perfect witness of all-judging Jove.

What we are all desirous of is that both the condemnation and the applause should be well founded,
well considered, and well regulated.   But I am here
only concerned with the methods and regulation of
the condemnation.   Personally, I have not the least
objection to being hissed.   Considering that the
three occasions on which I have met with a public
demonstration of this order have been brought
about by passages in my plays that, whatever
their faults or their unintentional offensiveness,
were at least deliberate, were deeply felt, were
carefully thought over, and were written in all
good faith and earnestness—these things considered,
I am unable to blame myself for their unlucky
reception or to lay it to heart.   "I had rather be
damned," says Shelley, "with Plato and Lord Bacon,
than go to heaven with Paley and Malthus."   I
would not willingly offend any single person among
my audience ; indeed I would, at some violence to
my own convictions, remove any scene that would
hurt the natural reverence of any spectator.   But
how little any real feeling of reverence has to do
with the matter I have already pointed out in this
Review some years ago.   And, considering what

things have been most vociferously applauded on our modern stage, one might take some credit to oneself for being blamed ; for surely it is better to be blamed for work either good or bad than to be praised for work that is transparently bad.

I must own that I think it is very often a slightly irrational feeling that prompts an audience to hiss, a survival of that frame of mind which induces certain islanders to go out every evening and howl and hurl their darts at the sun simply because he is going down. Our minor philosopher says there is something to him ludicrously inconsequent and comical in the whole method whereby we set about securing good plays. And to hiss a man who has spent perhaps some five or six months in the stupendous task of trying to please two thousand people, each of them with different tastes, notions, ideals, prejudices, whims, and standards, simply because he has failed to satisfy them all at all points, seems a little uncharitable and discourteous, as well as illogical. Besides, hissing in many cases defeats the end for which the audience has come— that is, if that end is the consideration of the play and not the hunting of it down. What would be the result if the next exhibition of the Royal Academy should be opened simultaneously to public and critics, and every member of the public who had paid his shilling should be permitted, without giving any reasons, to stick his umbrella into any part of any picture that he did not like ; while at the end of the view it should be *de rigueur* for the whole body of the Academicians and exhibitors to run the gauntlet between two rows of the public ranged on

each side from the top of the Academy steps to
Piccadilly, the public being entitled for their shilling
to express their approbation or their disapprobation
in any method short of personal violence? What
would be the result? No doubt the art-loving
public which the occasion would be sure to bring
together would have sufficient good-manners and
respect for themselves not to interfere with many of
the best works, or to allow their neighbours to interfere with them wantonly, if they could help it. But
if some Tartuffe claimed his right on behalf of
public morality to plunge his stick into every nude
figure on the walls, and if some doctrinaire claimed
his right on behalf of art to annihilate every canvas
that did not illustrate his theories, and if the critics
were compelled to judge these tattered and mangled
remains as if they embodied the artist's full intention,
is there any doubt that the greatest injury would
gradually be done to art, and that in the long run
nothing would be safe of survival but what was of
assured respectable mediocrity and dead conventionality, that having a thousand times proved inoffensive to the British philistine might be relied
upon to prove inoffensive once more? I do not
say that nothing else *would* survive, but that nothing
else would be *safe* of survival. The entire tendency
would be to stamp out originality. Originality is
always more or less offensive and shocking and
debatable. Artists would naturally say, " I cannot
afford to waste six months on painting a picture
that the first comer, however prejudiced or ignorant,
may plunge his umbrella into and thereby make me
the laughing-stock of the whole artistic world. I

must paint something that will please everybody—
and sell."

Can any one doubt the folly of such a system ?
Yet this is precisely a parallel to the method in
which plays are judged. I am not disputing the
general substantial justice of first-night verdicts. I
am not bringing wholesale charges. I am not deny-
ing that there is very great fairness, very great
generosity, very great enthusiasm on first nights in
many instances. I am only pointing out a law of
tendency, not perhaps very marked in its operation
or its immediate results, nay, very frequently quite
obscured and apparently contradicted by immediate
results. If I tell a man who goes to Monte Carlo
with twenty thousand pounds that if he keeps on
playing long enough he will inevitably become bank-
rupt, I do not accuse the bank of cheating. He may
win once, twenty times, a hundred times, and may
laugh at my prophecy. But if he perseveres, that
very small advantage the bank retains will work to
results as certain as the multiplication table and
gravitation, and he will be ruined. So it is on our
stage. There is a law of repression, of restraint, of
gentle but irresistible suasion towards small, foolish,
cockney ideals. And gradually we all get tuned
that way. Thus an author, in planning a new piece,
is tempted to make it his first business not to give
full play to his own views of life, his own knowledge
of human nature ; he is under the ignoble necessity
of making it his first business to remove everything
that can possibly offend the most untrained cockney
intellect. One line, on a first night, that presents a
view of life foreign to that which obtains in Tooley

Street or Gotham, may so upset three wrathful gentlemen from Tooley Street or Gotham, who may chance to be in the house, that they may conceive themselves bound by the sternest sense of duty, by all they owe to the drama, to themselves, to the public, and to Tooley Street or Gotham, to protest against the piece, and, as far as they can, to prevent its being heard, or heard of, again. They are quite within their rights to protest, and so far as in them lies to uphold Tooley Street or Gotham standards, but unfortunately the piece has to be judged almost entirely by that first-night performance. And it is very obvious that while the electric light, or the three gentlemen from Tooley Street are behaving themselves in an eccentric manner, no examination of the author's work is possible. But in the one case the fault is laid to the electric light, in the other to the author. It is only a very strong, calm, shrewd judgment that can remain " unshaken, unseduced, unterrified " under such conditions, and penetrate to the author's meaning—that is, if the author happens to have any. And it requires some courage to pronounce a verdict in favour of a piece in face of the fact that very probably the public, hearing of the first-night reception, will take it for granted that the play is a failure. An author dares not risk anything. How can he show his heart when he knows that the tongs are waiting to tear it out from him, and flay and shrivel it ? How is any great work in modern drama, not to be done, but even to be attempted ? We are scarcely likely to achieve any very great work ; but imagine what its reception might be unless it was sheltered by a great name and a great position on the part of the producer! A few years ago, at the Bristol theatre, I happened to sit next to a good-natured, common-sense old sea-captain, whose course of reading and previous theatre-going had not extended to the play in performance. The play was *Hamlet*. As it proceeded he became more and more puzzled as to the motives of the plot and characters, and he entreated me to explain them to him as he went along. However, the exigencies of the case did not permit me to enter into an exhaustive analysis of the play, and in the middle of the performance he left the theatre, swearing. This may prove that *Hamlet* is a bad play, and that the first piece of clap-trap that catches the public is a good one. Or it may prove, what is almost undreamed of in the art of the stage, though it is so thoroughly recognised in all other arts, that the first rough two-foot rule of common-sense that the first comer may take out of his workaday pocket, though a perfectly reliable instrument for its own business, is scarcely the kind of measure to apply to a water-colour of Turner's for the purpose of seeing how near he approaches to nature in his portraiture of a mountain. The two-foot rule is admirable for measuring deal planks, but in the case of the picture it only proves Turner to be contemptibly, ridiculously wrong. And the knowledge that the two-foot rule is to be applied only tends to prevent an author from touching anything that may demand rather a different kind of measure.

Further, another reason why great forbearance may be asked from an audience on a first night, so far as a final judgment on the author's work is concerned, lies in the fact that a play is not a certain,

definite, stereotyped, irreversible thing. A play is
fluent, flexible, wayward, protean. Any given representation of any play is only one of a possible thousand, all varying more or less, all of them more or
less embodying the author's ideas, so that he could
hardly say of any one of them that it was not what
he intended. But the very slightest difference of
balance, of relation, of proportion, of selecting this
actor instead of that, of putting up with this actor
when that cannot be had, may make all the difference with the public. So curiously subtle are the
conditions that make for success. The most that
can be said of any first-night performance is that,
out of a thousand possible varying productions of a
play, this particular one is, or is not, satisfying or
likely to be popular. But a new play is always
judged as if the author's share of it were there
definitely imaged once for all, graven in the rock.

Again, there are very wide variations of the same
play, even when played by the same company, on
different nights. At rehearsal a play shifts from
morning to morning. One day everything seems to
go well : there is life in the piece, life in the actors,
and the whole thing gives an impression of reality.
The next day everything is flat, the piece seems
formal and mechanical, the actors mere puppets, and
the whole thing is lifeless and wooden. And very
often it seems that the failure or success of a piece
is due to the same causes that make it go heavily
or brightly at rehearsal. And if very great forbearance may be asked for the play on the first night,
much more may it be asked for the actors and
actresses. An author can keep out of the way, and

if he is fortunate to have a healthy, sanguine temperament, he can appraise a first-night's failure at its due value ; but the actors and actresses are bound not merely to face that dread ordeal, they are bound not merely to walk on hot bricks, but to perform a very delicate artistic operation all the while. While the house is with them, they are buoyed up in their task ; but the moment they feel there is an antagonistic spirit in front, however small a portion of the audience it may pervade, it is quite impossible for them to keep their self-control and do justice to themselves and the author. Imagine a person whose occupation makes him peculiarly sensitive to the least breath of praise and blame, which cultivates his nerves to the utmost point of refinement, called upon to enact a scene of great passion or transcendent emotion for the first time, with the knowledge that the three wrathful gentlemen from Tooley Street are offended, and are only waiting for the slightest slip on his part to make their indignation echo through the house. How can a man give voice to the passion that is in him under such conditions ? How can he miss reaching his aim by at least that short span which separates the sublime from the ridiculous ? Yet he too is judged as if his performance were a piece of statuary, carved once and for all, instead of a breath—an inspiration. Perhaps it is unfair to urge the state of fright and abject nervous terror which seizes even some practised performers on a first night. It will be said that unless a person has calm, strong nerves, he or she ought not to enter a profession that so eminently demands them. But there are very many delightful performers, whose services the stage would be the poorer for losing, who are completely paralysed by our present system of judging plays, and to whom a first night means days, and even weeks, of agonizing anticipation and after depression and prostration. And very often the performers have to suffer for the author's sins. It seems a pity that some other method for visiting condemnation upon the author could not be devised, or at least some other time and place. A pillory on Hampstead Heath for three hours on the succeeding day would scarcely be practicable, yet it would be a wiser punishment than our present one.

Again, our present system of judging plays often tends to stereotype conventionality as much by its injudicious praise as by its injudicious censure. In many respects a first-night audience, enthusiastic, sympathetic as it is, is intensely conservative. Just as to lawyers law grows to mean chiefly, not equity or justice, but a strange esoteric game of thimblerig according to their rules ; just as to clergymen religion grows to mean chiefly, not righteousness and keeping the commandments, but a wrangle about candles and deportment and millinery, so the theatrical mind is apt to deify its own arbitrary technicalities, and to take them for the essence of the matter. Nothing is less understood even by a first-night audience than the nature and limits of the necessary conventions of the stage. It is curious to notice when once a formula has gained acceptance how eager a first-night audience is to perpetuate it. And this while all the time it may be genuinely anxious for something new within the artificial and narrow limits of that formula. At the Exhibition of 1851 it was asked why there was not a greater freedom and variety in the designs of lilac prints, these designs being confined to a few childish geometric patterns. It was replied that other designs had been printed, but would not sell because the old women who wore lilac prints had got certain patterns stamped on their brains, and would not submit to any variation of those patterns. How potent is the operation of a similar law among first-night audiences may be gathered from a glance at recent theatrical history. In serious drama during the last ten years one great formula has prevailed, the melodramatic formula. As the personages, the motives, the situations, the sentiments of melodrama have gradually become more stereotyped, more lifeless, more mechanical, so the applause of first-night audiences has become more emphatic, more unstinted, more unhesitating. And it is not the first-night audiences who have been the first to perceive that the formula is outworn, but a section of the poor, old, stupid public itself. The victim has declared that his nose has not been cut, though he has been assured on all sides that it has. The first-night receptions have been as noisy and triumphant. All that contributed to the success of former pieces has been duly served up again : the hero has been as superfluously and impossibly virtuous, the villain has been as superfluously and impossibly vicious, the sentiments have been as forced and cheap, the playwright's skill has been as deft and ingenious ; but the more unanimous and assertive the first-night success, the less has been the public response.

I think I may claim to have shown a fair case for consideration when I say, that, while very gratefully acknowledging the great generosity of first-night audiences, their enthusiasm, their quick intelligence in technical matters, their kindly feeling towards their favourites, the fact that their verdict is supposed to be final, conclusive, and exhaustive, sometimes acts as a drag and a bar to the development of our drama.

What is the remedy? To fill the house with friends on a first performance? I can conceive nothing more distasteful to an epicure of praise than the noisy, mechanical plaudits of a claque. Away with all dodging of public opinion, all incense of "bought hallelujahs," all hole-and-corner methods of getting a verdict! Since the public opinion is what we seek, let us court it openly and without fear. But let us at the same time recognise that a first-night audience by its composition cannot be entirely representative, and indeed is often quite misrepresentative. We, who are first-nighters, lay too much stress upon our judgment.

I have no patent pill to offer for the disorder I have tried to diagnose. Natural remedies are the best. I think, then, the very greatest forbearance may be asked for all work that is of avowedly serious aim. A burlesque, a laughable farcical comedy, anything that the public will naturally run after, may be left to take care of itself. It sometimes seems that both the press and the public are inclined to make every allowance and indulgence for work that confessedly means nothing, and has evidently not cost the writer a sincere thought or a moment's

G

observation of life ; while to work of deeper import and intention a different standard is applied. It is, of course, very flattering to be told that one is judged by the severest standard. One hears a great deal about these two different standards. Some transparent masterpiece of clap-trap and insincerity is produced amid universal acclamation. " But surely you wouldn't wish to be judged by the standard that showers praise on such work as that ? " No, but why judge any work by such a standard ? Why confirm that poor gallery boy in his natural love of bathos and his foolish cockney ideals of life ? Why confirm the great middle classes in their stock notion that the true hero of nineteenth-century life is a prodigiously virtuous person, who gets falsely accused of murder or theft by transparently artificial means, who is proved innocent by the same transparently artificial means, and is then dowered with lots of money, and left to settle down snug and smug with his brother British philistines for the rest of his life ?

One may be allowed, then, to beg the greatest forbearance for all work that, however faulty in points of technique, however opposed to the accepted formulæ of the day, does yet aim at painting a phase of life, or at tackling some vital type of character, or at illustrating some great passion, in a serious and straightforward way. It is strange how much more an audience is attracted by the painting of manners than by the exhibition of passion. Unless a great passion is greatly rendered it merely convicts the author of using violent language which seems at once too feeble and too forcible for the situation. Strong things on the stage are lamentably weak unless they are strongly and convincingly rendered.

Again, we may beg a large measure of suspension of judgment from a first-night audience. It is the sign of a small, narrow, uncultivated intellect to be certain it has found finality. It is children and savages who demand instant solutions and explanations of everything, and are satisfied with sudden, extreme judgments dictated by their passions and prejudices. We may, then, ask the three wrathful gentlemen from Tooley Street or Gotham to be quite sure a play is worthless before they condemn it, to be quite sure that three other gentlemen from Tooley Street or Gotham, coming with a calmer mind on a calmer occasion, may not perhaps like the very things that they are so anxious to condemn.

And we may ask that body of young men students—so earnest, so intelligent, so anxious to advance the best interests of the drama, so ready to show their love of it by the sacrifices they make of their time and convenience to support it—we may perhaps ask them to keep an eye on the three gentlemen from Tooley Street or Gotham, and not to let them hinder the advancement of the drama in their desperate anxiety to enforce Tooley Street or Gotham standards and judgments. And, above all, we may labour to inoculate the great public with the truth that first-night performances must, from the nature of things, be merely tentative, temporary, inconclusive, and sometimes quite deceptive. We may urge the truth that a play is judged on a first night from the point of view of its conformity to the accepted technicalities and conventions of the passing day, and from its Joseph-Surface-like quality of pleasing everybody, and getting well spoken of by everybody. But it is very often found out afterwards. And the public may be asked to place only as much confidence in first - night decisions as a knowledge of this justifies.

It may be said that the question of getting a modern national drama with high artistic standards is not worth troubling about, and that things are well enough as they are. But surely, with all the money that is lavished upon forms of amusement whose best virtue is that they are harmlessly stupid and totally inoperative, with all the time and money that are devoted to the cultivation of that costly wax exotic, Italian opera, a little sacrifice of time, of patience, of money may be asked for the fostering of some higher and sincerer form of modern English drama than is at present in vogue.

IV

REALISM AND TRUTH

(A Letter to the *New York Dramatic Mirror*, 19th April 1890)

IT was with some surprise that I saw myself
described in one of our leading English dailies the
other day as a realist and a champion of realism on
the modern stage. Within the previous month, in
responding for the drama at a public dinner, I had
named "beauty, mystery, passion, imagination" as
the four chief qualities to be searched for in a play ;
and on another occasion I had counselled playgoers
who hungered for real life to go into the streets
and get it. But perhaps the labelling of some
of my plays as "studies of English life" had
confused the writer of the article, and had led him
to suppose that such a description necessarily proclaimed the author a realist.

It is indeed most difficult for a dramatist to
convey to his hearers what is his precise standpoint,
and what are his main views of human life. The
novelist stands outside his characters and talks to
his readers as he goes along, and, by a thousand
confidences and asides, defines his exact relations to
his puppets and their exact orbits in his scheme of
human life. But no such liberties are permitted to

the playwright, and on our side of the Atlantic a
general resentment is felt against a dramatic author
who ventures to hint to the public that his work can
possibly have any other aspect or significance than
can be immediately seized upon and perfectly comprehended by the first gentleman in the gallery who
has paid sixpence to have an evening's fun.

The distinctions between realism and truth on
the stage are a perpetual stumbling-block to the
uneducated playgoer, as are also the distinctions
between the cheapest, stalest devices of the hack
playwright and those necessary conventions which
even the greatest dramatist must frankly surrender
himself to and accept.

The uneducated playgoer goes to a theatre and
sees a real lamp-post and a real London street. He
goes to another theatre and hears a gentleman in
antique dress soliloquising in blank verse. He
recognises certain features of the lamp-post and
certain features of the London street, but soliloquies
in blank verse are palpable and egregious impossi-
bilities. He thinks that the lamp-post and the
London street are "real life" and that Hamlet is
not. He does not closely observe that the lamp-post
is a profile of thin wood or cardboard, nor is he
disturbed by the monstrous portent that the London
street keeps swaying to and fro in all its six stories
according as gusts of wind blow at its back from the
stage-door. To him the London street and the
lamp-post are nearer "real life" than Hamlet. He
knows no difference between realism and truth.

I wish every playgoer could know all the tricks
and illusions of the stage from beginning to end. I

wish that he could be as learned in all the devices
and scenic effects of the stage as the master-carpenter.
Then, perhaps, he would begin to understand that
the real business of the dramatist is not to stupefy
and mystify him with shallow, empty, realistic effects,
and that scenery is only useful in illustration and
strict subordination to the movement and development of human character and passion.   And having
learned how trumpery and secondary realism is in
scenery, he might go on to learn the far harder, yet
equally necessary, lesson that realism is just as
contemptible in dialogue and construction as it is
in scenery.

How silly are the reports sometimes sent to
theatrical papers of unintelligent theatre-goers mistaking the scene on the stage for real life, and shouting
to the actors !   What a mistaken view of their art
must those actors have who consider that the hisses
paid to them in the character of villains are an
acceptable tribute to their exertions !   Compare the
noisy, ill-judged, misplaced applause of provincial
audiences with the eager, unerring enthusiasm and
appreciation of the audience at a professional
matinée, where, so far as the acting goes, every one
knows the precise means by which an effect is
produced, and therefore knows the precise reward it
should receive !

Truth and realism are as distinct, and in some
respects as antagonistic, in a modern drama as they
are in poetic tragedy.   To all hungerers for " real
life " on the stage it must be replied—" Why pay to
see profile lamp-posts and canvas houses when lamp-
posts with cubic instead of superficial dimensions

and houses with solid foundations can be gazed upon all day long without a fee ? "

The fact is, all realism is only, as Carlyle puts it, getting on a three-feet stool to look at the stars. You certainly do get three feet nearer to them. That cannot be denied.

The most stupendous difficulty, the most outrageous convention, meets the realist on the very threshold of the theatre.   For the purposes of the stage, human lives have to be woven into a consecutive story, and this story has to be chopped into three or four acts of an average three-quarters of an hour each.   There may be, indeed there are, dramatic *moments* in the lives of all ; there may have been dramatic scenes of *two or three minutes* in the connected lives of two or three people ; but never in this world was there anything approaching to a dramatic *three-quarters of an hour* in the lives of half-a-dozen or a dozen people, passing in such a way and with such a volume and variety of incident and emotion as to be satisfactory or even endurable in representation to a modern audience. Note, too, that the scenes which can be rendered in precise imitation of real life are the poorest, the weakest, the least suggestive, the least dramatic, the least interpretative, the least illustrative of human life *as a whole.*   Therefore the realist has to accept this astounding convention to start with ; and having accepted it, why should he hesitate to accept a host of minor conventions, provided that they advance the dramatist's main business, the exposition and interpretation of human life and character ?

There could not be a greater condemnation of

realism on the stage than the fact that in proportion as its advocates succeed in practising their theories their plays lose variety of character and action, decrease in the quantity of human life and emotion represented, fail in the qualities that give a permanent interest and value.

The rejection of stage realism is not antagonistic to the most severe, the most faithful, the most searching, the most *truthful* portraiture of modern life. That Zola is wrong is no reason that Bulwer-Lytton and Sheridan Knowles and the legion of stucco blank-verse writers are right. A total inability in a modern playwright to paint his neighbour across the street is by no means a sure qualification for his painting truthfully ancient Greeks and Romans and the heroes of antiquity. Shakespeare painted kings and demi-gods and heroes because he knew how to paint the ordinary men and women of his own day. His foot is sure in heaven and hell because it is also sure in taverns and lanes, and at Warwickshire sheep-shearings, and amongst the roaring mob of the streets.

What a splendid rebuke to modern realism is conveyed in the few hundred lines at the end of the second act and the beginning of the third act of the Second Part of *Henry the Fourth*! First we get the tavern scene at the Boar's Head, a bit of the frankest, most uncompromising realism——the Prince and his fellow-roysterers done to the life with photographic fidelity, but with such a gust and wealth of comic creation ; such vivid, riotous quickening and marshalling of the sordid details and disreputable personages into a masterpiece of jocund, careless, glowing, bacchanalian revelry ; such delightful rough-shod triumph over virtue, morality, respectability, and responsibility, broken in upon only by the grave, compunctious reply of the Prince to Peto's message :

> By heavens, Poins, I feel me much to blame,
> So idly to profane the precious time.
>
> .   .   .   .
>
> Give me my sword and cloak.   Falstaff, good-night !

—such sustained warmth and vigour and joviality as quite redeem the scene from the imputation of mere realism.   What a reproof to the modern clamour for ugliness, vice, and disease for their own sakes ! Every stroke is real life itself, as fresh as if it came straight from the hands of God ; and what a final impression of sane, genial, human existence it leaves ! (Compare, in passing, this tavern scene with the other inimitable picture of the grossest, lowest tavern life, Burns's " Jolly Beggars.")

To return to *Henry the Fourth :* the moment we are out of the Boar's Head Tavern, Shakespeare snatches us up into the third heaven of poetry and philosophy. The wearied, sick usurper, Bolingbroke, addresses his magnificent reproach to sleep, and on the entrance of his counsellors, breaks into the yet more beautiful lament of baffled statesmanship and tired ambition —lines that seem to breathe the final word alike of the king, the poet, the statesman, the philosopher, and the geologist :—

> Oh, God ! that one might read the book of fate ;
> And see the revolution of the times
> Make mountains level, and the continent
> (Weary of solid firmness) melt itself
> Into the sea !   And, other times, to see

The beachy girdle of the ocean
Too wide for Neptune's hips ; how chances mock
And changes fill the cup of alteration
With divers liquors !

"Not much like real life," the modern realist
would say. And a moment or two ago we were
sprawling and rioting in the Boar's Head in the
worst of company ! Pass on, and note in passing
Warwick's speech beginning, " There is a history
in all men's lives,"—pass on—the scene changes—
down we come to earth again—and a moment after
the poet in his fine frenzy has well-nigh shaken off

the loosened globe from her long hinge : [1]

he is quietly back in Gloucestershire, listening to the
silly cackle of Justice Shallow. After the most profound speech of Bolingbroke's, hear Justice Shallow's
discourse on the deepest concerns of humanity !

Shallow. Oh, the mad days I have spent ! And to see how
    many of mine old acquaintances are dead !
Silence. We shall all follow, cousin.
Shallow. Certain, it's certain, very sure, very sure ; death, as
    the Psalmist says, is certain to all ; all shall die.
    How a good yoke of bullocks at Stamford fair ?
Silence. Truly, cousin, I was not there.
Shallow. Death is certain. Is old Double of your town
    living yet ?
Silence. Dead, sir.
Shallow. Dead ! See, see ! he drew a good bow, and dead !
    . . . How a score of ewes now ?

Realistic enough in all conscience, and yet not

---

[1] The splendid defiance in the fifth act of *Sejanus* scarcly rings like
Ben Jonson. Whose were the " second pen " and the " happy genius "
he speaks of in the preface ?

mere realism.   Realism is the mere letter of art that
can never profit without the spirit.   Shakespeare
could paint the sheer, hard, bare facts of life as
truthfully as Zola, and did so paint them, but with
infinitely more suggestion and relation.   But he never
rested in them, or thought them of value in themselves.

It is the same with Turner.   Ruskin has pointed
out what infinite pains Turner took to paint the
exact stratification of rocks, the exact ramification
of the branches of trees and their exact relations to
their trunks.   Yet he only used his knowledge as
Shakespeare did ; he never rested in it or made it
the main end of his painting.   And it was only
when Turner was challenged on the score of truthfulness that Ruskin took up the cudgels and showed
that his pictures were painted with a perfect knowledge of the realistic side of his art.

"For my part, I don't see nature like that," said
a realist, standing in front of a canvas that Turner
had smothered in a tempestuous blaze of lovely
colouring.   "I don't see nature like that," croaked
the realist.   "No," replied Turner.   "*Don't you wish
you could ?*"

V

THE SCIENCE OF THE DRAMA

(Reprinted from the *New Review* for July 1891 by the kind permission of Mr. Archibald Grove)

To ensure immediate success in play-writing only two rules need to be observed : " *Don't fog your audience*," and "*Don't bore them*." And as the latter rule covers the former, the science of successful play-writing may be broadly defined as the science of not boring playgoers. But then playgoers have such widely different tastes, and there are so many thousand different and contrary ways of boring and amusing them !

In England at the present moment our theatre-going public is most heterogeneous in its composition. Every audience in every West-End theatre will be found to contain a large number of persons whose notion of amusement is as delightfully ingenuous as Joe Gargery's when he wrote to Pip, " Wot larks ! " In the same audience will be found a sprinkling of those latter-day super-subtle pleasure-seekers who do not begin to enjoy themselves until the shades of ugliness and dulness have wrapped them impenetrably round. Vain is it to charitably implore these good people not to bore themselves,

when they reply that in boredom is the very avatar
of delight. It is curious to watch these strenuous
efforts to copy those wild asses of the Hebrew
prophet who tried to get nourishment by snuffing
up the east wind.

But leaving out of consideration the extremes of
ignorance and simplicity on the one hand, and of
eccentricity, perversity, and insanity on the other,
and taking a survey of the ordinary, everyday
English audience at the present moment, it is still
almost impossible for a playwright to estimate the
immense variety of tastes, prejudices, and sympathies
he has to encounter and deal with. The Puritan
dread of the theatre is still widely spread and
astonishingly operative, and tends to shut out the
hope of the immediate foundation of a school of
English drama at all commensurate with the strength
and depth and complexity of our national character.
One has only to compare the recent bitter utterances of Mr. Spurgeon about the theatre, his wholesale condemnation and excommunication of the
Church Universal because some parsons go to the
play, with the rebuke he administered to his congre-
gation a week or two afterwards for being too
respectable, and for not winking at anybody on
leaving his chapel on Sunday mornings,—one has
only to compare these two amazing utterances from
the same lips to gauge the terrible depths of
absurdity and unreason into which the Puritan
prejudice plunges its victims. It is true that great
crowds of raw theatre-goers half emancipated from
this prejudice are coming to our plays, but they are
coming timidly and fearfully, with cramped and

narrowed minds and quite infantile judgments in dramatic matters. We have no great traditions amongst our audiences. We were all of us, authors, actors, and playgoers, brought up in a small, feeble, artificial school. It will take many years to establish a sound tradition amongst the great body of playgoers. Again, the lateness of the dinner-hour has squeezed us into a narrow two hours' compass or thereabouts as the average length of a play. And further, the fever and hurry of modern London life, its dull, incessant toil and gloom, have tended to spread abroad the strangely false idea that the one end of the theatre is—not to show us our lives, but—to take us out of them! This view of the stage may be convenient to those writers who will not give long years to the patient observation of life and to the mastery of their art founded upon that observation. And it may also be convenient to playgoers who are equally impatient and careless and ignorant. But its complete acceptance by authors and public is the grave of the drama.

I have hastily recounted one or two of the disadvantages and discouragements that the modern English playwright has to face and suffer from, or conquer if he can. It is pleasanter to turn to the advantages and encouragements. The theatre is very fashionable with the classes; it is immensely popular with the masses. The long years of peace have given abundant prosperity to the country, while the increasing value of time makes it an economy to pack our pleasures into the shortest intervals of our business. If it takes fifteen or twenty hours to read a sensational novel, and only three hours to see a sensational play, the playwright is clearly a benefactor of the same order as the patentee of a time-saving invention. If it be urged that it would be a wiser economy of time to save the three hours also, with the additional beneficial result of setting free the playwright to pursue some such healthy agricultural occupation as breaking stones or hoeing turnips, then the playwright is surely within his right to resent such an impertinence, and to bid the reformer turn his attention to other purely ornamental or wasteful vocations, such as stockbroking, horse-racing, and the promulgation of the tenets of those one hundred and ninety-nine out of our two hundred sects whose doctrines are clearly wrong ; though, dramatically speaking, this last reform would be a withdrawal from English life of its one vital, perpetual, and always present element of comedy. I trust no one will suspect me of jesting on so serious a subject as the English drama. If such a trial as that recent one of the Bishop of Lincoln does not prove the existence of a mysterious law of compensation, amounting to a special providence, whereby the deficiencies and weaknesses of modern English playwrights in the realm of comedy are continually supplemented and remedied by the extraordinary antics of our spiritual teachers, then I think it would be difficult for any one to bring forward a valid proof or a lucid definition of any special providence whatever.

To return. The material prosperity of the English drama was never so great as at the present moment. Such vast crowds have never assembled in so many theatres, and such large rewards of money and popularity have never been showered upon managers, authors, and actors. These crowds are, as I have said, highly composite, being made up of persons of all classes, all ages, all religions, all opinions, all tastes, all grades of general and dramatic education. And they themselves, the final judges and critics of our work, are the subject-matter of it! The wealth of dramatic material in modern English life is prodigious. The dramatist stands overwhelmed before its richness, its variety, its never-ending kaleidoscope. I have just used the word "dramatist" for the first time in this article. The standpoint I have indicated in the last few sentences is rather different from that of the popular playwright. But it suggests the dramatic author's perpetual dilemma, which is this: "How shall I, while writing a play which will be sufficiently popular to bring in at least seven hundred pounds a week to cover my manager's expenses—that is, which shall attract to some extent all these persons of different tastes—how shall I yet preserve that removed attitude which stands quite apart from all their passions and prejudices, and contemplates them as something external and objective? How shall I get the whole body of playgoers or some considerable portion of it to take up, or even to comprehend, this attitude of spectator, which is the true dramatic attitude? They are full of the heat and business of life, they are the actors in the real scene which I am only mimicking; how shall I get them to abdicate their leading parts and step down and become mere spectators?" Imagine this great drama of politics, religion, commerce, philanthropy, marriage, and intrigue, which is being enacted all over England to-day. The only condition upon which a dramatist can make full use of it is that he shall be allowed to stand outside of it, treat the whole of it impartially, and gather around him a large section of the public who will also lend themselves to this true dramatic view. The brightest sign for the future of the English drama is the fact that during the last ten years a growing number of theatre-goers have learnt to appreciate this condition, without which no English drama is possible. We are at present in a state of very rapid transition. But no playwright can say to-day, what I think he might honestly, though perhaps mistakenly, have said ten years ago, "There is not a large enough section of the English theatre-going public sufficiently interested in dramatic art as distinct from mere entertainment, sufficiently adept in that most interesting of all studies, the study of humanity, to make it worth while for a playwright to risk his reputation by attempting to give them a representation of life, instead of the stale devices of the theatre that they are used to and love so well." No playwright can say that to-day. We have abundant proofs that there is a sufficient section of the public justly resentful at seeing the great drama of humanity used only to set off the petty tricks and artifices of the theatre, justly anxious to see the theatre put in its proper secondary place as an exponent and displayer of its great exemplar, the drama of human life. It all lies in that. We can rely, I think, upon a great increase of this advanced and critical body of playgoers. Upon them largely will depend the future of the English drama.

If much may be hoped from the increasing critical power and intelligence and numbers of those playgoers who do know and care, much may also be hoped from the stupidity and carelessness and genial irresponsibility of the far greater number of playgoers who do not know and do not care. In the long run those who do know and love what is right in stage-work will have their own way and will carry the great, careless crowd with them. It is curious to note the recent change everywhere in the expressed opinions regarding the contemporary drama. Such a conception of the drama as is here swiftly sketched, namely, that of a national art, definitely related to the great intellectual movements of our time, dealing largely with large themes and questions of moment, instead of copying certain small, silly or funny temporary aspects of everyday life—such a conception was ridiculed, deprecated, and scouted on all sides six or seven years ago. But in spite of constant opposition and misrepresentation it is being gradually adopted, and its assumption has been at the root of whatever recent dramatic progress has been made.

It will be noticed that I have throughout steadily maintained the necessity of a considerable amount of popular support as the foundation of any possible school of drama. This implies a large amount of concession and compromise at times. The wise statesman does not attempt to make laws too far in advance of the moral and intellectual condition of the people. Nor does the wise playwright forget that play-writing is very rigorously limited in similar respects. This is, as I have shown, the perpetual dilemma of the dramatist. Play-writing only exists by virtue of immediately pleasing a large section of the public. If it does not do this it has no *raison d'être* whatever. There are many disadvantages and limitations in casting a work of imagination in the form of a play. The one great advantage is that it can be instantly exhibited in the most striking and vivid manner to the populace. Apart from this, it would have far greater chances, and allow its creator a far larger intellectual sweep and flexibility, in another form. Let any playwright, whose vats are bursting with an immortal vintage too good to be tapped at once by some tolerably large section of the public, be earnestly counselled to bottle it and cork it up for posterity in some other than the dramatic vessel.

Shakespeare and Molière are the greatest dramatists of their nations. They are, and were, also its most popular playwrights.

> The fault, dear Brutus, is not in our stars,
> But in ourselves, that we are underlings !

I believe it was understood that this paper would deal chiefly with the technical and mechanical side of play-writing. And I started it with some such intention. But the larger issues at stake carried me aside, and I have not been able to return to my original subject. And it is really of far more consequence that these larger issues should be stated and understood, than that the mere petty details of the craft should be exhibited, to nobody's great delectation or instruction. The practical side of carpentering is to be learned by apprenticing oneself to a master-carpenter for seven years and working at the bench. At the end of the time doubtless much remains unlearned. The practical side of play-writing is to be learned by watching the same plays night after night, and continuing this drudgery for twice seven years. At the end of the time much will remain unlearned. So it was hardly likely I should be able in the limits of this paper to deal exhaustively with the technique of my art. I hope I shall be forgiven for dwelling on another side of it, which should be of far greater importance and interest.

" I place the Stage next to the Church," said a lady to me the other day.

" Why put it second ? " I asked.

VI

THE LITERARY DRAMA

(A REPLY)

(Reprinted from the *New Review* for January 1892 by the kind permission of Mr. Archibald Grove)

UNDER the above heading in the December number of this Review Mr. H. D. Traill took thirteen pages to prove that no such chimera has ever existed. The Greek drama was not drama in our sense of the word, while in all other dramatic schools, from Shakespeare and the Elizabethans to Dumas and Pailleron, the literary and dramatic elements in a play have never been fused : they have only been superposed. " He who says ' literary drama ' says ' picture-statue,' says ' flat-relief,' says ' miniature-fresco,' or connects in a kind of centaurine union any other two mutually exclusive forms of art."

Finally, in a parable, we poor modern dressers and jerkers of the puppets that fret their little hour upon the English stage of to-day, are bidden to be satisfied with our mechanical skill in constructing and exhibiting our marionettes, and not to try and shove in amongst our betters, the poets and essayists. In the earlier part of his essay Mr. Traill seems disposed to allow to play-writing the dignity of an art ; but having triumphantly slaughtered the pretensions of Shakespeare, Congreve, Goldsmith, Sheridan, Hugo, Augier, and Dumas, and finding himself confronted with nothing but the wretched corps of living English playwrights to do execution upon, he becomes possessed with a benevolent contempt corresponding to the abject appearance of his adversaries, and tells them to rest in their " mechanical skill and the contemplation of their money-takings."

If Mr. Traill had confined his criticism to those modern English plays that have recently appeared in print, he might possibly have made out a good case against the aspirations of the modern English drama to call itself " literary." Though, indeed, the play that provoked his article, *The Times*, gave me a very keen delight in witnessing it, and I read it afterwards with far more pleasure than I have read some of the Elizabethan and Restoration plays which are yet accounted good literature.

But Mr. Traill will have it, not merely that the modern English drama is not " literary " at present, but that it never has been, and never can be. I propose first to examine the arguments whereby he seems to convince himself that we have never had a literary drama. The two most obvious English pretenders to be literary dramatists are Shakespeare and Sheridan. Their claims examined and dismissed, the rest of the fry are easily disposed of.

Mr. Traill makes the astonishing statement that of Shakespeare's plays only eight will draw money audiences, viz. *Much Ado about Nothing, The Merchant of Venice, As You Like It, Richard the Third, Hamlet, Macbeth, Othello,* and *Romeo and Juliet.*

Mr. Phelps actually put on thirty-four of the thirty-seven reputed Shakespearean plays, and retired honourably, if not with a fortune, at least with greater financial credit than attends the close of more than half of modern managerial careers. A very large fortune has recently been made by *The Winter's Tale*, while *The Taming of the Shrew* has also drawn large money audiences. On the whole, one would be well within the mark in saying that fully one-half of Shakespeare's plays are actable to-day, and under favourable circumstances will actually make money for the manager. Of what modern playwright's revivals can so much be affirmed? Mr. Traill says, " It must surely be a little disconcerting to the believers in the literary drama to reflect that the most ' literary' of all dramatists is far from being the most successful." On the contrary, I can say that Shakespeare still draws more money than any living playwright, and is more frequently played than any of them. " Compare," says Mr. Traill, " Shakespeare's record with the record of the late Mr. Dion Boucicault." Very well, let us compare it. They were both successful authors in their day ; both wrote for their own immediate public, and both were well rewarded for it. And when Mr. Traill reminds successful modern playwrights of Milton's five pounds for *Paradise Lost*, it is surely just to remind Mr. Traill of Shakespeare's comfortable fortune made out of popular play-writing.

In October 1889 Mr. Dion Boucicault's plays were sold by auction. The whole of the rights of fifteen plays realised £586 : 5 : 6, an average of

£39 : 1 : 10 each play, the highest play being sold
for £152.   Probably the average length of copyright in the plays would be about twenty years.
The copyright of *Hamlet* alone for twenty years
would be worth several thousands of pounds.   If a
new actable tragedy of Shakespeare's, worthy of
being placed alongside the great four, were to be
discovered, it would be worth a fabulous amount in
acting rights.   A posthumous play of Boucicault's
would scarcely find a purchaser.   And Shakespeare
has been dead nearly three hundred years.   What
will Boucicault's plays be worth in three hundred
years ?   Or, for the matter of that, the plays of any
of us ?   Across what tenantless and silent Sahara
will our dust be blown, or in what iron hills of oblivion will our bones lie sealed, when the buds grow
red and " mild winds shake the elder brake " in the
April of 2200, *Romeo and Juliet's* six-hundredth
spring-time ?   I assure Mr. Traill that the acting
rights of Shakespeare's plays, if they could be
secured, would be valuable to-day out of all comparison with Dion Boucicault's.   So much for the
money test.   I dealt with it first, because I longed
in passing to salute the holy, comforting, *bourgeois*
doctrine that the universe must be eternally right if
our own shop is prosperous.

To come to the literary test.   Mr. Traill quotes
certain speeches, such as the Queen Mab speech, the
Seven Ages speech, the Sleep speech from *Macbeth*,
and he says, " These are not dramatic ; these are not
the characters speaking ; it is Shakespeare himself
speaking, with a disregard of dramatic propriety as
sublime as the poetry he pours forth."

Yet in representations of the plays these speeches are invariably listened to with the deepest attention, and generally secure the warmest applause of the evening. Whether or not they are dramatic, at least they have the sovereign theatrical merit of not boring the audience. Of course they are not realistic. They are not exactly what would have been spoken on the occasions. All through his article Mr. Traill insists on the necessity for absolute realism in stage-work. He even rates Shakespeare for not being a modern realist. Pressed home, Mr. Traill's argument is, "You must be absolutely realistic ; nobody in real life ever did talk literature ; therefore you can never be literary." Now, if one comes to absolute realism, it does not exist on the stage or in any other art. If Mr. Traill would read Dion Boucicault's plays he would find that their serious passages are in *fact* as little like what would really be spoken as Shakespeare's, while in *truth* and *suggestion* and *power* there is of course no comparison. Comedy scenes both in Shakespeare and Boucicault are frequently an almost exact reproduction of real life. Any one who practises writing for the stage very soon becomes aware that in writing comedy, which busies itself with the infinite littleness and emptiness of human life, quite different methods and conventions have to be observed from those observed in writing tragedy, which employs itself with the immense importance and meaning of human life. There is a wonderful instance of the juxtaposition of these two methods (or perhaps they are moods rather than methods) in the closing scene of the second act and the opening scene of the third act of the

Second Part of *King Henry the Fourth;* [1] but any reader of Shakespeare will recall a hundred examples.

To return to Mr. Traill's instances. Are the Queen Mab speech and the Seven Ages speech essentially undramatic? The gay rhetoric and banter of the Queen Mab speech are surely not alien to Mercutio's temperament, and the middle-aged philosophy of the Seven Ages is surely most suitable to Jaques and the place and the occasion; while the splendid Sleep speech in *Macbeth* is one of those things that make it a great tragedy, and not a vulgar facsimile of a murder on the artistic level of the exhibitions in Madame Tussaud's Chamber of Horrors.

"But it is not dramatic," says Mr. Traill. Then nothing can be dramatic that is not realistic. But is this so? Do not these speeches lift great actors to great heights of passion that could never be scaled by realistic language? Could any exact reproduction of the actual words likely to be used on such occasions image forth the volcanoes and whirlwinds and maelstroms of Lear and Othello? To take the first instance that occurs:

> Had he a thousand lives, my great revenge
> Had stomach for them all.

Would it be more dramatic to say, "If I catch the blackguard I'm damned if I don't kill him," which is something like what would actually be said on such an occasion? Are the love scenes of the late Mr. T. W. Robertson and the late Mr. H. J. Byron more "dramatic" than the love scenes in *As You Like It* and *Romeo and Juliet?*

[1] See *ante*, pp. 89-91.

To sum up on all that portion of Mr. Traill's article which deals with the literary drama of the past : I think if he will carefully examine the matter he will come to the conclusion that he has unwittingly tumbled into the realistic fallacy. And the realistic fallacy, pushed to its logical conclusion, denies the necessity of any art at all. Its championship is what we expect from the average modern young man, but not from an Oxford scholar.

I come to that part of Mr. Traill's article which denies to poor living playwrights any pretensions to be artists at all, and places their vocation on a level with the Punch and Judy man in the street. The attitude of literature towards the modern drama is very amusing. Nearly every man of letters in England has written, or is writing, plays, and not one has succeeded. And thereupon literature belabours the modern stage, and pours contempt upon it and upon those who are practising upon it. What if the modern stage retorted upon modern men of letters with the following simple equation ?

The intellectual force which Mr. Eminent Man of Letters puts into his play $=$ The intellectual force which the same Mr. Eminent Man of Letters puts into his poetry and essays.

But

with this amount of intellectual force Mr. Eminent Man of Letters produces a play which, both as literature and stage-work, is immeasurably inferior to the average work produced by current playwrights.

Therefore

writing a play is an intellectual operation which is incomparably more arduous than writing poems and essays upon which a goodly literary reputation is built.

If it be said that my second proposition cannot be sustained, I can refer objectors to the managers of London theatres. It is common to hear London managers speak of the quite childish plays sent in by men bearing names of high repute in literature. Doubtless their failure is to some extent due to a want of knowledge of stage-technique. But I am convinced it is far more largely due to a lack of that vivid and intense power of imagining, realising, and condensing which is necessary to success in drama. And I claim that this power or faculty is an intellectual one, and, if Mr. Traill will allow me to say so, that it is not quite of the same order as the power and faculty required for the successful exhibition of marionettes. It will be noted that I have not claimed that it is a " literary " gift or power. To thoroughly inquire into the literary possibilities of the modern drama would require far more space and time than I have at my disposal. Of course it all depends on the exact definition and limitations of the term " literary." In Ben Jonson's *Bartholomew Fair* the rawest and rankest slang of the day is freely used. Yet I suppose the play, and many of the Elizabethan dramas where the same thing occurs, would not be denied a place in English literature. It is sufficient for my present purpose if it is conceded that the art of writing modern English drama is, or should be, an intellectual art. For if it is intellectual it can scarcely be utterly devoid of literary form. It is impossible to imagine a drama of high intellectual excellence that shall not be to some extent "literary," as it is impossible to imagine a drama of high "literary" excellence that shall not be a work of intellect. I am not juggling with words. My only desire is to obtain some recognition and definite status for the art of play-writing. The *Times* has lately given three columns and a half to the eulogy pronounced by a French statesman on a recently-deceased French dramatist. How strangely different is the status of the playwright in England! Any effort to claim an intellectual standing for the art that represents, or should represent, the whole of our national life, is met on this side of the Channel not only with the jeers and hootings of the uncultivated, but is also derided and frowned upon by men of culture like Mr. Traill. Surely the best, perhaps the only, safeguard against the success of all kinds of bunkum and clap-trap on the English stage is the custom of publishing our plays. We may not as yet have written plays with a distinct literary "note," but the knowledge that we shall be "read" as well as "seen" must tend towards the cultivation of a literary form. Yet the recent publication of certain plays has met with curious antagonism from the most unexpected quarters. Mr. Comyns Carr, in a letter to the *Speaker*, has ridiculed and belittled the practice. Says Mr. Comyns Carr: "There is something almost 'suburban' in this feverish desire of our playwrights to be literary." I was at first unable to understand Mr. Carr's use of the word "suburban" in this connection. It seemed to me a strangely infelicitous term to apply to an attempt to bring some kind of style and form into the art of play-writing. " Suburban," when it is not used in its strictly derivative sense, means " raw, formless, straggling, unfinished." And I was much puzzled by Mr. Comyns Carr's choice of the word, till a certain minor philosopher assured me that " suburban," in Mr. Carr's sense, has no relation whatever to the subject under discussion, but is employed to indicate a condition of intense mental and artistic self-importance in the person who uses it. The mere mention of the word " suburban " in this sense at once does away with the necessity for argument.

It is only in the drama that one is counselled to go down to the crowd and cram them with any rubbish that they clamour for. It is not so in music, or in painting, or in any of the other arts. We should think it strange if, because of the immense circulation of the *Family Herald*, the *Sunday at Home*, and *Tit-Bits*, it was denied that there was or could be any such thing as English literature. We should think it strange if, because of the success of some music-hall song, it was denied that there was such a thing as the art of music, and musicians were advised that the conditions of musical composition were such that they had better resign all ambition and drench the mob with street melodies. We should think it strange if, on account of the vogue of some gaudy chromo-lithograph, painters were advised that their art was a wretched thing, not worthy of an instant's thought beyond the money that could be made out of it. No, it is only the playwright who meets with such eccentricities of criticism and advice.

And the mischief is that there has been just sufficient truth in such criticism to give it currency.
English play-writing *has* largely been an affair of
mob-verdicts, of picture-posters, of big capital letters
in advertisements, of sitting on bandboxes, of sensation and trickery of all kinds. But if it is still
difficult to draw the line between dramatic art and
popular amusement, yet that line is growing more
and more definite. A large section of the public is
palpably dissatisfied with the old theatrical tricks,
the childish unrealities, the feeble prettiness that
amused the last generation, and is demanding from
its playwrights that the English drama shall be a
faithful picture of the realities of life, and shall
traffic in a large way with the large issues that are
shaking mankind. There are, of course, immense
forces ranged in favour of theatricality and convention. The strange thing is that an English playwright should be called upon to combat these forces,
inch by inch, for dear life ; that instead of being
allowed to pursue his calling with a sure feeling that
his work will speak for itself, he should be obliged
to take up arms perpetually for the mere right to
shape his work as he pleases, and to have control of
that for which he is compelled to accept the responsibility.

It will be noticed that I have not contended in
this latter portion of my article that our modern
English drama is " literary " in the sense in which
the Elizabethan drama is literary. How far it can
be a literary product is a matter for future discussion. But that it has literary possibilities quite
equal to the modern French drama cannot be denied.

And if we can engage the best intellects of the day to take a delight in the drama as an art instead of a mere pastime, there is no limit to its influence and scope. Fortunately, a wider sphere seems to be opening for the modern drama. The very gallery boy is beginning to perceive that all this trumpery clockwork of mechanical situation and theatrical device is utterly lifeless and barren, and has no more to do with reality than the toy men in a child's Noah's Ark.

The real question at issue is between the theatre and the drama. Shall the theatre bend the drama to its service and force it to remain servile, inoperative, childish, formal, conventional, the after-dinner bauble of the upper classes, the silly police-romance of the pit and gallery? Or will the drama be able to say to the theatre : " No, human life is a larger thing than the theatre, and the theatre can be powerful only in so far as it recognises this, and allows the chief things in a play to be not the cheap, mechanical tricks of the playwright, the effective curtains, the machinery of cleverly-devised situations, but the study of life and character, the portraiture of the infinitely subtle workings of the human heart."

Our best hope is that a larger and larger section of the public is beginning to find out this truth. And perhaps by and by we may be able to convince even the gentlemen in the gallery.

Briefly, the modern English drama needs to be established on a sound intellectual basis first, and then we may begin to ask ourselves what literary adornment may be employed upon it. But in the meantime eminent literary gentlemen must not be contemptuous of those who are fighting a tough fight against all the giant forces of theatricality, conventionality, indifference, jealousy, folly, and ignorance, that they may gain a little secure foothold where the art of portraying our national English life can be practised without the terrible necessity of immediately pleasing the first big, ignorant crowd. We may not succeed. The English theatre may drop back into imbecility, impotence, disrepute, and paralysis. But if it has any future as an art, if it ever becomes operative in the life of the nation, it must come the way I have indicated. It cannot *grow* towards conventionality, towards tricks, towards violent and outrageous situations, towards stage-device and illusion. There's nothing but death before it that way. If it lives and flourishes, if it *grows* as an art, it must draw its nourishment from the spiritual and intellectual forces of the nation, not from the stale air of the footlights. And the English drama is beginning to tap these great reservoirs and to find nourishment there. And its enemies and false friends rage. But it holds its way.

[I have been invited by Mr. Henry Arthur Jones, with his usual courtesy and friendliness, to re-read the foregoing article and make such comments on it as it may suggest to me. This offer of a reply is a generous one, and the temptation to accept it is great. But I feel that to endeavour to re-argue my whole case within the limits of a couple of pages would be hardly doing justice to myself, while to exceed these limits would perhaps be doing something less than justice to Mr. Jones's readers. On the whole, the briefest possible re-statement of my position seems the utmost I can attempt.

Let me begin, then, by admitting that the theses which I propounded and undertook to defend in the article to which the foregoing is a reply was, designedly and for a sufficient reason, a little too broadly stated. If you wish to combat a theory to any purpose, you must " draw " its advocates; and to do that it may be advisable to go somewhat further than would otherwise be prudent in your attack upon it. It was with this motive that I insisted, in terms more absolute than were warranted, on the completeness and continuity of the divorce of literature from the drama. To affirm, or at any rate to imply, as I perhaps came near to doing, that the strongest dramatic and the highest literary effects are *never* combined even in Shakespeare, is no doubt to approach perilously near to paradox ; and Mr. Jones had only to open his *Othello* to light on a refuting passage. Nevertheless I still maintain that the combination in question is comparatively rare even in Shakespeare, and I hold as firmly as ever by the less sweeping proposition that nearly all the greatest Shakespearean utterances are heard at moments when the path of poetry diverges most distinctly from that of drama, and when the poet, to our eternal gain and gratitude, has followed the former. And I repeat that this is proved by the fact that these are the very passages which are the most remorselessly " cut " in representation, and that even when they escape the blue pencil of the stage-manager, the actor shows his sense of their want of dramatic fitness either by slurring them over altogether, or by delivering them in a manner as glaringly inappropriate to the poetic spirit which animates them as it is undeniably appropriate to the dramatic emotion of the scene.

In the prose play the divergence between the literary and the dramatic form of expression is of course less marked. There literature and drama undoubtedly meet oftener, and continue longer together, in the same regions of thought and emotion, and share a much larger common vocabulary. But two languages do not become one in mere virtue of the fact that their respective dictionaries contain a certain number of identical words; and I still contend that literature and drama speak not one language but two. Near the end of his reply Mr. Jones somewhat shifts, or appears to shift, his position, and says that he "has not contended in this latter portion of his article that our modern English drama is 'literary' in the sense in which the Elizabethan drama is literary; but (he adds) that it has literary possibilities quite equal to the modern French drama cannot be denied." But it can be denied; and I do deny it. I maintain that it has been otherwise willed by that fate or fortune which determines the history of languages, and which has in the course of the last three centuries carried colloquial English — by which I mean not slang and slipshod, but the speech of the educated Englishman who seeks to express himself with as much accuracy as will escape pedantry, and as much force as stops short of the rhetorical—to a far greater distance from literary English than that which divides, if indeed any does divide, colloquial from literary French.——H. D. T.]

[I should be treating my guest with rudeness if I inquired what are the "greatest" Shakespearean passages which are "remorselessly 'cut' in representation." I will therefore content myself with saying that I cannot recall them. I can cordially agree with Mr. Traill that many of Shakespeare's *sweetest and most beautiful* passages (such, for instance, as the famous one beginning " O Proserpina !" in *The Winter's Tale*, and the "temple-haunting martlet" speech in *Macbeth*) do not get over the footlights with any effect.

I think, however, if a strict examination is made, it will be found that the fusion of drama and poetry is tolerably constant throughout Shakespeare, and that, in what are generally allowed to be his "greatest" speeches, as a rule the "greater" the speech, the more complete is the fusion. It is true that this fusion of drama and poetry is, as Mr. Traill observes, very "rare" in literature ; but this rarity arises from the truth which I am trying to enforce, namely, that dramatic work of all kinds demands that the furnace in which it is cast shall be heated sevenfold, to a very Nebuchadnezzar's white-heat, before that necessary fusion can take place which binds in one perfect golden image for ever the utterance of the writer and the utterance of his character. If any one doubts this let him make experiments. At bottom the dramatic " cry " is the lyrical " cry " uttered from the depths of another soul.

It will be allowed on all sides that Shakespeare was poetic. If he were not also dramatic throughout, how comes it that he has so hidden himself in his characters that we know next to nothing of him, and never see him except by a blurred side-reflection? How much we should know of Byron, of Burns, of Wordsworth, of Shelley, of Tennyson, even if we had nothing but their poems to know them by !

However this may be, I can only tender my grateful thanks to Mr. Traill for having honoured my book with his reply. And I may also express my great satisfaction that scholars and critics of his standing are beginning to occupy themselves with the modern acted drama.—H. A. J.]

VII

THE BIBLE ON THE STAGE

(Reprinted from the *New Review* for February 1893 by the kind permission of Mr. Archibald Grove)

THE Apostolic distinction between things lawful and things expedient may be conveniently called to mind in considering the suitability of representing Biblical characters and incidents on our stage. Those who deny its lawfulness must either prove that the Bible has no relation whatever to men's lives and conduct, in which case it lies outside the dramatist's concern ; or they must show reason why this great storehouse of human experience, of man's joys and sorrows, loves and hates, hopes, fears, and aspirations should be locked to the dramatist and freely opened to the painter, poet, and musician. It is useless to answer that virtuous dwellers in Peckham and Camberwell would be shocked if moving stories such as those of Saul, David, Joseph and his brethren, Jacob and Rachel, Esther and Vashti, the Prodigal Son, and many others, were worthily put upon our boards. For this answer only provokes the further question as to what is the value of the notions of Peckham-cum-Camberwell upon any art matter whatever. Our English drama sprang from mystery-plays, which were quite widely

allowed without any thought of irreverence. And virtuous persons from Peckham and Camberwell might
even to-day quite conceivably stuff their heads with
prejudices against religious pictures and religious
sculpture and religious architecture—as indeed their
ancestors did—as stuff them with prejudices against
religious stage performances. It is not a matter of
judgment or reason, it is only a matter of prejudice.

Throughout that great perpetual comedy which
the Spirit of the Universe provides for the infinite
delectation of his elect in the present condition of
religion and religious affairs and professors in England;
throughout that constant succession of most varied
scenes, here a Bishop of Lincoln judgment, and there
an epileptic dance to General Booth's pipes and
tabors ; here a churchyard riot over a dead Dissenter,
and there low comedian Spurgeon railing at the
stage ; at one moment a Church congress fixing its
barometer at rain or fine, and piously imagining that
it regulates the weather; at another Mr. Gladstone
and Professor Wace swallowing the whole herd of
Gadarean swine with the ease of a conjurer swallowing a poker — O my brother Englishmen, do step
out of the ranks for a moment and look at this
medley, motley rout of your own notions and whims
that you have deified and called by the name of
religion ! Do look at yourselves ! See what tricks
and antics you are playing before High Heaven !—
throughout all this whirling march of fantasy, and
humour, and comic incident, beyond all conception
of playwright's brain, no group gives a keener relish
to the cosy observer than the group of British art
and literature blessed and anointed by the dew of

British Gospel grace and the oil of British godly
zeal!

It never could be to the advantage of the English
drama to make one of that group and get itself
blessed and anointed along with the religious
magazines and religious etchings and engravings.
Though doubtless there would be a huge harvest
of wealth and popularity to be reaped if by chance
our great religious public took to saving its soul
through the medium of religious melodrama as it
now saves its soul by means of cheap religious prints
and serial stories in the *Sunday at Home*. One cannot contemplate such a development of our theatre
without a shudder. But though it would be a great
pity if our stage became an additional grotesque apparatus for saving souls, I see no reason why a drama
founded on one of the Biblical themes I have named,
or on kindred ones, should not be done at one or
two of our best West-End theatres—that is, done
from artistic motives, and without any suspicion of
saving anybody's soul in the matter. Not that I
object to people saving their souls, even at the theatre
if they wish, but there are different ways of doing it,
and I would prefer not to save mine through the
medium of religious chromo-lithographs, or religious
magazines, or religious melodramas. I do not say
I would rather be damned, but I would make it a
matter of careful deliberation.

In the present state of public taste there would
be very grave danger that a religious drama, if it
were successful at all, would thrive for the same
reasons that have made certain religious pictures
a permanent London institution. I am considering

the danger to art, not the danger to religion. Religion never can be in any danger. One might as well try to do something to help gravitation as to help religion. As if any of us could escape from it!

So far as doctrines and dogmas are concerned, the stage need not for a moment trouble itself about them. The drama has a larger sway and sphere than any doctrine or creed, a more instant and piercing appeal to the heart.

In presence of the great verities of the soul, in presence of such tremendous issues as are raised in *Faust* and *Macbeth* and *Agamemnon*, all the cobwebs that were ever spun by priests to veil the Infinite are blown into air and nothingness. Zeus or Jehovah, Prometheus or Christ, Buddha or Mahomet, Satan or Furies, Calvin or St. Francis, Newman or Wesley, Rome or Jerusalem, Westminster Abbey or Little Bethel—the drama neither defends nor decries them, neither affirms nor denies them, neither blesses nor curses them, but uses them as it wants them, accepts all their shibboleths, gives them currency, and smiles at them. The drama has to do with realities, not with words. What has Shakespeare to do with the Reformation? What has our modern drama to do with the stale, withered husks that our two hundred sects fodder themselves on?

But I see no reason why the great human stories of the Bible should not be utilised on our stage. I am speaking here with the utmost reverence for a Book, or rather Books, which I have dearly loved and constantly studied from my childhood, which have been my classics, and which will, I hope, when our nation has purged its eyesight so as to be able to understand them, continue to be " a master light of all our seeing." It is with the greatest love for these Books that I hold it to be quite lawful to treat certain of their stories upon our modern stage. Lawful, I say—the question of expediency is one that must be applied to each individual case as it arises. The English theatre could not possibly make a worse use of the Bible than the sects have done, or misunderstand it so completely.

VIII

THE FUTURE OF THE ENGLISH DRAMA

(Reprinted from the *New Review* for August 1893 by the kind permission of Mr. Archibald Grove)

WHAT will be the future of the English drama? What will be its near future — the future that depends on the authors, the actors, the audiences, and the critics of the day? Will it have a larger future in the generations of Englishmen to come? A glance at the last ten or twenty years may perhaps show us where we are going. Twenty years ago a *Westminster* reviewer considered that the drama was virtually a dead art. In the earliest ages it had been the guide and religious teacher of mankind; then it had been his friend and companion; to-day and for the future it could be no more than his bauble. And certainly the English drama of that day justified the reviewer in making such a prophecy. That part of it which was not merely translation and emasculation of the French drama was surely the feeblest artistic product ever brought forth by a great nation. Of the society comedies of last generation it may be said that they tried to represent those aspects of 1864 English drawing-room life which were not worth representing at all. They never concerned themselves with any greater issues than how the daughter of a stage tradesman could be received into the family of a stage nobleman ; their characters had neither sex, nor philosophy, nor religion, nor passion, nor manners. But they used to say funny theatrical speeches. The stronger drama of twenty years ago was mainly derived from the French. But in later years—about 1880—a school of English melodrama arose which held sway for nearly ten years. To-day it seems to have lost its influence and power of attraction.

Briefly, the changes in the English drama during the last twenty years may be summed up as follows :—

(1) We have almost ceased to translate and adapt from the French, and to-day it is as unusual for our leading West-End theatres to play French adaptations as fifteen years ago it was unusual for them to produce original English plays. At the time of writing the Garrick Theatre is the only leading theatre in the West End where a French adaptation is being performed. The Lyceum, Haymarket, St. James's, Court, and Criterion Theatres are all playing original pieces by English authors. To all appearances we shall in the future rely less and less upon the French drama. We may, indeed, claim that at last we have a school of modern English drama.

(2) The dramatic intelligence of our audiences has been awakened during the last ten years, and to-day we appeal to a slightly more intellectual public than did the dramatists of last generation.

The feeble witticisms and puns of that time would scarcely be endured by any single West - End audience to-day. In the last generation the great body of playgoers had not emancipated themselves from Puritan prejudices. They came to the play very timidly, and without any standards or means of forming a judgment on what was offered to them. They came to the theatre as a pastime, as an alternative to the Christy Minstrels or to Madame Tussaud's ; and their general state of mind and intelligence was akin to that of the public who were captured by the announcement that " Rosherville was the place to spend a happy day." With the theatre-going public on this level, there was, of course, no hope for the production of any artistic dramatic work ; all drama and all comedy of a high order were impossible, all serious treatment of life and character was banished. And even so recently as 1884 a storm of resentment and disapproval followed a very mild attempt to place on the stage a study of English Dissenting life. It was held that such subjects were not suitable for the theatre ! We have travelled far the last ten years. This improvement in the intelligence, and in the critical faculties, and in the insight and judgment of the great playgoing public is, I think, likely to continue in an increased ratio. There is almost certain to be within the next few years a decided raising of the standard of dramatic entertainment all round.

(3) The distinction between the theatre as a funny entertainment and as a mirror of life—that is to say, the distinction between popular amusement and dramatic art—has been gradually growing

more and more definite. The one important fact for an English playwright to recognise to-day is this, that in the midst of the vast, heterogeneous, careless, indifferent mob of playgoers and amusement-seekers we have a smaller but yet considerable circle of cultivated and intelligent playgoers who are interested in the drama as an art and as a study of life. At last, after years and years of preaching, of coaxing, of criticising, of discouragement, of baffled effort, of abuse and misrepresentation, those who have been fighting the cause of dramatic art as opposed to popular amusement can claim that they have won the day. This smaller section of cultivated playgoers is likely to be largely reinforced from the greater public. As playgoing becomes more and more of a national habit, playgoers will find more and more amusement and interest in watching a study of life rather than in following a funny entertainment. And although it is possible to-day even in the stalls of our best West-End theatres to meet with otherwise intelligent and cultivated people who have as rudimentary notions of wit and humour as the before-mentioned Olympian deities, yet the process of cultivation is likely to continue, and we shall find larger and larger audiences to whom strong and serious work will appeal with certainty of instant recognition.

(4) Whilst this line of severance between dramatic art and popular amusement has been made more definite during the last few years, there has been a concurrent movement in the opposite direction, and the music-halls have made more and more successful invasions of the theatres. Thus, while

some half-dozen West-End theatres have established themselves as homes of dramatic art, many of the other theatres have lent themselves to the encroachments of the music-hall and variety entertainment. So popular, indeed, did the music-hall become last season that some of our leading critics were afraid that its attractions would supersede those of the theatre, and drive the drama out of the field. But such fears are quite groundless, and already the attractions of the music-hall for the fashionable world are on the wane. The drama stands in no permanent danger from the music-hall. No doubt music-halls will continue to be immensely popular with the vast crowds of amusement-seekers. So far as the music-hall entertainment consists of impersonation of character by comedians, it may be recognised as a low and simple and unspecialised form of drama. (I use the word "low" in the biological sense, as the naturalist would apply it to the unspecialised types of life.) There are many clever and popular comedians on the music-hall stage, and they are very justly welcomed upon the boards of many of our theatres. So far as the music-hall is concerned with impersonation, it has no possible line of progress except towards the drama : towards more complex, more specialised, and more heterogeneous forms of dramatic entertainment. In the demand for the legality of music-hall sketches one sees the proper line of development for the music-hall, so far as it is related to the impersonation of character—that is, to the drama. So far as the music-hall is not concerned with impersonation, but with feats of juggling and other entertainments, it has, of course, nothing to do with the drama, and is apart from our subject. But the real line of cleavage to-day is between some half-dozen leading West-End theatres and all the rest of the places of entertainment, call them theatres or music-halls.

(5) I have already touched upon the increased seriousness with which authors and audiences approach the ordinary subjects for stage - plays. Not only have the ordinary subjects been treated in a more serious and daring manner, but many matters that ten or twenty years ago were considered to lie outside the sphere of the theatre altogether have been dealt with during the last few years. In a period of growth and development it is interesting to note how fresh shoots spring up on all sides. It seems likely that the English stage will gradually and successfully assert its right to deal quite fearlessly and impartially with all the questions that are shaking, and vexing, and penetrating the mind of the nation. Religion, politics, science, education, philosophy, are all likely to be dealt with on the English stage during the next generation. While watching this expansion of the British stage and its successful assertion of its claims over all the body, the mind, and soul, and spirit, and heart of man, it is instructive to notice the failure of every attempt to ally dramatic art with the realistic portraiture of disease, and decadence, and physical degradation. There is something irresistibly comic in the loving and painful endeavours made by one or two sincere, well-meaning critics to persuade us that the sordid delineation

K

of the ignoble physical distresses of sordid and ignoble people is the final and crowning aim of dramatic art. In the future of the English drama nothing is surer than that the art of emptying dustbins will be seen to be the art of the dustman, and the art of anointing pustules will be seen to be the art of the hospital attendant, and both of these necessary operations will be regarded as outside the sphere of the dramatist rather than as the chief and desired goal of his most daring ambition. The cult of the sunflower was amusing and harmless; the cult of the toadstool would be offensive, if it were not ludicrous.

(6) The gradual transition of the English drama from a popular amusement to an art has been accompanied by certain correlative changes in the methods of its appeal to the public. No theatre of importance now disfigures our street hoardings by hideous picture-posters, and it is to be hoped that the day is not far distant when the English theatre will be able to entirely dispense with all such distressing reminders of its existence.

I have thus briefly tried to indicate the immediate future of the English drama, and the direction in which it is likely to travel during the next generation. In the next few years it can hardly fail to grow in strength, in authority, in influence, in sincerity, and to make firm its relations with all that is best and soundest in our artistic and intellectual life. It is perhaps unwise to prophesy further. But one cannot help asking whether it will not be a still greater and wider influence in our national life in the generations to come. The more the

Church becomes an archæological museum of fossil dogmas, the less hold and command will it have upon the religion and morality of the nation. If the Pulpit loses its power, will the Drama take its place?

DR. PEARSON ON THE MODERN DRAMA

(Reprinted from the *Nineteenth Century Review* for October 1893
by the kind permission of Mr. James Knowles)

DR. PEARSON, in the wide sweep of his recent prog-
nostications about *National Life and Character*, has
given several pages to the consideration of the future,
or rather the impossibility of any future, that lies
before the drama.   Those of us who are therein
concerned and interested may perhaps be allowed
some feeling of pride at being noticed at all in a
work of such philosophical pretensions as Dr. Pearson's.
Twenty years ago it would have been almost impossible for a philosophical or sociological forecast to
have glanced at anything so trivial as the future of
the English drama.   As well might it have concerned itself with the future of the rag-doll or Noah's-
Ark trade as a possible make-weight in social progress
or degeneration.   It is most gratifying to notice how,
during the last ten years, the drama has been weaving connections with all the roots and supports of
our national life—with science and religion, with art,
philosophy, and literature.   In the present instance
our pride, indeed, is somewhat tempered by the fact
that out of 344 pages Dr. Pearson gives only about

seven to the drama, and that those seven are filled with lamentations over its decline and assertions of its demise beyond all hope of resurrection.

Now it seems to me that Dr. Pearson's is the typical attitude of many cultivated minds towards the drama ; and while such an attitude is general, dramatic progress is much hampered and delayed. Therefore it is worth while to examine carefully Dr. Pearson's statements, opinions, judgments, and conclusions.   He begins well by acknowledging the power that the stage has to vivify and to bring out, as it were, in letters of fire, the meaning and design of the author.   He says: " Hardly any one derives as much pleasure from reading a play as from seeing it well put upon the stage.   Even a very ordinary cast of actors, giving only the trivial stage tradition with no original renderings, will present one of Shakespeare's plays in such a way as to stimulate or instruct a critic."   Excellent !   But then in the very next sentence he goes on to say : " Unfortunately the age is no longer tolerant of work with a high aim."   So far as this refers to Shakespeare it is scarcely true, for Shakespeare's plays have drawn far larger houses and commanded longer runs in this generation than they have ever drawn and commanded before.   They have been the subject of more exhaustive comment, and I cannot think— although this must remain a matter of opinion — that they have called forth less loving or less intelligent appreciation.

But Dr. Pearson continues : " It has become a proverb that Shakespeare spells ruin, and the exceptions to this are where popular actors give the stage version more or less infamously garbled, with such gorgeousness of costume and surroundings that the mind is diverted from the words to the presentation." There is in this sentence a heap of contentious matter, and I think it lays Dr. Pearson open to a charge of grave, though unintentional, misrepresentation. Who has infamously garbled Shakespeare in these days ? The tendency of this age is to restore the text of Shakespeare, to preserve it superstitiously. Shakespeare was, indeed, " infamously garbled" in the days of Garrick, Kean, and the Kembles ; but surely it would puzzle Dr. Pearson to substantiate the implied charge of " infamously garbling " in these days. When Dr. Pearson blames the present gorgeous mounting and lavish scenery, it seems to me that, to a great extent, he contradicts what is surely implied in his first admirable sentence about the stimulation and instruction to be gained from seeing a play " well put on the stage." Evidently Dr. Pearson desires that pieces should be " well put on the stage." But what is being " well put on the stage " ? I think a good general definition would be that a piece is " well put on the stage " when it is so mounted that the scenery and accessories illustrate and sustain the author's meaning, and do not disturb the spectator, either by their inadequacy, poverty, and unsuitability on the one hand, or by their over-elaboration, ostentation, and irrelevance on the other. Dr. Pearson's phrase about " the mind being diverted from the words to the presentation " is, I think, an unhappy one. The only way in which Dr. Pearson could secure that his mind, in a theatre, should not be thus diverted from the words to the presentation would be to shut his eyes. In any stage representation whatever, no matter whether the scenery is good, bad, or indifferent, the mind is constantly playing round both words and scenery. There is a profound significance in the ordinary expression we use in speaking of a visit to a theatre. We always speak of going to "see" a play, never of going to "hear" it. "Have you 'seen' Salvini's Othello?" "Have you 'seen' Irving's Iago?" "Have you 'seen' Tree's Hamlet?" We never go to "hear" a play or an actor. So I think Dr. Pearson quite mistakes the relations that should exist between words and scenery. One would, indeed, desire first of all to hear beautiful language fitly and appropriately spoken with all due emphasis and pause and music. Bad elocution—the slovenly and ignorant management of the voice—is the crying sin of our English stage to-day. How many actors have we who can speak a blank-verse speech so that a critical auditor, hearing it for the first time, can tell what its metre is, and where its lines begin and end, or, indeed, whether it is verse or prose, and not some amorphous jumble of both?

So that, granted it is of the first importance that the author's words should be exactly measured and correctly delivered, yet this alone is not enough: the eye must be satisfied too. Words and scenery should be perfectly married. Now Dr. Pearson, of course, will reply that he wants the play to be "well put on." But to this generation, that means "gorgeous costumes and scenery." Now that we playgoers have become used to these beautiful settings, we should be certainly more distracted and disturbed by their absence than we are by their presence. Any one who remembers Salvini's last performances of *Othello* at Covent Garden will also remember the hideously inappropriate and vamped-up scenery that all through the evening poked fun at the tragedian's grandest efforts, and shrieked at the spectator, defying him to indulge in a moment's illusion. Now better Salvini and his hideous green-and-white modern furniture than a bad Othello and the most perfect *mise-en-scène*. But why not Salvini and a beautiful setting? Surely this would have been less "diverting" in Dr. Pearson's sense. A cavil at gorgeous mounting seems to come more fittingly from a crushed tragedian of the old school than from the lips of a liberal and broad-minded scholar. I am persuaded that if Shakespeare lived to-day he would rejoice in the beautiful illustration of his plays that is now always accorded to them by the better West-End theatres. The chorus in *Henry the Fifth* is surely a safe guide to his desires and aspirations in the matter of mounting a play. Of course elaborate mounting does not absolve the manager from other and perhaps higher duties to the drama ; but the careful and artistic setting which plays receive to-day at the hands of some four or five West-End managers is, I assure Dr. Pearson, most welcome to an author, and I cannot help thinking that it is also a most valuable illumination to the play. Of course the setting of plays to-day is so utterly different from the Elizabethan setting that a revival of a Shakespearean play often necessitates some rearrangement and cutting of scenes. But if I may venture upon what will doubt-

less be called an amazing piece of impudence, here
again I fancy Shakespeare would be very tolerant.
He was a consummate master of stage-craft, and had
the keenest sense of what was effective on the
boards.   But he was far more than this.   In spite
of all their crudities and of their adaptation to wholly
different modes of stage-setting and stage-management, his plays yet remain masterpieces, not, indeed,
of paltry nineteenth-century theatrical device and
trickiness, but of sovereign, constructive, dramatic
skill.   They still contain the best lessons in stage-
craft for beginners.   The design of Sardou is to the
design of Shakespeare as the design of a gimcrack
eight-story boulevard "residence, with every fitting
complete," to the design of a Gothic cathedral.

But in certain respects Shakespeare's plays, being
written for such wholly different conditions, do need
some slight rearrangement and curtailing before they
can be made acceptable to a nineteenth-century
audience—nay, before they can be presented at all.
Will his blindest worshipper assert that, supposing
Antony and Cleopatra were to be represented to-
morrow, it would be more reverent to Shakespeare
to play thirteen scenes in one act with constant
changes and interruptions, and constant noise of
carpenters shifting the scenes and properties, than to
prune and dovetail the act, so that without altering
its drift and main design, the spectators might be
allowed some repose and continuity of interest in
what was set before them?   It is impossible to
suppose Shakespeare is raising any objections in
the shades to what is being done to and for his
plays on the London stage to-day.   Nor would

he, I am persuaded, bring any charge of "infamous garbling" against the later producers of his plays who have thus adapted them to the present necessities of stage representation.

But Dr. Pearson also accuses the present age of being intolerant of work of a high aim because the works of Shakespeare's contemporaries are not placed on the stage. Now how many Elizabethan plays can be put on the stage to-day in a manner that would please even their most fervent admirers? The first condition of any enjoyable representation of any play is that it should be acted to a full house. Whatever other merits a play may have, if it has not this sovereign one of adaptability to the actual stage, of possibility of representation in such a way that its course of action and the motives of its characters shall be clearly intelligible to an audience, its place is not on the boards of a theatre. Now the very great majority of the Elizabethan plays are simply impossible on the boards to-day, with our present development of the art of scenic illustration and costume. They would all of them cost enormous sums and infinite care and patience to produce, and they would draw perhaps one full house of votaries. The second night the theatre would be empty, not because this age is no longer tolerant of work with a high aim, for *Hamlet* is played more frequently, and is on the whole more popular, than any modern play. They would fail to draw because, with all their wild power and beauty, their magic and grandeur, their lightning and music, their incomparable dramatic situations, their stores of passion and poise and clash of character, they so generally lack that sustained harmony and unity of design and that sure, instinctive, impregnable foothold of world-wide morality which make the great Shakespearean plays so universally popular, and assure them their deathless renown as the acknowledged dramatic masterpieces of the civilised world. That is, Elizabethan plays outside Shakespeare fail, or would fail, on our regular stage to-day, and with our present playgoing public, not because of their high and great qualities, but because those qualities are marred and obscured by imperfections in design and puerilities in the conduct of the story. They fail, not because they are too good, but because in certain very important stage qualities they are not good enough. For instance, it would be impossible to put certain scenes in Marlowe's *Jew of Malta* before any cultured English audience without provoking shouts of derisive laughter. But if we are not likely to see any elaborate productions of the Elizabethan plays outside Shakespeare, I think we shall occasionally witness very interesting and creditable performances of some of them. The Independent Theatre gave a performance last season of that most beautiful of all tragedies, excepting only Shakespeare's, *The Duchess of Malfi.* And excellent work is being done by the university students at Oxford every year. They might with advantage turn their attention one year to some Elizabethan play outside Shakespeare. I do not know what impassable limits have been set to their annual dramatic excursions by "strict age and sour severity," but if I am not daring the censure of dread unknown powers I would suggest the performance of one of Massinger's plays. *The City Madam, The Bondman,* or *The Fatal Dowry* would make a very interesting experiment. Indeed, outside Shakespeare, Massinger has left us a series of plays that could be placed on our modern stage with less alteration than those of any other dramatist of that age. There is hardly one of them that has not a succinct plot which so far as structure goes could be easily adapted to our theatre of to-day. Though, of course, as a poet Massinger is not in the first flight of the Elizabethans. I think, in the matter of our old dramatists, I have made a good answer to Dr. Pearson's assertion that " unfortunately the age is no longer tolerant of work with a high aim."

When Dr. Pearson comes to modern dramatic work he shows a delightful confusion of thought and vagueness of accusation which make his judgments quite typical of outside cultivated modern opinion on the drama. On p. 165 he says : " We find that the serious work of modern times is never even regarded. Shelley, Browning, and Tennyson are experimented on from time to time, and put away almost instantly ; Byron's name has not recommended his dramas ; Swinburne has never been tried." Then afterwards he says : " Dramas like *Manfred*, *Luria*, and *Erechtheus* are little more than splendid collections of passages reflecting the subjective moods of the poet." Just so : they are not dramas at all, at least they are not plays. Then why should the age be censured for not producing them ? Shelley, Browning, Tennyson, and Byron do not fail on the stage because they are poets ; they fail because they are not dramatists. One has only to take any chance page of Shakespeare and

note the infinite variety and volume and involution
of *objective* action and character—set forth in poetic
language, it is true, but in language that can be
instantly seized and understood by the man in
the pit—to know why Shakespeare succeeds as a
dramatist and why Byron and Browning fail. And
it is scarcely true to say that Tennyson has failed.
I know of nothing more flattering to the modern
English drama than the intense interest latterly shown
by Tennyson in the theatre, and the pretty, touching stories that are told of his eagerness to win a
success on the boards. His attitude in this respect
differs very much from that of some of our minor
poets, who are never tired of exclaiming how contemptible is that avocation of modern playwright
which they have assayed, and how dirty are those
laurels that they have failed to win. Both attitudes
are, however, equally flattering to the modern drama.

But Tennyson has achieved a very great success
during the last season, and stands a good chance
of being continuously reproduced. There was
" nothing for tears," " nothing but well and fair,
and what might quiet us," in that beautiful death
with his dearly - loved *Cymbeline*—" the play of
plays, which is *Cymbeline* "—by his side. But its
circumstances make doubly poignant the regret that
our great poet did not live to see the production of
Becket and the magnificent impersonation of the
prelate by Mr. Irving. Further, Dr. Pearson says
that the success of Bulwer-Lytton and Sheridan
Knowles " seems to show that the public is really
tolerant of the drama only when it is bad." But
here again Bulwer-Lytton and Sheridan Knowles

succeeded not because they wrote bad poetry, but because they wrote actable plays. And because they wrote fustian literature, they have been found out, and their verse plays are virtually dead on our stage to-day. Mr. Daly's recent revival of *The Hunchback* will surely be the last time such an attempt will be made by a West-End manager of high standing. Indeed, the disrepute of Bulwer-Lytton and Sheridan Knowles to-day is one of the most hopeful signs of the renascence of the English drama.

I think if Dr. Pearson will re-examine his position he will admit that the charges he has brought against the age of intolerance of dramatic work with a high aim are really not to be proved by the facts he quotes, and, indeed, cannot be substantiated at all.

Again, Dr. Pearson seems to think that all great situations have been used up, all great characters exhausted, all great themes treated. This reminds one of the strange fear that haunted John Stuart Mill's early life, that the notes of music being limited to seven, no great future development was possible to the art, but only eternal imitation and repetition. Wagner appeared soon after.

Once more, Dr. Pearson says : " The world everywhere is more orderly and reticent than it was, and less suited to theatrical effects." Perhaps so, and our drama will accordingly follow suit. Already we see a great reduction of gesture and mere ranting on our modern stage, and actors convey their meaning by quieter and subtler methods. But this does not mean the extinction of the drama. Our future drama will doubtless copy the manners and methods of the age : we shall have less gesture but not less feeling, less friction but not less power, less theatrical effect of voice and bearing but not necessarily less drama.

To sum up, I believe that the English drama has never since the days of Elizabeth had such a chance of establishing itself as a national art and as a great power in our national life as it has to-day. Of course very little has been accomplished as yet. Nothing has been garnered yet, and very little has flowered. But the ground has been prepared, and the seed sown. I believe that the work of the last ten years is bound to be immensely productive in the future. The great theatre-going public is no doubt stupid, and careless, and indifferent; but we have to-day a sufficiently large inner public who are keen, alert, discriminating, and highly appreciative and cultivated. And the bigger public is good-natured enough and stupid enough to be led anywhere.

It is most amusing to hear cultivated men like Dr. Pearson, who know neither our difficulties, nor our aims, nor our circumstances, nor how great and many-sided is the stress of the battle we are waging —it is most amusing and most exasperating to hear them talk vaguely and superciliously about the impossibility of any good coming out of that Nazareth, the modern English theatre.

Constantly some of our best literary men do try to write a play for the actual stage to-day, and when they do not succeed they shrug their shoulders and say to their friends, " There ! You see what a contemptible thing play-writing is ! How absolutely it is beneath the notice of any self-respecting man of letters."

The mere technique of a modern English play is as fine as the deftest goldsmith's work. This is quite apart from the dialogue, but without it the best dialogue is of no avail. In all that has been written about the drama of late years I only remember one passage that shows any grasp of the difficulties of dramatic work, or any insight into the relations of dramatic to other literature. This passage is contained in a recent article on Lessing by Mr. T. W. Rolleston :—

The discipline of the drama seems to give, as nothing else can give, a strong, athletic, sinewy fibre to the literature which has passed through it. It is easy to see how this comes about. A drama is a *doing*, an action. Place the poet under the necessity of making the passion with which he deals visible in *action*, and that an action which must strike an audience as natural and appropriate, and it is obvious that the passion is at once submitted to a severe test of its genuineness. Nothing that is artificial and hollow will pass muster here, and no mere magic of expression will avail to hide that hollowness if it exists. Hence the severe psychological study which the drama exacts—the wholesome necessity of keeping closely in touch with fact. Again, mark the conditions under which alone a drama can make a successful appeal to an audience —the variety it demands, and the conspicuous unity of action which it no less strictly demands—what a training in composition is here involved ! Finally, it is an essential condition of the drama that the author shall keep himself out of sight. He must not comment, he must not explain or justify ; he must gain the right moral and the right æsthetic effect by the bare presentation of what his audience will accept as a rendering of Nature. In dealing under these conditions with a great and moving theme, what a power of concentration, what a mastery of expression, what delicacy of judgment are involved ! As a piece of artistic training it has precisely the same effect as it has on a human character to be forced to wrestle with the grim realities of life. To be told " words, intentions will not avail you here—show what you can *do*," is bracing to the strong in the measure of their strength, disastrous to the feeble in the measure of their weakness. And it is the drama above all forms of literary art which lays upon the poet that severe and wholesome ordeal.

I have quoted this passage at length because it really explains the failure of so many eminent literary men to write a play. In addition to the inherent difficulties of all dramatic work, there are just now many passing currents and side-winds of modern public feeling to be understood and allowed for, many shoals and sandbanks of prejudice and cliquism to be left on one side. But land is in sight at last.

NOTE.—What an ironic comment on Dr. Pearson's prophecy, less than two years ago, of a vast and almost universal tropic empire for China, is her present helpless condition at the feet of Japan.

X

A PLAYWRIGHT'S GRUMBLE

(Reprinted from *To-Day*, December 1884)

The highest thing that art can do is to set before you the true image of the presence of a noble human being. It has never done more than this, and it ought not to do less.—RUSKIN, *Lectures on Art*.

FROM my study window the hillside slopes down a quarter of a mile to one of the prettiest and most old-fashioned of Buckinghamshire villages. The red-tiled roofs, subdued by lichen, just overlook the orchard trees, or throw up a brightish-red chimney here and there, where the branches hang low enough to give them a peep, or half or wholly hide amongst the tall spreading elms ; the clean blue smoke lazily smears the deep masses of dark-green foliage ; the noble church-tower, with its " never sere" garland of ivy, rises four-square and dominant above the irregular house-tops, commanding them with its heavenward purpose, as the precepts of its religion command the waywardness and fickleness of human life ; haystacks and corn-stacks dot the shorn fields; all through the year men are pursuing in their turn the healthy primal tasks of tilling and sowing and reaping, those blessed occupations that, as Keats says, Deity delights to ease its heart of love in holding peaceful vay over. The wooded hills shut in a bit of as yet untainted English landscape, not greatly changed, one is pleased to think, during the two hundred and twenty years that have gone by since Milton took refuge here close by, in the time of the great plague of London. There is no railway within five miles; no gas, but plenty of clean air; no water-companies, but plenty of clean water. There is scarcely a view that does not make a picture, and the human life that is framed in this setting has all the outer conditions of health and happiness.

The whole scene is typical of the greater part of English life fifty years ago. A few generations back it would have been impossible to have wandered out from a town and not to have lighted upon many such scenes; in a few generations to come, at our present rate of progress, such a scene and such conditions of healthy human life will be almost impossible throughout the length and breadth of England.

Loftier and stronger and more dulcet voices than mine have raised this cry and have vainly urged Englishmen to save England. Think of it, my countrymen! Thirty millions of us, the richest nation in the world, so rich that twenty-nine millions of us cannot afford pure air or pure water or unadulterated food! English life growing more monotonous and more stereotyped in its dull, weary, mechanical routine every day; as one of your teachers has it, " the higher classes hopelessly materialised, the middle classes hopelessly vulgarised, the lower classes hopelessly brutalised," the insatiable locust of industrialism devouring every green thing, men turned into machines for producing and selling with the most exhausting labour of body and mind all the cheap and worthless produce of modern life ; a whole London Directory-full of us mainly toiling with infinite pains to solve the eternally barren problem of how we can most easily live *upon* each other, instead of asking ourselves the fruitful question of how we can most effectually live *for* each other. Just think what the type of English life threatens to become, and then think of the despair of the playwright who approaches it with Ruskin's words in his mind, " The highest thing that art can do is to set before you the true image of the presence of a noble human being. It has never done more than this, and it ought not to do less."

Those of us who have been at the Health Exhibition this summer may have watched the open admiration of the visitors for the representation of the street of Old London. Dismal dwellers in suburban regions were open-mouthed in their loud praise of the beauty of a street picture that was once as common in England as gas-works and telegraph posts are to-day.—Good folks, with all our vain bluster of money-making this last fifty years, this England of ours is rapidly becoming a very intolerable dwelling-place, except for the lucky few of us. Imagine in two centuries' time a representation of a typical modern English street of to-day, and ask whether it could ever awaken a moment's interest or admiration in any living breast. Unless indeed by virtue of the glorious gospel of free-trade, free and glorious permission to speculative builders to ravage and desecrate England, we shall by that time have reached such a refinement of ugliness and

impotence in architecture, that even our Dalston of
to-day will by comparison shine divinely beautiful,
and our Clapham shed its parting benediction of
hoary loveliness upon a degenerate twenty-first century.

The test of any social state is not its power to
shelter and teem with hopeless, sickly, impoverished,
degraded millions, but its power to produce, in however restricted quantities, average happy, healthy
individuals ; not its power to compel hecatombs of
human organisms into dull, blind uniformity of
ceaseless toil, but its power to allow free men free
development of character and choice of healthy
labour. What can be more striking than the difference between the average Englishman of two generations ago, as any country-bred middle-aged man
can recall him from memories of childhood, and the
probable average Englishman of two generations to
come, the typical Englishman we are menaced with,
when railways and steam tram-cars shall have done
their perfect work, and having provided us with
means of going everywhere at a moment's notice,
shall have left us no longer any place worth going
to or stopping at ?

But perhaps it is more saddening to look upon
the pleasures of the multitude than upon their toils.
On a recent first Monday in August I had the
double misfortune of being out-of-doors on a bank
holiday and at a railway terminus in the east of
London. Crowds and crowds of white, unwholesome
faces, pinched, anxious, haggard, keen with discontent, or jaundiced and petrified with melancholy,
by reason of a ceaseless hand-to-hand fight with

starvation ; plenty of coarse, witless jesting but little real mirth : not one thoroughly merry and healthy English face did I see amongst all those myriads. I saw no real happiness but only fierce anxiety, flurry, restlessness, scrambling and crowding into third-class carriages to be whirled away for a few miles for a few hours from deadening barren toil to deadening barren pleasure—will any one say that these men's grandfathers, at work in some late hay or early harvest field on such an August day fifty years ago, were not happier and healthier and every way in a more enviable condition than their descendants taking their pleasure on this bank holiday? Was not the workaday life of those days better than the holiday life of these?

Are not the types of peasantry that Burns and Wordsworth drew more noble, more manly, more healthy than the type of working man our modern civilisation has created? And still we go about to make the village life of England impossible, and still we glorify the agencies that are turning England into one dull, stifling town, with all the houses alike dreary and ugly, and all the lives that are lived in them alike weary, stale, flat, and unprofitable.

Forty thousand John Brights preaching till they are black in the face the divine gospel of free-trade in useless, unhealthy labour, shall never persuade me that we are journeying towards the millennium on our present track.

How can it be so when each year sees more and more of the country spoiled and devoured and rendered unwholesome for healthy human existence?

The gauge of the value of any human life or

any group of lives is its capacity for heroic art-
treatment. How spontaneously the Elizabethan
drama rose from the national life of England in the
sixteenth century—how spontaneously the brilliant
and corrupt comedy of the Restoration rose from
the brilliant and corrupt court of Charles II ! It is
always to be remembered that Shakespeare inter-
preted ancient heroic life through modern heroic
life—he painted Greek and Roman heroes so well
because he had English heroes ready to his hand.

There is no possible way of weaving great
modern plays unless the playwright be supplied with
the raw material of great modern lives. While the
bulk of English lives are petty and suburban, so too
must remain the bulk of modern English plays.

Where is the playwright to find his models ? Is
he to eschew modern life and evolve some fairy
world and fit it out with unnatural beings from his
own imagination ?

That, doubtless, is a temporary way out of the
difficulty, and an age sick of itself, an age grown
weary of itself, will fly as readily for relief to unreality on the one hand as it will to sensation and
gross realism on the other. But there will never be
any final resting-place for us in unreality, whatever
glamour we may throw around it. Virtually the
only scene and time for any really living drama for
us is England and the nineteenth century—

> Not in Utopia, subterraneous fields,
> Or some secreted island, Heaven knows where,
> But in the very world which is the world
> Of all of us—the place where in the end
> We find our happiness, or not at all !

Yes, and where we find our dramas, or not at all! And there will never be much poetry in our dramas till we put a little more into our lives.

After all, perhaps the worst and most fruitless way a workman can spend his time is in grumbling at his tools, and here is one playwright who has been finding fault with the conditions of his art, instead of resolutely setting himself to discover, amidst all that is unlovely and dull and mechanical in modern society, that secret aspect of beauty and those admonitions of faith which almost every human life that is lived unfolds to the careful searcher—that touching of all our later days, close-pent in the aimless warfare of city-life, with pencillings of the divine light that shone about us in our infancy when, "trailing clouds of glory," we came hitherward "from God Who is our home."

CHALFONT SAINT PETER,
Oct. 1884.

THE DRAMATIC OUTLOOK

(An Inaugural Address delivered to the Playgoers' Club on Tuesday evening, 7th October 1884. Reprinted from the *English Illustrated Magazine* for January and February 1885.)

BEFORE I begin my address I should like to express the pleasure I feel in speaking on the affairs of the drama to such an audience as this. To be a member of this club implies a devotion to the interests of the drama for its own sake, not as an idle amusement for a vacant hour, but as the serious and fine art which has for its end the portrayal of all the varying passions of the human heart and all the chances and changes of life—a devotion which takes practical shape in your constant attendance, oftentimes at great inconvenience, at all first-night performances, and in your discussion of them week after week. But it is not as *lovers* only of the drama that I am pleased to be with you : it is as *judges* also of the drama that I am glad to have an opportunity of talking over its prospects with you. I hail the formation and continuance of this club as a very hopeful augury for the future of the English drama.

The verdicts passed on a new play are often so contradictory and fluctuating, there is so much uncertainty alike in critical and professional as in public taste, that a body of opinion formed by a circle of habitual playgoers after deliberation and debate must be of great value and weight to authors, actors, managers, and the general public.

With so much of a preface, I will proceed to my address; and I will ask you to please forget, and to let me forget, any small efforts of my own, and come amongst you as a playgoer to discuss with playgoers the prospects of the drama, what direction the present movement of public interest is likely to take, and how far it can be governed and controlled, and forced to take a right direction. And I will ask you to forgive me and have patience with me if I am wrong in thinking you would wish me to deal with this matter in the most serious and earnest spirit of which I am capable.

I suppose the first thing that would strike a stranger coming to England to report on the present condition of the drama would be the enormous and ever-growing popularity of the theatre with all classes. I suppose the next thing that would strike him would be the comparative scarcity of original modern plays of high excellence and serious import. (As I shall constantly use the word " serious " throughout my address, I may as well explain that I use it as opposed to " farcical " and " burlesque," and not as opposed to " gay " and " cheerful "—thus, in this sense, *The School for Scandal* is a serious comedy.) Mr. Stopford Brooke says, " With Sheridan we may say that the history of the English drama closes." Mr. Matthew Arnold says, " I see our community turning to the theatre with eagerness, and finding the English theatre without organisation or purpose or dignity, and no modern English drama at all except a fantastical one." Again, "We have in England everything to make us dissatisfied with the chaotic and ineffective condition into which our theatre has fallen. We have the remembrance of better things in the past, and the elements for better things in the future." Mr. George Henry Lewes says, "That our drama is extinct as literature no one ventures to dispute."

It is true that all these criticisms were written some years ago, and in the meantime a tendency towards a better state of things has begun to show itself. But at present it is only a tendency, a symptom, a foreshadowing. And looking to what has actually been accomplished in the interim, it is doubtful whether, in its literary aspect, either of these distinguished critics would see reason to alter his language in speaking of the stage of to-day.

But we need not go to such authorities as those I have quoted for confirmation of the intellectual poverty of the modern drama. It is a matter of everyday newspaper comment that managers cannot obtain satisfactory original plays of home-growth, and it is a fact that the manager of our leading comedy theatre has produced only one original play of English authorship for the last eight years, and is now contemplating a revival of a French adaptation ; while, if at the end of any recent year we have turned to the summary of the plays produced during the previous twelve months, we must have been forced to confess that, though the reapers have been numerous, the harvest of good, sound, ripe grain, fit for the nourishment of human brains and hearts, has been miserably small. I hope you will acquit me of coming to you with any desire to carp and find fault for its own sake. It would be far pleasanter to stand here and prophesy smooth things to you, to congratulate you and the general body of playgoers upon the splendid succession of modern plays you have been privileged to see, and to congratulate my brother authors and myself and our managers upon the splendid sums of money we have put in our pockets; to point to the crowded houses, the enthusiasm, the runs of several hundred nights, and to ask triumphantly, "When has the drama seen such prosperity?"

And indeed there are just now many reasons for hopefulness and congratulation in the condition of the drama, and though there are also many reasons for fear and anxiety, there are none for despair. But while so little has been done and so much remains to be done to place the modern English drama on an equal intellectual footing with its sister arts, to establish an authoritative school of modern English dramatic literature, it would be a fatal mistake to rest in and be thankful for what has already been attained. As yet our hands have barely touched the plough-shafts, and it is not time to chant harvest thanksgivings. No, if we wish really to further this cause of dramatic art in England, I think the best frame of mind for us all—managers, authors, critics, and for you who are the vanguard of playgoers, the tasters for the general public—I say the best frame of mind for us all to get into, and to remain in for some time to come, is a state of wholesome, watchful discontent.

I have spoken of the comparative scarcity of modern original plays of lasting value, and I have also mentioned the cause to which I think this barrenness may be traced—the want of an authoritative school of English play-writing.   I do not mean a large building with titled patrons, and printed rules, and paid professors.   I do not ask for the erection of forcing-houses for English plays.   I only beg for thorough weeding and digging.   We have a school of English poetry, of English music, of English landscape, of English portrait-painting.   In each of these arts there are definite, severe rules and tests of excellence, there is a bar of trained and educated opinion ; and it would be as impossible for a man to win sudden distinction and influence and great wealth upon some utterly worthless piece of work, as it would be for him to produce a work of great merit without receiving something like adequate recognition.

But is there any such security for the reward of conscientious dramatic work, or any such safeguard against the successful perpetration of incompetence and imposture ?   I can only assure you that the success or failure of any piece at any theatre is to all human judgment a complete lottery, and is as impossible to predict as to predict which side a penny will fall uppermost if you toss it into the air. All that one can be certain about is that it will fall definitely on one side or the other : there is no middle course ; either flat success or flat failure is tolerably certain.

It is quite possible that some bit of dramatic quackery may be produced to-morrow, and by virtue

of extensive advertising, or practised stage-management, or sensational scenery, or clap-trap surprise
tricks, or by its containing some vulgar catch-word,
or by hitting some transitory mood or folly of the
populace, or by virtue of some unforeseen but
equally unworthy attraction, may draw all London
to a theatre for a twelvemonth; while it is quite
possible, that by reason of its not satisfying some
unforeseen and perhaps ignoble appetite of the public,
a play of lofty aims and literary workmanship may
utterly fail; though it is only fair to say that a
good play is much less likely to fail than a bad one
is to succeed.

But the success of a bad play works a far
crueller and deadlier injury to dramatic art than the
failure of a good one. The failure of a good play
is at worst a negative evil. Not for a moment need
the author of any sincere and well-attempted work
bewail that it does not take such an immediate hold
upon this great fickle public as is implied in these
days by theatrical success. With the examples
before us of all the great poets who have had to
endure neglect and contempt and evil criticism, what
can it matter that any dramatic work this age is
likely to produce should also have to endure a
season of adversity and censure and misunderstanding, and win its way to immortality, if it win it at
all, by slowly living them down? No, the failure
of a good play is a very small matter. Good work
is eternally recuperative and self-assertive; it cannot be choked or trampled out of life. But the
success of a bad play works far-reaching, immeasurable harm to dramatic art. It confirms the public

in their carelessness and in their natural taste for pretentious, superficial work. It confirms the manager in the hideous belief that pecuniary success can be won only by more and more consulting the more debased taste of his patrons. It confirms some authors in the bad practice of writing down to the public, and it confirms other authors in their despair of ever being able to obtain a hearing for their best work. Worst evil of all, the success of a bad play blocks the way, and makes it impossible for good work to get a hearing. For remember that, while any number of pictures may be painted, and any number of poems published, there can be only a quite limited number of plays produced—that is, produced in such a manner and with such an attention to detail, to stage-management, and to other accessories, as to give them a fair chance of success. We cannot have a greater number of plays than we have theatres of repute to give them a home.

I ask you to consider very carefully the meaning and the causes of this uncertainty attending the production of a play. How is it that when author, manager, and actors have all done their best there remains such a terrible margin of doubt whether all their efforts have not been in vain, and whether the piece will hit, I will not say the taste, but the favour of the public ?

Take the case of a landscape-painter of recognised talent and position. He paints a picture for this year's Academy ; he gets so much money, so much praise, and is criticised in such and such a way. He will paint a picture for next year's Academy, putting into it the same amount and the same quality of thought, and study, and handiwork, and he may safely reckon that he will receive much about the same reward of money and appreciation. He may be a little underpraised or underpaid one year, and a little overpraised or overpaid another year, but there will always remain for steady, conscientious work on a certain level a certain steady average reward that, subject to very slight variations, he can almost certainly depend upon.

But how is it with a dramatic author?

It is most humiliating for any one who has attained any small measure of popular favour to be obliged to confess that immense public success in the drama of to-day may be much more nearly allied to such widely-spread crazes as in recent years have afflicted our nation concerning the fate of Jumbo and Mr. Arthur Orton, than to any worthy kind of renown built on a lasting and solid foundation.

I do not say that any great theatrical success will ever be totally devoid of merit, but I do say that it may possibly have no higher merit than that of tickling vast crowds of pleasure-seekers. As long as theatrical success is doomed to partake in some measure of the nature of a public craze, and is fanned and fostered by such means as keep alive public interest and excitement in ignoble events and catastrophes of the passing hour, so long must the drama forfeit and forget its natural dignity as an art, and descend to brawl and shout in the market-place amongst its brother vendors of quackery, and its brother exhibitors of monstrosity. And so long will authors and managers remain without compass or rudder, without guarantees that bad work will fail, or that good work will succeed.

An author writes a play, and finds, somewhat to his surprise, that he makes the fortune of a manager and the reputation of a theatre ; with the same good intentions and the same level of workmanship he writes another play, and to his much greater surprise finds that he ruins his manager, the prestige of the theatre, and his own reputation. Instead of being tolerably certain of a moderately fair reward for conscientious work, he does not know whether all his months of labour will be repaid only by hisses and hootings, or whether they will bring him enormous applause and profit. I ask whether that art can be in a healthy condition in which its professors and experts are so completely at a loss that they do not know before production whether a play is good or bad, and whether, if it be good, it will succeed ; an art in which everything is so precarious, whimsical, drifting, and uncertain that the final verdict of goodness or badness is registered by some spasmodic and irresponsible impulse of popular caprice. What is the meaning of this uncertainty, this startling inequality in the results and rewards of a playwright's work ? Does it mean that there is no absolutely good or absolutely bad dramatic work ? that there is no such thing as a good play except that which by some lucky accident may hit the unaccountable and momentary fancy of the public, and no such thing as a bad play except that which, by the lack of some happy combination of circumstances, may fail immediately to draw crowds to the theatre ? Are you content that the test of success in the drama shall be an affair in which blind chance and zealous bill-posting shall play the arbiters?

Because if it is so determined, all that one can do is to leave the matter alone, for all that one can say is but a darkening of counsel by words where no knowledge can be obtained.

But I do not think you will rest content in the easy explanation that popular success is the only test of the excellence of dramatic work. I think you will agree with me that there is an absolute good and an absolute bad in play-writing, and that this may be found out with tolerable certainty, and may be maintained in spite of a popular verdict to the contrary—nay, that it is our duty to assert this standard of excellence until we have redressed the present grievous uncertainty and inequality which attends the production of plays, or at least have done all in our power to redress it. Observe how this uncertainty tends to demoralise and disconcert the efforts of authors and managers. The reward for a successful play is very great; there is a prize of perhaps many thousands dangling just above our heads which may be won by months of patient study and labour, but which is just as likely to be won by the execution of some astonishing, sensational somersault.

But what an author who respects himself and his art should desire is not the chance of scrambling in the gutter for a prize of £10,000, but the assurance that his honest work will be fairly valued, and will bring him honest bread and cheese.

Now I think that all who are interested in the drama are concerned to bring about a condition of things where rewards may be tolerably certain and equal, where good work may be fairly assured of instant recognition and sufficient but not excessive remuneration, and where bad work may be always sure of instant condemnation and bankruptcy and transportation to limbo.

In other words, we are concerned to break down the formation of a *ring* of dramatic authorship, and to establish a *school* of dramatic authorship. And this school of dramatic authorship cannot exist until and unless there is a body of educated, cultivated opinion for it to appeal to, and be judged by. While the English public remains capricious and fitful in its judgments, English authors will remain capricious and fitful in their work.

I think the Playgoers' Club may become a powerful instrument in the formation of a body of educated public opinion on dramatic art. You have already enormous power in your incorporate capacity as first-night playgoers. For my own part, I think that power has been in the main wisely and generously wielded. If first-night audiences have been sometimes righteously severe on bad plays, I can remember, and remember most gratefully, certain occasions when they have been, perhaps, more than wisely enthusiastic over some very middling ones. But great as your power is as individuals, I think you may grow to have still greater power in your corporate capacity. When it becomes known that those who take the most earnest interest in the drama have banded themselves together to promote the study of that art, and have resolved to inquire amongst themselves what is a good play and what is a bad one, and why one play is good and another is bad, and having obtained whatever knowledge is available on the question, have resolved to diffuse it, and have raised a certain standard whereby plays shall be judged, and have determined to encourage all sincere, earnest, and workmanlike plays, and to condemn with the strictest rigour all slipshod, insincere, pretentious make - believes of plays—when this becomes known, I do not see how this club can fail to command immense weight for its decisions, or to become an increasing centre of influence and authority upon the questions it deals with. I do not know the exact scope and limit the founders of this club proposed for it ; what I do know is, that if its members are conscientious and alert in the prosecution of its best aims, this Play-goers' Club may become one of the leading forces in changing for the better the whole tone and complexion of the English drama of the future.

Our drama is just now in a state of rapid transition ; it is popular with the masses as a recreation and a spectacle, but it has not won for itself a steadfast position as an art. Fifteen years ago we had a nearer approach to a school of authorship than we have now. What is called the teacup-and-saucer school of the drama was then in the ascendant. When authors and actors had exactly copied and reproduced the littlenesses of social life, they were thought to have attained perfection. Great passions were eschewed, because they were felt to be out of place in a drawing-room. Moreover, it was observed, and truly observed, that in modern life, and especially in polite life, great emotion is studiously concealed and repressed, and conveyed not in poetry, but usually in very commonplace language indeed. Finally, we began to doubt whether there was in modern life any capacity for great passion or emotion. At any rate, if these did exist, it was felt their representation on the stage would be somewhat disturbing to family audiences, and might endanger our placid enjoyment of our elegant teacups and saucers. The essential weakness of that school is found in the fact that it never occupied itself with any greater theme than a contrast of manners between a vulgar, usurping middle class and a decaying aristocracy. This is the keynote of the whole school. Throughout its whole range, humanity has no greater problem to solve, no deeper question to ask itself, than how the prejudices of these two classes can be best soothed and accommodated to each other. The essential strength of that school is found in the improved stage-management, the attention to minor details of accuracy, and the greater air of *vraisemblance* which it has imparted to almost every modern play.

A distinct vein of Mr. Robertson's influence runs through almost every comedy, and even through almost every melodrama that has since been produced; and it was doubtless necessary and helpful to the formation of a future school of English drama that this phase of rendering English life should be passed through. But it is impossible to disguise from ourselves that that school is passing away, and that the next step forward for the English drama does not lie in that direction. It is with the drama as it is with painting: the greatest and worthiest and most enduring things cannot be rendered in exact copy of nature. As Ruskin says: "You can paint a cat or a fiddle so that it may be mistaken for real life, but you cannot paint the Alps in such a manner." So it is with the human passions. Certain commonplace aspects of human life may be rendered on the stage in exact reproduction of real life. Their value or worthlessness in a play will depend upon the dramatist's treatment of them, and upon their juxta-position in his scheme. Certainly the dramatist cannot afford to neglect even the smallest facts of human nature, the most ordinary talk, the most everyday occurrences. For even these, by judicious contrast and blending, may be touched with a sense of eternity, and like some frail, delicate shell imprisoned in the rock, may endure, wrapped round with the everlasting hills.

Thus in Shakespeare, while at one moment we are overhearing the most ordinary gossip of ordinary English life, the next moment we are caught aloft to see all the vast procession of humanity, and all the kingdoms of the earth, and all the hells that lie beneath men's feet. It is this very contrast, this sudden shifting of standpoint, which gives value to the startlingly faithful painting of common, every-day life in Shakespeare.

And unless it is touched with this sense of eternity, wrapped round with the splendour of heroism, and imbedded in what is primary and of everlasting import, the mere reproduction on the stage of the commonplace details of everyday life must always be barren, worthless, and evanescent. Because a thing has happened in real, everyday life, is no reason for putting it on the stage. Humdrum

is one of the infinities. Nothing is so untrue and
so unreal as ultra-realism. You may station yourself in Cheapside, in Regent Street, or in Seven
Dials, and if you are of a discerning mind, you
will probably learn more about human nature in
one single hour than you will learn from a hundred modern plays. The commonest street incident
may give birth to thoughts that " lie too deep for
tears," and suggest as " obstinate questionings " and
as deep perplexities as troubled the soul of Hamlet
or of Job. But that is no reason why a manager
should send his scenic artist to Regent Street or
Seven Dials, and, having provided himself with a
canvas and pasteboard representation of an aspect
of bricks and mortar that is not worth representing,
should then engage a hundred supers to represent an
aspect of humanity that is not worth representing.
No ; there is but one thing that is worth representing
on the stage—the heart and soul, the passions and
emotions of man. All else is secondary, subservient,
useful only as it helps to that end. When a dramatist
has deafened and terrified us with a thousand explosions, he has done nothing ; when he has surprised
us with a situation, he has done nothing ; when a
stage-manager has marshalled his thousand supers,
and drilled them into graceful attitudes and imposing
processions, he has done nothing ; when a scenic
artist has painted for us miles upon miles of Atlantic
Ocean, we are yet unsatisfied, or we should be.
When a dramatist has shown us the inside of any
one human heart, he has done all. I said just now
that the greatest passions could not and should not
be rendered in exact imitation of nature, and that so

rendered on the stage they become valueless and untrue. Nature has endless space and eternal time at her disposal; she can give three-score years and ten to her weaving of a man's life; she can fill in every petty detail and elaborate to its utmost every character. But the dramatist has at most three hours to paint for you a dozen or twenty characters. He has therefore to be vivid, succinct, selective. He cannot show you all the varying aspects and truths of character; he can show you only the most important aspects and the most vital truths. Heroes in real life do not talk in blank verse; they never did. Yet it is eternally true and right for Macbeth and Lear to speak in blank verse, because in this way their characters are aggrandised, dignified, exalted, and dissociated from all that is transitory, mean, and inessential. Macbeth speaking blank verse is far more real, more true to nature, than a modern young man making love on the stage in exact imitation of the way he makes love off the stage. The one is an eternal verity of lasting import and consequence to humanity; the other is a comparatively worthless fact which has no lasting significance. I wish to press this point upon you, and to ask you to dwell upon it——namely, that a mere exact copy of any incident, or the reproduction on the stage of things as they occur in real life, is not being true to nature in the best sense. Nay, if it excludes the higher truths and grander aspects of character, it may be called being false to nature. I will illustrate what I mean, and I will beg you to ponder over my illustration, and apply it in any modern instance that may come under your notice.

My assertion is, that being true to nature on the stage is showing you the inside of the human heart, and to do this effectually it is oftentimes necessary to sacrifice petty, inessential *vraisemblances* of time and place. The frequent use of the soliloquy in Shakespeare is a continual illustration of this, and you will find throughout his plays constant violations of actual facts to gain essential truths of life and character. I could give you scores of instances of this ; the one that first comes to my mind is in the last act of *Richard the Third*. You will remember that on the eve of the battle of Bosworth Shakespeare makes Richard and Richmond pitch their tents within three or four yards of each other. Consider what an effect this absurdity would produce on a first-night audience of to-day ! What a howl would ascend from all parts of the house at so palpable a violation of all rules of probability. And at first sight it is very improbable, and absurd to the verge of childishness. But think it over. What is it that Shakespeare wishes to enforce in this scene ? All through the play the tyrant has been acting in magnificent derision of conscience. He has done evil, not like Macbeth, timidly, compunctiously, fitfully, shudderingly, but exultingly, proudly, wilfully, eagerly. He has gloried in trampling out the landmarks of right and wrong. He has not stifled his conscience ; he has laughed at it. Is he to escape ? No. In this last hour conscience finds him, seizes him asleep, asserts her " sovereign sway and masterdom," and dips his last earthly rest in a live, insupportable, inescapable horror more bitter than an eternity of doom. But this revenge of conscience can be better shown in contrast ; and further, Shakespeare has another truth to show—namely, that the same agencies, the same powers, the same thoughts and memories, the same events that minister terror and foreshadow destruction to Richard minister peace and assurance, and foreshadow victory to Richmond. He wants to brand into us this eternal truth, that the universe is set and tuned to bring final terror and dismay to evil, and final comfort and victory to good. Therefore he boldly sweeps away all considerations of actual space and locality, and daringly commits himself to the palpable absurdity of placing Richard's tent quite close to Richmond's. Does it seem so very absurd to you after all ?

I have given you this instance because I wish you to understand some of the difficulties under which a dramatist labours in the present day if he dares to make the higher truths of character his chief study in place of the meaner facts of actual occurrence. And I also wish if possible to get you to take a somewhat different view from that generally taken by the playgoing public as to what is meant by a dramatist's being true to nature.

If you will have patience with me a little longer we will inquire what hopes there are of the foundation of a school of modern English drama, and what tendencies and aims we should encourage and foster, and what tendencies and aims we should discourage and condemn.

We will put aside farcical comedy, burlesque, and comic opera, and deal only with plays of serious intention. Not that any one of us, myself least of all, would wish to exclude or to frown upon any of the lighter forms of dramatic entertainment. We are all glad to escape from the sterner aspects of life, and after a day's toil it is pleasant to take refuge in plays that shelter us snugly from reality and that frankly own there is nothing in life worth caring two straws about. In our present social condition, with the stress of business pressing more hardly upon us year after year, it seems to me that the general public will always run more eagerly after these lighter forms of entertainment than any other. Their natural taste may be safely trusted to prompt them in this direction.

But the finest possible succession of farcical comedies does not mean a school of English dramatic literature, and as for burlesque, it can only flourish in perfection alongside and following a vigorous growth of serious drama. Without good, sound original plays there can be no good burlesque ; a bad serious play burlesques itself.

Our great need is, then, for a school of plays of serious intention, plays that implicitly assert the value and dignity of human life, that it has great passions and great aims, and is full of meaning and importance. Now that is a view of human life which it needs some courage to present to a theatrical audience of to-day. There is a certain spirit of raillery abroad, which tends to frighten serious writers from their work. I think it is an immense loss that certain of our best writers, men who by their talent and culture are capable of giving to the theatre works of sincere study and lasting literary value, men who are qualified to take the lead in any movement for a demand for sound original plays—it is a bad sign that such men are employing their pens on farcical comedies and burlesques. And the reason is that it is becoming more and more difficult to get an audience to accept a serious play in the spirit in which it is meant. The same difficulty does not threaten, or only in a minor degree, plays which make no attempt to deal with life truthfully and honestly. Where all is avowedly absurd, avowedly outrageous and impossible, there are comparatively few opportunities for ridicule. When a play starts by frankly declaring that there is nothing sacred in life, it is safe of the approval of all the empty-headed, empty-hearted, empty-souled part of the audience.

To write a play of any kind is most difficult, harassing mental work ; how difficult, only those who are employed in it can know. But it is far more easy to write a play that trifles with human affairs than a play that deals seriously with them, and success is more easily snatched, though perhaps not so surely held, in trifling than in dealing seriously. Consider what the word "theatrical" has grown to mean in the English language. It means "false, hollow, sham, gaudy, empty "—that is to say, every play that is brought out has to combat a vague, general impression that all things "theatrical" are in some sense an imposture, a deception. A picture is as much a make-believe as a play ; it is no more real life than a play ; but consider the difference that is implied in the adjectives "pictorial" and "theatrical," consider the stigma that the ordinary acceptation of this word "theatrical" naturally and inevitably fastens upon every play. Now the reason of this is that the higher purposes of dramatic art

have, to a great extent, been lost sight of in the
attempt to trick the public into believing that what
they see on the stage is real life.   Every artifice has
been used to impress and delude them with this
false idea ; enormous scenery and effects have been
pressed into the service ; audiences have been
deafened with explosions, scorched with houses on
fire, terrified with railway collisions, shipwrecked,
deluged, bombarded, put to every conceivable peril,
all to enforce the ignoble and totally false and
inartistic notion that what they are seeing is actual
fact.

And now at last there is a growing class which
is finding out that it is not actual fact, but mainly
tinsel, pasteboard, and flummery.   And these wise
and clever people are taking enormous credit to
themselves for their discoveries, and are pluming
themselves upon their knowingness and superiority
to the poor deluded creatures sitting around them
who are taking it all in as actual fact.

The evil is, not that what is known and should be
known and felt to be make-believe and suggestion
is so known and felt, but that the vital and essential
realities of dramatic art, the literature and character-
drawing of the author, the emotion and expression of the actor, are also assumed to be false and
hollow.

I suppose we have all of us at times been carried
away by some fine bit of emotional acting, and in
the midst of the tide of our answering emotion,
while we were rendering with full hearts the tribute
of our tears or our applause to the actor who had
swayed us, we have suddenly been chilled by the

stare of some empty-headed person regarding us
with an air of benevolent pity as much as to say,
" How green you must be to be taken in with this
stuff! Look at me! I can yawn and twirl my
moustaches while that poor beggar on the stage
tears his heart out, because I know what bosh and
make-believe it all is."

There is no greater curse to the stage to-day
than the swarm of heartless, brainless, supercilious
theatre-goers who come not to be amused, to be
touched, to be interested, but to show their immense
superiority to the poor deluded fools who are amused,
touched, and interested. Three or four of them in
prominent places will damp and chill and spoil the
evening's amusement of a whole theatre. Barbers'
blocks and milliners' dummies would be an inspiring
and appreciative audience compared with them. I
can conceive many reasons why an intelligent man
should stay away from the theatre. I can conceive
no reason at all why he should come, except for the
pleasure of admiration. It is so easy and cheap to
laugh ; it is so easy and cheap to destroy. It took
centuries and men of profound genius to build
Westminster Abbey, but any fool or madman can
with a pound or two of dynamite blow it to atoms
in a few minutes.

What I wish to impress on you is this, that any
play which professes to deal seriously with human
life is sure to have a ridiculous side if you like to
search for it and dwell upon it. There are plenty of
absurdities in *Hamlet*—you all remember Voltaire's
criticism of it, a criticism which is quite incontro-
vertible from his point of view. *Paradise Lost*, too,

looked at from the standpoint of modern life, is the
most foolish and improbable concoction ever penned.
Now if these great and eternal creations have an
absurd side which a modern audience would be sure
to seize upon, how much more likely is it that the
comparatively feeble and ephemeral productions of
to-day should also have a ridiculous aspect.

And if in any particular place the interpretation
of a play is weak or false or indefinite, this absurd
side is sure to peep out, and the author's meaning
is not merely obscured or missed, but sometimes
directly misstated.   Now so far as concerns the
growing unwillingness of all educated playgoers to
believe in the reality of a stage-play, the tendency
to regard everything theatrical as a palpable deception which it is a very clever thing to have found
out, so far as regards the wise people who come to the
theatre to air their knowledge that it is all a sham
and a make-believe, there is but one way of dealing
with this spirit, and the sooner we recognise it the
better, because then we shall understand the position,
the only possible sure position, which dramatic art
can take up and keep fast in the future.   I will beg
you to follow me very closely here.   The great
majority of playgoers come to the theatre to be
persuaded that what they see is actual life ; and the
falsity of this position is growing daily to be proved
by the fact that the more advanced and constant and
educated section of playgoers is less and less inclined to accept it as actual life, while the ribald
and sneering section of the community is taking a
great delight in having discovered with all the profound penetration of Bottom in *A Midsummer Night's*

Dream that " Pyramus is not killed indeed, and that he, Pyramus, is not Pyramus, but Bottom the weaver," and that " the lion is not a lion, but Snug the joiner."

Now I think if you agreed with the remarks I made in the earlier portion of my address, upon what is being true to nature on the stage, and that the aim of the stage is to present, not the passing and unnecessary facts of actual occurrence, but the eternal and necessary verities of life and character, if you agreed with me there, you will agree with me when I state the second proposition which I am most anxious that you should accept, namely this :—Everything that tricks and deceives playgoers, or that attempts to trick and deceive them, into believing that what they are seeing is real life, instead of being a representation, a transcript, an abstract of real life— everything that so imposes on them is false, ignoble, unworthy of art, and must sooner or later be surrendered and abandoned.

Why is it that the more plays a man sees the less he is moved and interested, unless there is a false notion at the bottom of play-seeing that it is intended to be taken for actuality ?—which false notion a constant playgoer gradually sees through. Amongst constant playgoers, and especially of late years, there is a growing delight to ridicule the necessary conventions upon which all serious dramatic art is built ; and you may see the consequences in the fact which I have before mentioned, that our best writers are gradually leaving the higher walks of the drama and turning to farcical comedy and burlesque. Surely if there is a sound foundation to the drama, the more a man goes to the theatre the more real he ought to feel it to be, the more inclined he ought to be to lend himself to the necessary illusions and conventions, to accept them and to take no further notice of them, that he may give all his attention to winning interest and enjoyment from the author's work.   Is this the spirit in which many among a modern audience approach a play?   Or do they not rather approach it with an idea that it is all sham and make-believe?   I am sure you, as earnest playgoers, must have observed and regretted this temper in many modern first-night audiences. Now there is only one way of combating this spirit. Let it be boldly understood and conceded once for all to these clever people, " This discovery which you plume yourself so much upon making is what all true dramatic art starts with ; we do not wish to trick you into taking it for real life ; in certain super- ficial facts it is and always must be very different from real life ; many obvious, inessential resem- blances to real life, which any shallow brain can perceive, are slighted and omitted : many deep-lying, not very obvious, but yet very important truths are elaborated and dwelt upon, and placed in the strongest light.   You jeer at the play because it is not actual life as you have scanned it.   Just so ; it is not meant to be actual life—it is only meant to be reflective, suggestive, illustrative, indicative of real life."

I think a frank declaration and understanding of this principle is necessary for any future develop- ment of the drama.   Let us recall our own educa- tion as playgoers.   At first we accepted it all as real and actual, the scenery and effects no less than the passion and emotion of the actor and author. But as we grew experienced and observant, and had more leisure to bestow on details, we began to scent that a great deal of it was very unreal indeed, and we have continued to find out that more and more of it is conventional and make-believe, and farther and farther removed from life. Speaking generally, we may say we have found out that scenes and occurrences are contrived on the stage to impress the greatest numbers of careless superficial observers and ignorant playgoers as being real life; but the more we look into the matter, the more we are convinced that they are not real life, but only pretensions and illusions, purposely meant to trick the vast majority of casual playgoers, who are imperfectly educated upon the subject. And pondering further on the limitations and conditions of the art, we arrive at the conclusion that it is impossible for the stage to give all the fulness and variety and multitudinous aspects and details of real life: it can only select, and hint at, and suggest, and seize upon a few perennial and essential truths that do not always lie upon the surface of the actual facts.

Every audience is composed of a crowd of playgoers in all stages of this gradual process of education and disillusion. And the most habitual playgoers are of course the most unbelieving in the deceptions of the stage. But we want all playgoers to become habitual playgoers; and with the theatre growing as it is to be more and more popular, we may expect in each audience a greater and greater proportion of habitual playgoers. But when all playgoers become hardened habitual playgoers there will be nobody left to accept the illusions of the stage, or, to push the matter to its utmost absurdity: when the drama has attained its greatest popularity, nobody will believe in it.

So you see I have taxed your patience and brought you all along this weary road to-night only to lead you up this blind alley. How shall we get out of it?

Let us go back a few steps. Along with the gradual process of disillusion and disbelief in the more palpable unrealities and superficialities of the stage, if we have really loved the drama, we have found a growing belief in, a growing conviction of, the lasting reality of certain attributes of stage work. If all playgoers were enlightened to the state we have imagined, if they had full knowledge of all stage tricks and devices, if they had been hardened by constant exposure till they were proof against all surprises of the playwright, the stage-carpenter, the lime-light man, the scenic artist, what foundation would there remain for the drama? What are those qualities of a play which must endure, which neither time, nor familiarity, nor the spirit of ridicule so rife among us can shake? Why, precisely those qualities which have been the foundation of every good play since the world began— great and lofty conceptions of human life embodied in an interesting tale, in real flesh-and-blood characters, and in fitting language. These things will always remain as the never-to-be-destroyed essentials of the drama—a great idea, an interesting tale, the faithful portraiture of character and literary power.

Here at last we have got upon firm ground, and there can be no secure future for the drama except in this direction and in the development of these attributes. With these assured, all scenic illusion, all tricks of situation, all mere noise may be banished, and we shall never feel the loss.

If I were asked to name two cardinal tests for discovering the merits of any play, I would suggest those of "character-painting" and "literature."

And for this reason, no matter how great an idea a play may have for its foundation, that idea cannot be conveyed, nay, it is ruined, unless it is conveyed in adequate language. And no matter how interesting a tale a dramatist may have, it is also ruined to any thinking mind unless it is conveyed in fitting language. Moreover, the question of an interesting tale is one which everybody can judge of without possibility of error. A child knows whether it is interested or no. An audience cannot be deceived or go wrong upon this point.

Therefore the two remaining tests, the two vital tests, of the goodness of a play are, "Is it literature?" "Does it truly paint character?" And these are just the tests upon which an average modern audience is apt to be careless, or ignorant, or mistaken. So long as an audience is interested or excited, or imposed upon by scenery or dresses or stage-effect, it is very careless of the actual words that are spoken. If the language is not glaringly false or inappropriate, an audience does not trouble its head upon the matter. But when it does trouble its head to pay attention to the language, it is attracted by what is forced, smart, meretricious, falsely-splendid, rather than by what is simple, severe, and natural. The literary tastes of an average audience may be gauged by the fact that no book or poem written above a certain level of literary skill ever attains that wide, immediate popularity which is a necessary accompaniment of stage success—those books and periodicals which have the widest sudden circulation are rarely of any lasting literary value ; they are at best non-literary.

Further, our fine mother-tongue seems lately to have lost, and to be still losing, much of its native dignity and music and power. We seem to be entering upon one eternal, universal carnival of slang. It is impossible for any one who has studied the essentially strong, devout, sincere, and earnest English character at its sources ; who in childhood has heard the English language spoken in everyday life in all its sincerity, purity, and vigour ; who knows and has studied the magnificent capabilities of this instrument of speech which our ancestors have forged for us—it is impossible for such an one to view without the bitterest pain and dismay the parallel degradation of English character and English speech which is rapidly taking place. For the degradation of the English tongue implies the correlative degradation of the national character. Out of the fulness of the heart the mouth speaketh. You know what a great power this spirit of foolish banter and slang is in London life. Nothing is attempted in a truthful and earnest manner but up comes this evil monster and spits its blistering froth of filthy familiarity over every fair and reverent deed, and nothing is left that is sacred, or mysterious, or even decent. I know how hopeless it is to contend with this spirit—one might as well

> Send precepts to Leviathan to come ashore,

or

> Bid the main flood bate his usual height.

But none the less is it our duty as playgoers to protest, however hopelessly and helplessly, against this blatant invasion and perversion of our mother-tongue, against the senseless cunning that finds an evil double-meaning in every innocent expression, and to demand that on the stage our language shall retain its native grandeur and simplicity and honesty, as it is also our duty as Englishmen—and a duty of the greatest importance—to look to it that, so far as we ourselves are concerned, the wells of speech which Chaucer and Spenser, which Shakespeare and Milton drew from, shall be kept pure and undefiled.

The other test of a good play is fidelity of character-drawing. On this matter too an audience is careless while it is amused and excited, or if its attention is aroused, it is apt to be ignorant or mistaken. Again, an actor's personality sometimes immensely aids and vivifies an author's sketch, while at other times it deadens and destroys it. It is almost impossible to see an author's meaning except through the interpretation given on the stage. A play is oftentimes so nicely balanced that the excess or deficiency of interest gained or lost by one of the characters may totally destroy its equilibrium, and render it impossible for an audience to see the author's intention ; while again, the immense force and vitality with which some particular actor is able

to invest a part often saves what is worthless from
condemnation and contempt.

It is often said, and it is a current axiom in a
theatre, that the test of a good play is, " How will it
act ? " That is doubtless to a great extent the test
of a popular play ; but I would urge that the test of
a really good play is, "Can it be read as well as acted?"
It may act well and be thoroughly worthless, except
as a spectacle or a joke—it cannot read well to any
jury of cultivated minds unless it is a piece of
literature.

Now doubtless there is sufficient rough, shrewd
sense among a general audience to make them
tolerable judges of broadly-marked, forcibly-drawn
conventional characters. They like their virtuous
people to be very virtuous, their villains to be
very villainous, and they like their comedians to
make them laugh by any possible means. But
directly an author attempts sheer, hard, truthful
character - painting he ventures upon dangerous
ground with a general audience. The best and
sincerest character-painting is subtle and unobtrusive, and hardly declares itself. You may recall
what I said a little while ago, that the dramatist
has only three hours to draw a dozen or twenty
characters, while nature can give seventy years to
one. Therefore he has to crowd into those
few minutes all that he considers it necessary for
you to know of the character he is drawing. You
will find scores of this instant, direct presentation
of character in Shakespeare, where in a few speeches
he tells you as much of a man as you could gather if
you had lived with him for years. But then you have

to pay the most earnest attention to these speeches, and turn them over and over again in your mind. Human nature is the most interesting, but at the same time the most difficult and complex, subject you can study, and many facts of character which at first sight appear of great prominence and importance are found afterwards to be secondary and unimportant. Now the chief truths of character are those which are most historical, which look before and after, which not only tell you what a certain man is, but tell you how he has grown to be so, and hint at what he is likely to become. Here, as in many other places of my address, I am translating from the rules of art that Ruskin laid down forty years ago in his *Modern Painters.*

Indeed, if you will but study him, you will find that much of what he has said there may be as usefully applied to the criticism of the drama as to the criticism of pictures. So true is that fine saying, which I think is Michael Angelo's, "There is but one art."

The chief truths of character are those which are most historical. I will give you an illustration from Goldsmith which I daresay will be fresh in your memories. You remember old Hardcastle drilling his household in anticipation of visitors. He particularly cautions them against laughing when he tells any of his stock tales to his guests, whereupon Diggory exclaims, "We must laugh, master, if you tell that tale about grouse and the gun-room—we've laughed at that any time this last twenty years." Whereupon old Hardcastle, highly flattered, says, "Well, that is a good tale, Diggory; you may laugh at that."

Observe the painting of present character in these two speeches, the genial weakness of old Hardcastle, so lovable, so truthful, so natural, illustrating in the kindest and tenderest way the everlasting truth that human nature is always ready to be turned from its purpose by a little adroit flattery. But observe also that these two speeches open up a vista that practically shows you all that is worth knowing of old Hardcastle's life for the past twenty years, and also foreshadows what his life will be for the next twenty years, if he should live as long. The more you dwell upon them the more they suggest. But the next time you see *She Stoops to Conquer*, mark the effect of these speeches upon a general audience—they will not awaken any great roar of laughter, such as is caused in a modern piece by a stupid distortion of words, a verbal quibble, or a meaningless mistake of pronunciation. By the greater part of the audience their full purport will be quite missed ; they will scarcely strike home at all. They will count for nothing in the question of the success of the piece with a general audience.

Another reason why I urge that "literature and character-painting" should be accepted as the chief tests of a good play, is that without them a play has no lasting value at all. Mere ingenuity of situation, dramatic surprises, and complications of a story are at bottom worthless unless they illustrate and develop human character. They are in themselves of the same order of art as a conjurer's. The ingenuity that ex-pends itself in devising dramatic surprises is of the same order as that which expends itself in devising

Chinese puzzles. The ingenuity that expends itself in painting human character is of the same order, though it may not be a thousandth part of the degree, as that of Shakespeare or Molière. Again, every dramatic work of lasting value will stand these two tests of literature and character-painting, though it may not stand any other tests. You know that many of Shakespeare's works do not stand the test of originality of plot, of probability or even possibility of story, of dramatic situations at the ends of the acts, of neatness and plausibility of construction. They would be condemned on these points and upon many other points which are necessary to the success of a modern play. But they stand the tests of " literature " and of " character-painting."

Again, if in our visit to the theatre we have heard our fine native tongue nobly employed, and if also we have seen a little into the infinite secrecy and mystery of the human heart, at least we have garnered something for ourselves.

Of course I am not ignoring that very often we wish to go to the theatre, not to think, but to escape from thought. I do not wish to deprecate that attitude of mind in this over-anxious, over-wearied age. There is room enough, and there is a public large enough in London, to support the widest variety of theatrical entertainments, and that will be the healthiest state of the drama when they shall be all flourishing : the piece that makes us cry and think, the piece that makes us cry and laugh and think, the piece that makes us laugh and think, and last, but sure always not to be least popular, the piece that makes us laugh without thinking at all.

If I appear to have been somewhat one-sided in my advocacy of what I have called the serious drama, it is because I feel just now that it is in need of very earnest support.

I think it cannot be disputed, on taking a survey of the last thirty years, that the modern stage has not received its due share of recruits from the greatest writers of the age. We have many names of the first mark in every other department of literature ; we have no name of quite the first mark among the regular writers for the stage. Something of this is due to the great uncertainty which attends production on the modern stage, and something also to the fact that our best writers have not taken the pains to gain the immense amount of stage-craft necessary to write a successful modern play. I scarcely think we shall get the best available talent until there is something like certainty and equality in the judgments and awards. In reality we may say that the recent history of the English stage is comprised, and probably the immediate future history of the stage will also have to be comprised, in the following formula :—

No original play of lasting literary and human value has been produced. A few very good plays, many very middling plays, many very bad plays, have been produced ; and of these three classes some have been huge successes, some have been fair successes, some have been failures, according as the actor's interpretation, the popularity of the theatre, the uncertainties of public and critical taste, the temper of a first-night audience, the run of good or bad weather, and the thousand-and-one chances that rule the fate of a play, have determined. We must qualify this, however, by saying that once a play is started, and the attention of the public sufficiently drawn to it, there is some rough approximation to justice in the share of support it receives.

Probably for a long time to come play-writing will continue to be the matter of compromise and uncertainty that it is at present. " Will this hit the passing taste of the moment ? " " Will the critics see in it a great deal more or a great deal less than I intend ? " " Will they, that is especially the six or seven whose word carries weight, praise or damn it ? " " And if they damn it, will it be with faint praise or in that peculiar way that will send all London to see it ? " " Those first-nighters, who are after all the best judges of a play, will they take it seriously, as I mean it, or will they get into a laughing fit and jeer it ? " " What will make the success of the piece, the main interest or something I never thought of ? " These will continue to be, as they are now, the questions which an author will put to himself about any new play that he is writing. And while this uncertainty as to its reception remains, no author need feel very much elated at the success of his piece, or very much cast down at its failure.

One word about a term of late much quoted, much misused—the " elevation " of the stage. We have heard so much about this recently ; it has been used in such questionable quarters, and has become such a cant phrase, that one shudders to mention it.

If the English drama to-day is all that it should be, all that its lovers could wish, and if it is likely to continue in that happy state, there is no need of this club, and of your spending your time in debate upon what is already perfect and unimprovable. But I think we all of us agree that the modern drama is not quite in that state of desired perfection. Therefore to some extent it needs alteration and improvement. That idea is at the very foundation of the existence of this club. In the early part of my address I asked you to be very severe to all slipshod, careless, and palpably insincere work, but to no other. I now ask you to be most tolerant, most lenient to all work of evidently sincere intention, from whose pen soever it may come.

That is the first condition of our getting the best work from any author; and we want every author to give us his best, in all sincerity and in all confidence that it will be received in the same spirit in which he meant it. And we want our best authors to be employed upon the best work of which they are capable. Good plays cannot be written singly; they can be written only in an atmosphere of good plays, and amongst a crowd of writers of good plays.

We will not use the word "elevate," as it has lately got into such bad repute, but we will still declare that some innovation is needed in the drama.

If I were asked to name the kind of influence most needed on the stage to-day, I should say an influence akin to that which Wordsworth brought into English poetry at the beginning of this century, the influence of naturalness, simplicity, thoughtfulness, sincerity, of sheer, hard, straightforward devotion to nature and truth. Wordsworth's methods and training and temper were essentially undramatic, therefore I do not suggest that they should be brought into the modern drama. But the advent of his spirit, his homeliness and cleanliness of moral air, his stern, simple grandeur, his love of all the sanctities and charities of life, his faithful portraiture of English character at its purest sources—these and their adequate prominence on the stage would in time work as great a reformation amongst us as Wordsworth effected in poetry.

But alas! as you know, Wordsworth was voted dull and babyish by an age that found its highest ideals of poetry realised in the false, unnatural splendour of Byron's and Moore's Eastern tales.

I will finish with a quotation from one of Wordsworth's sonnets, especially as it is suggested by one of the finest and most wonderful passages in Shakespeare.

You all remember the scene in *Macbeth* where Duncan comes to Macbeth's castle, and Banquo's speech about the temple-haunting martlet that had built its nest upon every "jutty, frieze, buttress, and coigne of vantage": a speech in itself full of the highest poetic beauty, which yet, however, as two of our poets have pointed out, becomes lighted up with a terrible import and suggestion when we think upon the innocence and security of the birds under the castle roof, and then remember the infernal scene of murder that is about to be enacted within the walls. Wordsworth, recalling those few lines of Banquo's, and avoiding all thought of their dread foreshadowing significance, has written a sonnet where he refers to them and works out the pretty fancy that a certain class of writers hang their nests of clay, never meant to endure, upon " coignes of vantage," while the flattering zephyrs of popularity play round them. But soon the nests come tumbling down, dust for oblivion ! Then, with his magnificent self-assurance in the work he was doing, Wordsworth writes the lines with which I close—lines that were full of rebuke to that age when poetry had so long remained content to be a thing mainly of words and artifice, and had almost ceased to have any concern with nature, lines that are full of support at all times to all art-workers of honest endeavour, and that are a sure guide to the highest qualities and permanent value of any piece of art :

> To the solid ground
> Of Nature trusts the mind that builds for aye,
> Convinced that there, there only, she can lay
> Secure foundations.

ON BEING RIGHTLY AMUSED AT
THE THEATRE

(A Lecture delivered originally at Bradford, Yorks, on Sunday afternoon, 13th November 1887)

I HAVE so far conformed with the prevailing custom of Sunday as to choose what I may call a text, a heading for the remarks I am about to make on the theatre.

A passage from Sainte-Beuve, the great French critic, quoted by our great English critic of literature, Mr. Matthew Arnold, in his *Essays on Criticism*, seemed to suggest a suitable subject for an hour's talk with you this evening. It runs thus as rendered by Mr. Matthew Arnold : "'In France,' says M. Sainte-Beuve, ' the first consideration is not whether we are amused and pleased by a work of art or mind, nor is it whether we are touched by it. What we seek above all to learn is whether we are *right* in being amused with it, and in applauding in it, and in being moved by it.'"

I want you to take a few glances at modern English playgoing in the light of this maxim of Sainte-Beuve's.

I am afraid you are booked for a dull afternoon.

That great master of English fiction, our wise and manly Henry Fielding, in one of those delightful initial chapters to the books of *Tom Jones*, remarks that whenever his readers found him dull they might always rest assured it was with some profound purpose. If you find me dull this afternoon I will ask you to credit me with some profound purpose in my dulness. It is true that when I have finished you may not be able to discover exactly what that purpose was, but by that time the lecture will be over and you will be free.

I suppose you are all theatre-goers. I will assume that you are. Your presence here is sufficient evidence that you are kindly disposed towards the drama and its representatives. It will not be necessary for me to enter into any defence of the drama, or to take an apologetic tone for what I am doing this Sunday afternoon. Such meetings as these are symptoms of a growing feeling that whatever is necessary or helpful to the development of any part of man's many-sided nature is to that extent sacred, and may very properly be the occupation of his best hours of leisure and recreation. I say then that I am not here to defend the drama or to apologise for speaking to you on a Sunday afternoon about the interests of the theatre. Believing as I do, and as your coming here shows that you do, that all moments and functions of life are sacred, Saturday no less than Sunday, play and work no less than devotion and psalm-singing—believing this, we may very well leave the suitability of our subject to-day to be wrangled over by those who, notwithstanding some very plain testimony on the point, have never yet

O

been able to accept the dictum that the Sabbath was made for man, and not man for the Sabbath.

As for the drama itself, I will take it for granted you are agreed with me that "The greatest glory of England is her literature, and the greatest glory of her literature is her drama." I am aware that a modern playwright places himself in a very awkward position when he reminds his audience that we have a great national literary drama. It might be more politic for him to sneer at Shakespeare's clumsy construction, his want of originality in plot, and to prove that he could not write a modern play. But the fact remains that we have a great poetical drama, and also a series of very brilliant old comedies of the town-life of two centuries ago. We have also a modern drama—of a kind. I think you will go with me still when I say that with our cities becoming more crowded and our railway communication more developed every year, our theatres are likely to increase still further in influence and popularity. Some sort of a drama is necessary, and will be necessary for us while human nature remains what it is. The question is, What sort of a drama shall there be in England for the next quarter of a century?

I have assumed that you are all playgoers. I will go further and assume that you are all, what I hope you will become, confirmed, inveterate, insatiable playgoers of the widest and most catholic tastes, and the deepest and shrewdest critical insight. You will therefore please consider yourselves as representatives of all that is best and soundest, most loyal and most enthusiastic, most cultivated and most discerning in the theatre-going community to-day. I am pleased to address such an audience, and I shall consider that in speaking to you I am speaking, so far as my words may chance to travel, to the general body of English theatre-goers.

Now here we are face to face with one another, you as playgoers demanding what you think to be good plays, I as a playwright anxious, so far as my ability goes, to supply you. What sort of plays do you want?

That very distinguished amateur actor, Polonius, who, as you remember, tells us that he played the part of Julius Cæsar, classifies for us the different kinds of plays then in vogue as " tragedy, comedy, history, pastoral, pastoral-comical, historical-pastoral, tragical-historical, and tragical-comical-historical-pastoral." I observe that he makes no mention of melodrama, farcical comedy, burlesque, and panto-mime. Our modern theatre is largely supported by the latter four classes. Suppose we lump them with Polonius's list and we shall get a fairly comprehensive catalogue of the different kinds of theatrical enter-tainment. If I ask you as representative playgoers which sort of play you want, you, with your wide catholic tastes, will reply, " We want good plays of all sorts—good poetic and historic plays, good comedies, good tragedies, good melodramas, good far-cical comedies, and good burlesques and pantomimes." There is a saying one often hears from the lips of play-goers of all classes : " When I go to the theatre I want to be amused." And using the word " amusement " in its derivative sense, this instinct is quite right. The test of being amused is the primary test to apply to a play of any kind. The necessity of amusing, or, to avoid mistakes, we may say the necessity of *interesting*, his audience is the first consideration of the author. I am quite sure that, no matter how kindly you permit me to bore you as a lecturer, I must not trespass upon the same indulgence when I come before you as a playwright.

We will now glance again at Sainte-Beuve's maxim—" The first consideration is not whether we are amused, but whether we are *right* in being amused." Yes, but pardon me, M. Sainte-Beuve, we must *be* amused before we can ask ourselves whether we are *rightly* amused : if the work of art bores us to begin with, there is so far an end of the matter —we are neither rightly nor wrongly amused, we are merely bored. So to avoid ambiguity we will put the maxim thus : " The *first* end of a play is to amuse : the *chief* end of a play is to amuse rightly." But you reply, " If we *are* amused, if we go to the theatre and have a good laugh or a good cry, and enjoy ourselves, what do we want to bother any further about it ? What's the use of asking ourselves whether we were right or wrong ? What does it matter ? " If you were enjoying a certain course of living, and your doctor told you that it would gradually undermine your health, don't you think it would matter whether you continued it or not ? And it does matter, and it has a permanent influence upon your character and intellectual health, whether you laugh at this jest or that, whether you harden and wither your heart with witless drivel and imbecility, or whether you bathe and ease and enlarge it at such fountains of wise merriment as Sheridan and Goldsmith, Fielding and

Dickens, Cervantes and Rabelais. But I am sure that a representative body of playgoers, such as we are agreed that I am speaking to, will readily assent when I say that there is a right way and a wrong way of being amused, and that it is of considerable importance, both to the drama itself as an intellectual art, and to the character of its patrons, that they should know when they are being rightly amused at the theatre.

Now at last we are fairly launched upon our subject. All we have to do is to find out what is right and what is wrong, and why one way is right and another wrong. I use the word "amusement" here in its broadest sense. There were nine Muses, you know, and one of them was Melpomene. To-day, then, I use the word "amusement" to cover all the different kinds of pleasurable excitement that a theatrical audience can obtain from a play, whether of laughter or tears, sympathy with virtue or detestation of vice, delight in the author's work, the actor's, the scene-painter's, or the carpenter's. Generally your enjoyment of a play will depend upon several or all of these sources of amusement being harmoniously combined for you by a competent stage-manager. But I want to speak to you to-day about the author's share of the work, and I will ask you to forgive me the vanity of saying that I consider that the author's share of a theatrical entertainment is, or should be, its most vital and permanently important feature. I am aware that in England to-day, perhaps to a greater or less extent in all countries and at all times, it is the *actor* and not the *author* who attracts the public.

You go to see this or that popular favourite in some popular character, and his work and personality leave a definite impression upon you. You also go to see a popular play, a play that has obtained a great vogue, but you care very little about who wrote it, and in the majority of cases you don't know. A few of you here and there may go to see a certain author's work because of his name, but no author's career, in England at least, is followed with the same amount of attention that our best-known actors command. I am not saying this enviously. The immediate shout of popular applause, the direct responsive thunder of the acclaiming crowd to some sudden flash of his genius, is the actor's legitimate guerdon—alas that it should be so fleeting and insubstantial! We need not grudge the actor his rightful reward, so hardly won, so quickly lost. We need not scramble with him for popular huzzas. But alongside this devotion to and admiration of the popular actor, I think the English playgoing public may very well be solicited to study and examine very carefully the individual work and aims of the dramatic author. I urge that the more surely an author feels that he has some individual and personal authority with his public, that he is directly responsible to a trained and cultivated body of playgoers who are keenly watching every scene of human life as it comes from his pen, and referring it to a definite standard of criticism, the more likely he is to wake to the splendid duties and opportunities of his calling, and to give you the best that is in him. It is because our highest literary critics are continually reminding us of the intellectual poverty of our modern drama, of the absence from our contemporary stage of any searching and vital portraiture of our modern national life, that I beg from English playgoers a more strict and constant examination and recognition of the individual work and standpoint of the dramatic author, as the one element that can alone make a play permanently valuable, amidst all the haphazard circumstances that may make it temporarily successful.

Now I want you to ask yourselves what are to you the most important features in a theatrical entertainment. When you go to a theatre, what are the things that delight you the most? I suppose the most widely popular attractions to the English public are lively music, bright dresses, pretty scenes, beautiful faces and figures, graceful dances, catchy songs. I find that these things as a rule provoke the loudest and most frantic outbursts of applause. Well, we have owned to the most catholic tastes in these matters, and therefore I have not a word, except of the most cordial approval, to say of your enjoyment of these things. A first-rate burlesque or pantomime is infinitely better than a second-rate tragedy. Some of you will perhaps say that a second-rate burlesque is better than a first-rate tragedy, and in certain moods I don't know that I should be disposed to argue with you. But this at any rate we may affirm : that all delight and recreation to be derived from bright spectacles and gorgeous scenery and dresses are an unmixed good. I have put all these things first because they seem to give the most instant satisfaction to the greatest number of theatre-goers. But if you will reflect upon the enjoyment you have obtained from them, I think you will agree with me that if this kind of pleasure is the most vivid at the moment, it is also the most fleeting and evanescent. When you have heard a good joke at the theatre, you can chuckle over it the next morning. When you have followed a profound study of character, you can ponder over it for many days and compare it with your own observations of the human nature around you. But when your delight at the theatre has been obtained chiefly by the contemplation of scenery and figures and dresses, I don't know that any definite after-impression remains with you, except perhaps that your everyday working life seems very dingy and sombre by contrast. There is nothing to think about the next morning. And this leads me to propose this first general rule for you to take to the theatre with you : " All enjoyment that depends upon scenic effect, dresses, and group-ings of figures, though quite legitimate in its place, is of itself of an inferior, temporary, and compara-tively unintellectual kind." Scenic effects and illusions have no real dramatic value and signi-ficance unless they illustrate human passion and character. And they must be kept quite subordi-nate and in the background to that. For instance, when you go to see the play of *Macbeth* the chief thing is not that you should be dazed and half frightened by elaborate and weird witches' dances and grotesque supernatural effects. Your belief in these, your acceptance of them as real, only shows that you are not yet emancipated from the unscientific notions about the personality and bodily appearance of evil which your grandmothers held, and that you are imperfectly acquainted with the resources and the purely mechanical nature of theatrical illusion. The one thing above all others essential to you when you see Macbeth is that you should look deeply into the natures of the haunted murderer and his partner in crime. And the next thing is that you should take delight in the beauty and vigour and felicity of the language in which the legend is conveyed to you. Then, after that, and last of all, should come your enjoyment of the play as a perfectly-appointed and well-stage-managed spectacle. I do not mean to defend the slovenly mounting of plays. I think the stage should gladly press into its service every beautiful device and every ingenious illusion that scenery and costume can lend to it. But I want you as critical playgoers to understand the purely subordinate and merely illustrative character of all stage illusion and accessories. I will try to make this point clear to you.

I will suppose one night that you go to see a play that contains what we call a sensation scene—we will say, for example, an explosion in a coal-mine. And we will suppose that this is put upon the stage in such a realistic and substantial way as to make you forget you are in a theatre, and actually believe for the moment that you are witnessing the dreadful calamity. Now bear in mind that whatever might be the size and resources of the theatre, and whatever care and money might be spent upon the scene, it would in most of its essential features be quite unlike the reality. Many of its most vivid details—the strewn divided limbs, the darkness, the foul air, the horrible heartrending shrieks, the vast masses of earth rent and tumbling—could at best be only very imperfectly rendered, or altogether omitted. The next time you see one of these big sensation scenes, instead of watching in how many particulars it *resembles* the real scene, watch in how many more particulars, and these the most important, it *differs* from the real scene. But we will suppose that some of the more striking features of a coal-mine explosion have been so presented on the stage that you have temporarily mistaken them for reality. Well, what has happened? Merely this. You, a good-natured, simple-minded playgoer, have allowed some very clever carpenters, scene-painters, and property-men, with the help of half-a-dozen pounds of gunpowder and some big, irregular blocks of wood painted to look like coal or earth, to persuade you that you have witnessed a terrible colliery disaster. You have generously paid your shillings to be terrified by a purely mechanical arrangement of tumbling logs and gigantic fireworks that have positively nothing more to do with dramatic art, and nothing more dreadful in them, than the falling of a child's house of bricks, or the letting off of a squib or a cracker in your own backyard. And if you could examine the machinery that produced the effects, and were allowed to witness the scene night after night, at the end of a week it would probably affect you no more than these two ordinary homely events that I have compared it with.

I think that illustration ought to give you an idea of the value of scenic effect in itself.

Now the next night after you have seen this coal-mine scene we will suppose you go to another theatre and you see another play. And for the sake of comparison we will suppose that the play again treats of the miner's life. But what impresses you most in this second play is some homely scene in the miner's cottage—some lively picture of the terrible hardships or simple joys of the miner's life. There is no particular scenery : the four, or rather the three, bare walls and scanty furniture are the only background to the human figures. I don't stop to inquire whether you take the scenery for reality in this case, because now I am not dealing with the effect of scenery upon you. We have just considered that. What impresses you this time is some domestic episode, we will say the breaking up of the hitherto happy home through shame, or illness, or trouble of some kind. The scene is so well acted that you again mistake it for reality. You actually believe that the favourite son has robbed his employer, the favourite daughter left her home, the sick child will die because the necessary delicacies cannot be provided out of the father's small earnings. The tears roll down your cheek ; you feel hate against the wicked betrayer, sorrow for the broken-down father, pity for the poor wanderer ; or you dive your hand in your pocket, and you can scarcely help crying out, " It's all right—she shan't die—I'll send her round a basin of good beef-tea before I go to bed to-night."

What has happened this time ? You have been

deceived again—that's plain. That is the first thing that strikes you when you analyse your feelings the next morning. But you have not been so unworthily deceived this time. You have not quite the same sense of having been tricked. Your best sympathies, your kindliest feelings have been roused, and your heart has perhaps been made more tender and more ready to be moved by the next case of real sorrow or suffering that meets you. Also, you have not been merely deceived to a more worthy end, but you have been deceived by more worthy means. In the sphere of the drama, the artistic effort that deludes you by the semblance of human emotion is far higher and more legitimate than the artistic effort that deludes you by scenic effects. The counterfeited sorrow has been produced by higher artistic means than the counterfeited colliery explosion. But all the same, so far as you have allowed yourself to accept what you saw for an *actual fact* taking place beneath your eyes, you have been deceived, you have been taken in, and you have forfeited the highest pleasure that a stage representation can and ought to afford you. And this brings me to the second rule that I am going to ask you to take with you when you next go to the theatre. I will state it first and justify and illustrate it afterwards. It is this—

" A stage-play should never be mistaken for real life."

All art that deceives you into taking it for nature itself is inferior and comparatively worthless. I lately saw a drawing of Turner's called " Llanthony Abbey." Frail and beautiful, like the ghost of that

dead faith that built it, sequestered and decaying,
like its own religion, amidst the boundless disinte-
grating forces of undecaying nature, the abbey rose
under the everlasting hills, smitten with an unearthly
loveliness, consecrated afresh with those gleams that
never fell upon sea or land, a spectre, an exhalation,
a painter's dream of the scene it was supposed to
realise.   It was one of the most beautiful transcripts
from nature that I have ever looked upon.   But the
whole picture was not two feet square.   You could
never mistake it for a real abbey and real hills.
Some time before that I had seen in Paris a panorama of Paris at the time of the siege.   The whole
thing was so cleverly built and arranged that upon
entering you could scarcely persuade yourself that
you were not actually present amongst the horrors
of the war.   There were apparently real cannon,
real corpses, real soldiers, real snow, real bloodshed
in the streets.   It deceived you into thinking it was
real.   That panorama to-day, I daresay, is burnt up
or worn out ; thousands of people have been to see
it, and the only impression left upon them is the
remembrance of the cleverness of the artist who
tricked them into fancying they saw five or six of
the most evident and commonplace horrors and
incidents of the siege.   There was no suggestion,
nothing except just the few bare facts that the most
ordinary observer could have noted for himself without the least trouble in the first five minutes that he
glanced at the scene.   But Turner's picture remains,
and if its colours could be preserved it would remain
a heritage for the English nation as long as it shall
last, teaching them in Keats's words—

Beauty is truth—truth beauty, that is all
Ye know on earth, and all ye need to know.

Now that illustrates for you the comparative worthlessness of a picture that deceives you into accepting it for reality. But you will find it is the same in the other arts. For instance, you may be deceived into thinking that a cleverly-modelled wax figure is a human being, but you never mistake a beautiful statue for a man. An artist who respects himself never deceives you, never wishes to deceive you. He wants you to start fair with the same knowledge, the same judgment, the same frank acceptance of all the thousand conventions of his art, and the same understanding of its difficulties and limitations that he starts with.

Now let us apply our rule to the stage. I say you should never mistake it for real life. So far as you do, the more you go to the theatre, the more and more you will be disenchanted and find it stale and tricky. We have supposed that you have paid two visits to the theatre and have been impressed, the first time with a coal-mine explosion that you took to be real, and the second time with a display of emotion that you took to be real. We will suppose that you go a third time, and having previously read and pondered over the play of *Hamlet*, you go to see it performed by a master-tragedian. You already know its plot, so that you are not on the tenter-hooks of suspense as to what is about to happen. This gives you leisure and self-possession to attend to the beauty of the language and the unfolding of the character of Hamlet. The lofty metrical language at once forbids you to mistake the play for an actual scene of real life. In fact we will suppose that, having analysed your feelings on the two previous occasions, and having discovered that you have been deceived, you are resolutely aware all through the evening that you are listening to a play, and that never for one moment does it impose upon you that it is real life. Now what has most deeply impressed you upon this third occasion? What is the one thing that you carry away with you? The mystery and the philosophy of the character of Hamlet. You may have had other feelings aroused in the course of the evening—your love of beautiful scenery, your hatred of sin, and your pity for the sinner,—but we will imagine that the one great attraction for you has been the depth and mystery of that one central character. Now here at least you are on firm ground. I have indicated to you the highest and most enduring pleasure that you can obtain from a play. It does not vanish the next morning, or the next month. You can go to see the play again the next night, and you will find your pleasure increased. You can read the play again and again, and each time you can renew and intensify your delight. You are in touch with all the greatest minds of the last two centuries. You can attach your own guesses and thoughts about the character to your profoundest beliefs and doubts about the destiny of man and the mystery of the universe, and to all the speculations and theories of ancient and modern philosophers. The play of *Hamlet* asks afresh each time the riddle of human life. Now bear in mind that this particular pleasure you have derived from the play of *Hamlet* is quite distinct from those sources of amusement which we have recounted as most likely to captivate the inexperienced, thoughtless, and uncultured theatre-goer. And also it is not dependent upon—in its fullest degree it is opposed to—your mistaking the play for a veritable exhibition of real life.

But you say, " Are we not to have any colliery explosions on the stage? " I reply, " Yes, if they illustrate some scene of human devotion and heroism." " Are we to discourage the faithful and touching rendering of domestic emotion? " By no means. Lend yourself entirely to the great actor who depicts it, embark with him freely upon his sea of passion, stand with him in the heart of the tempest and the whirlwind he has created ;—and applaud him to the utmost of your hearts and voices. But as Shakespeare advises *him* at such moments to be entirely master of his passion, so must *you* too beget that inner artistic calm which keeps you constantly informed of the rightness of the grounds upon which your admiration is demanded, and the rightness of the means by which it is won. I will illustrate this by calling your attention to what frequently happens on our modern stage. We have recently had a numerous breed of very desperate stage villains. The cool, gentlemanly villain who gaily puffs his cigarette in faultless attire, as he revels in the contemplation of the most diabolical crimes, is at present the most widely-spread variety of the species. It is with some compunction that I own to having had a hand in the creation of this peculiar type. In the interests of public morality, you will be glad to hear that I have never in real life met with anybody quite so resolutely and gratuitously bad, so fertile in ingenious devices for the persecution of distressed virtue, and so callous and prompt in executing them, as the average modern stage villain. " The web of our life," says Shakespeare, " is of a mingled yarn, good and ill together : our virtues would be proud, if our faults whipped them not ; and our crimes would despair, if they were not cherished by our virtues."

But English playgoers in the main like their villains to be very villainous. They like their sympathies to be strongly roused and definitely centred. They relish an appeal to their feelings rather than an appeal to their judgment. And in all matters connected with the feelings, in all questions of conduct and emotion, the instinct of a popular audience is invariably right. And this keen sympathetic instinct is most valuable to the dramatist who knows how to seize it and guide it aright. But it sometimes stands in the way of the truthful delineation of character. It tempts the playwright to the creation of monstrosities of goodness and badness. He knows that the delivery of a virtuous sentiment by the perfect hero will be received with a storm of applause, and the perpetration of some unusually diabolical crime by the villain with hisses, while some clever and truthful stroke of character-drawing will be passed by in silence, unnoticed by the great bulk of his listeners. He dares not credit his villain with any redeeming traits, he dares not explain by what peculiar stress of circumstances the wretched creature became so enamoured of pure

P

and simple wickedness as to lose no opportunity of breaking all the precepts of the Decalogue from what the Americans call "sheer cussedness." Because he knows that this would interfere with the balance of sympathy, because he knows that what nine out of ten of his audience want is not a character to study, but a villain to hate and to hiss and to hoot. Now if you have followed my argument about the worthlessness of all art that intends to deceive you into taking it for nature, you will agree with me when I say that all demonstrations of hissing and hooting stage villainy, however creditable they may be to the moral sympathies of those who indulge in them, merely show that they mistake the real purpose of dramatic art. If the man has played his part well, applaud him ; if he has played his part badly, hiss him. But if you hiss him on account of the sentiments he has uttered and the deeds he has done, irrespective of how he has uttered them and how he has done them, you merely proclaim that your judgment and knowledge of theatrical matters are in such an immature and undeveloped state that they cannot distinguish between the man and the character he has played, between the stage and the real, outside life of the world. The only case in which you would be right to hiss certain sentiments apart from the acting, is when they are so embodied in the general drift of the play as to be contrary to the plain teachings of your moral sense, when they are so placed as to make the purport of the play, or of that part of the play, a direct offence against what you know to be right. But then it would be the author and the play against whom your judgment would be rightly aroused, and your hissing would imply a condemnation of them quite distinct from your feelings towards the actor. I am sure that the hissing of stage villains when they have played their part well is always meant in the most kindly spirit by the audience, and it is generally received by the actor as the highest compliment that can be paid him. And I do not wish to balk the current of generous enthusiasm which these demonstrations convey. But I should like to turn it into its proper channels. And therefore I venture to point out to audience and actor the quite defective sympathy with, and the misunderstanding of, the right pleasure which should be derived from the observation of a finished piece of acting which are implied in this method of rewarding it. The next time you see a villain playing his part well, applaud him as vigorously as you think his efforts deserve ; and this will show that your dramatic education is sufficiently advanced, and your dramatic judgment sufficiently balanced, for you to enter upon your examination of the play from the author's standpoint—from that point of view which, while never confounding right with wrong, or good with evil, stands artistically apart from both, and, with the omnipotence of the potter over his clay, moulds an Othello and an Iago, a Rosalind and a Macbeth, a Satan and a Raphael, with equal sympathy and delight.

On no account allow a personal feeling of detestation to take possession of you. This only shows that you have mistaken the actor's artistic effort for his possession of an evil nature.

I think that the modern stage villain is a creation to which you may very well be asked to apply the maxim with which we started. Now that you have got rid of your personal dislike for him, as I trust you will after this afternoon, you will be able to take a clearer and more unbiassed view of his character. Instead of hooting and hissing him, I hope you will direct your attention to examining him and understanding him. When you next see him "jumping on his mother" or poisoning his dear old uncle, the question for you will not be whether such conduct is sufficiently reprehensible to be visited by a storm of hisses, but whether in the first place the author has so imagined and vitalised his character as to make it likely that such a man, placed in such circumstances, would be guilty of such horrible deeds ; and, in the second place, whether the actor has so realised the character as to make it also consistent and credible. You are still to preserve your affection for your own mother and your own dear old uncle, but you are not to allow your domestic sympathies to be roused in such a manner as to blind you to fatal artistic defects in the conception and embodiment of the particular scoundrel who is at present supposed to be perpetrating these atrocious crimes in your presence. In other words, you are not to mistake it for real life. I am afraid you will think I have already insisted too much upon this point, that the stage is not to be mistaken for real life. But it is the one thing that I want to drive home into your memory, the one thing that I wish you always to remember upon entering a theatre. It is the first condition of all intelligent appreciation of stage-work that it should be rightly seen and known to be what it is, not nature, not real fact, but an abstract, a reflection, a suggestion, a seizure of one or two aspects of the million facets and million facts of nature. I will illustrate this for you before I pass on to my next rule. In that landscape of Turner which I have already spoken of there was a large stretch of country pictured on a canvas not two feet square. Now if the artist wished to give you all the facts of that landscape, he would have to employ a canvas as large as the scene itself. More than this. If you took a sufficiently powerful microscope, you would find that every morsel of land in that country-side was crammed by nature with facts too small for your natural eyesight to be aware of. Every bunch of moss upon the mouldering abbey walls would discover itself to be an immense forest alive with myriads of forms of animal life. You see at once it is quite impossible for the artist to render all the facts, or even a millionth part of the facts. What does he do? Frankly, he does not try to compete with nature, but with a few strokes of his brush he hints the essential features of the scene, gives you, so far as he can, its truth and spirit as they appeal to him, and leaves the facts to take care of themselves. And this is all the dramatic author can do in his sphere. No more than the painter can he vie with the infinite variety and mystery of nature. He cannot give you all the facts ; sometimes, indeed, he may have to sacrifice some very apparent but superficial facts for the sake of giving you what he considers important but perhaps not very obvious truths. And this is why any judgment that condemns a play upon the question of its representing or not representing the facts of everyday life is sure to be superficial and false.

Now I will pass on to my next rule, which is in some sense the converse, the complement of my last. We have seen that the stage is not real life. My next rule is—" So far as the stage departs from real life it is wrong." Perhaps you reply you cannot reconcile these two sayings. Well, they do not want any reconciling, they never fell out.

" But," you say, " Hamlet talks in blank verse, and nobody in real life talks in blank verse." If you come to the actual facts of the case, Hamlet spoke in more or less halting Danish prose. And Macbeth spoke a broad Scotch dialect. But Wolsey and Cranmer, who lived near to Shakespeare's time, of course spoke the ordinary prose of their day. Yet Shakespeare and Fletcher (for it is generally allowed now by the best scholars that the magnificent speech of Wolsey which we all used to recite at school, and many other portions of the play of *Henry the Eighth*, were written by Fletcher)—Shakespeare and Fletcher make their own countrymen of their own day talk blank verse as freely as Hamlet and Macbeth. " And this," you argue, " is very clearly a departure from real life." No, I don't think it is. Let us thrash the matter out. Take the case of Hamlet's soliloquies. We will suppose the actual Hamlet was something of the same cast of character as Shakespeare's creation. And he had something of the same reflections about death and human life, and they passed through his mind in some commonplace Danish prose of whatever period you may choose for the action of the play. He never spoke them out at all, but only thought them. Well, it is plain to begin with that if you are to know what is passing in his mind, he must speak it aloud. The soliloquy is therefore a stage convention, which you must accept, or you deprive yourself of much of that very valuable insight into character which depends upon knowing exactly how a man appears to himself, and what he thinks as distinct from what he says. Therefore to gain this insight, which is a very vital matter, you forget for the moment the comparatively unimportant fact that people do not generally soliloquise aloud. And thereby you considerably increase your knowledge of real life.

But having granted this use of the soliloquy, you say, " Why didn't Shakespeare give us the substance of it in some such ordinary English prose as might be supposed to be equivalent to the actual Danish prose that passed through the actual Hamlet's mind ? Would not that be nearer to real life ? " No, I don't think so. By lifting these vague, hesitating thoughts of Hamlet into lofty verse, by raising them above the trivial, petty commonplaces of everyday conversation, Shakespeare not merely gives you the essential purport of what passed through Hamlet's mind, but he gives you also the essential purport of what passes through every cultivated European mind when it employs itself in similar speculation. His words embody, not merely Hamlet's thoughts, but the thoughts of all the greatest minds that have occupied themselves with the same subjects. And this is done without the sacrifice of Hamlet's individual character. Though, as somebody has said, we are all Hamlets, yet Hamlet remains himself alone. Though Hamlet is typical of all humanity, yet he is distinctly Hamlet. He is, as every great and lasting dramatic character must be, at once an individual and a type. And in thus focusing and embodying the higher intellectual speculation of Europe in one character, Shakespeare has not been in any sense false to real life : he has, indeed, informed his work and his character with a larger and wider relation to real life, and given it a millionfold significance and adaptability by employing a noble verse-form which is at once felt to be removed from all that is petty, ignoble, commonplace, and unessential.

I hope I have convinced you, then, that although people in real life do not talk in blank verse, yet the higher aspects and aspirations of real life may be best conveyed in that form, and can sometimes be conveyed in no other. But there are certain plays of Shakespeare which frankly confess that they do not pretend to be pictures of real life or of the realities of life, such as *A Midsummer Night's Dream* and *The Tempest.* Much of the structure of these two plays is felt to be fantastic, and out of any direct relation to the actual experience of mankind. How do I reconcile this with my theory that when the stage departs from real life it is wrong ? Well, I readily own that much of the charm and beauty of *A Midsummer Night's Dream* is due to its pure fantasy. But what would that fantasy be without the introduction of the broadest and coarsest real life in the persons of Bottom the weaver and his friends ? Without this element of gross realism *A Midsummer Night's Dream* would not have much

more dramatic interest than Spenser's *Faerie Queen*.
Again, because *A Midsummer Night's Dream* is
essentially fantastic in its plan, you at once rate it
far below the great plays of Shakespeare that take
life seriously—*Hamlet, Lear, Macbeth,* and *Othello*.
Further, it takes a lower place amongst Shakespeare's
works than its companion play, where the scheme is
also frankly fantastic—I mean *The Tempest*. Why?
Because the supernatural agencies that buffet the
shipwrecked mariners in the enchanted island are
felt to be emblems and personifications of the stern
and awful powers of nature whose sport we are, in a
far different and higher sense than can be claimed
for the mischievous sprites in *A Midsummer Night's
Dream*. The wizard Prospero, viewed as philosopher and man of science, whose secret wisdom
harnesses and guides these mysterious forces of
nature for our benefit, is seen to possess a permanent
interest for mankind at large, and a vital relation to
our modern civilisation, which has no parallel in the
figure of Bottom the weaver, woven around with the
spells of the fairies. *The Tempest* is felt to be a
greater dramatic work than *A Midsummer Night's
Dream* in precise proportion as the fantastic architecture of its story is perceived to be fuller of
significance to humanity and more illustrative of
the actual dealings of real men and women with
the actual surrounding forces and elements of the
universe. In other words, *The Tempest* has a truer
and more serious relation to real life than *A
Midsummer Night's Dream*. But please to note
in passing that in *The Tempest*, as in *A Midsummer Night's Dream*, Shakespeare has balanced

his departure from actuality in the framework of his play by the introduction of scenes and characters of the most vivid and uncompromising realism. The celestial unreality of the story is redressed by the intrusion of the grossest earthliness and human animalism. Without this strong savour of real life, this reek of actual humanity, *The Tempest* would lose nearly all its dramatic interest.

Now I hope I have said enough to convince you that, even in plays which in structure and form diverge most widely from actual everyday experience, it is yet their relation to real life, their imaging of some permanent truth of human nature, that gives them their dramatic value, that makes them good plays. And unless they do image forth some permanent truth and reality, they are worthless. There is no kind of play that to me seems so barren, so dead, so wasteful of time as an imitation poetical play, a play that neither paints for you real life as it is, nor lifts you into that magic world where the facts of life become shadows and the truths of life become substance. I have instanced the play and character of Hamlet as types of true dramatic poetry, and I have tried to show you why they are so. If I were asked to give an example of a false, a would-be poetic play, and an imitation poetic character, I should mention (I hope I shan't shock you) the play of *The Lady of Lyons* and the character of Claude Melnotte. I am not now speaking of their merits as an acting play and an acting character. These merits, the merits of stage-craft in telling clearly and succinctly a very interesting story, are, I am ready to concede, very great. But the acceptance of *The Lady of Lyons* by the English playgoing public as a piece of poetry only shows that the great mass of theatre-goers have either the falsest or the vaguest notions of what poetry is. Or, to be more charitable, we will say they have such unconquerable longings for poetry that they are ready to swallow any gooseberry decoction and take it for champagne, provided it has got the champagne label on the bottle. If you will carefully read over the verse passages in *The Lady of Lyons* and compare them with the verse passages in *Hamlet*, you will see that the modern play shows beside the elder one like some pretentious stucco building of 1840 beside one of our great Gothic cathedrals. There is a saying of Carlyle's which I always apply to these imitation poetic plays—" Welcome the beggarliest truth rather than the royalest sham ! "

Compare the tawdry, insincere sentiment of that love scene between Claude Melnotte and Pauline with the sentiment of Robert Burns's love songs to his servant wenches. Compare it with the sentiment that dictated " Sally in our Alley." Watch the first pair of lovers you see together, the roughest and coarsest if you like. Try to guess what they are saying to each other, or, seeing that this is a matter of universal experience, perhaps you may have a stray adventure or two of your own lying handy in your recollection—compare them with the swollen bombast of the love scenes of *The Lady of Lyons*, and then tell me, if the author had set himself down to depict faithfully any real love scene between any two human beings, between a beggar and his callet, he would not have written something vastly more like nature and at bottom vastly more like poetry too. I say, if he had honestly studied the love affairs of the first shoeblack he met and rendered us a faithful account of them, a hundred to one he would have given us some vivid touch of natural poetry, worth all the empty rhetoric and bastard eloquence of a thousand Claude Melnottes.

The baldest facts are better than the finest imitation poetry. You see that, as in the earlier part of my lecture I tried to show you that the stage can never be real life, that it must never be mistaken for real life, that in many respects it must always differ from real life, I am now trying to enforce the equally important counter-truth that the stage must always be strictly founded upon real life, and that so far as it departs from this foundation it is weak and false. The dramatist can never truly draw any men and women but those he has lived amongst. Suppose all the records of English life in the sixteenth century were destroyed, and that Shakespeare's plays alone remained as the sole vestige of Elizabethan England. You would still be able to picture to yourselves exactly what kind of men the contemporaries of Raleigh and Sidney were, how they lived and spoke and bore themselves, and all the large, free life and proud spirit of our nation. You would lose the historical facts of the Spanish Armada, but you would know what manner of men those Englishmen were who shattered the yoke of Rome and Spain. The England of those times is pictured more truthfully and fully in Shakespeare's plays than it is in any history. At bottom all his heroes and all his characters are Elizabethan Englishmen. Now suppose that all traces of English nineteenth-century civilisation were to suddenly vanish, and that nothing were to remain of the England of to-day except the popular plays of the last twenty years. What sort of a picture would they render of our contemporary English life? No doubt an acute sociologist might be able to frame some idea of many of our habits and customs, and reconstruct some fragmentary scheme of the ordinary routine of an English household in the different classes of life that the different plays might deal with. But can we claim for our modern plays that they would collectively mirror English nineteenth-century life as the Elizabethan plays mirror English sixteenth-century life, that they would embody the spiritual and intellectual life of our nation to-day, that they would be in the highest, or in any sense, the history of our age? But if they do not do this, of what value are they? If the drama of any country and period does not faithfully picture the real men and women, the real everyday life of that period, it does nothing. Unless this is done you have no drama at all. When this is done you may have a vigorous poetic drama branching from it on the one side, and a school of farce and burlesque upon the other. But the root, the trunk, the living body of stage art is the truthful and serious rendering of the vital features of real everyday life. Whenever any art becomes effete, decrepit, moribund, there is but one medicine for it—" Come back to nature, to truth, to reality "; and so far as there is a living instinct in it, it must obey this call.

I think it is precisely this one quality of faithfulness and reality that the English stage lacks to-day.

I do not think that this age will witness any restoration of the poetic drama in England. We may get a few very beautiful and cultivated plays in blank verse that may be justly popular in their day and generation, but I do not think they will survive to have any influence upon future generations. I do not say that a great poetic drama is impossible in the immediate future : I only say that I think it is very improbable we shall get it. It would take me too long to give you the reasons upon which my opinion is founded. But I think it is quite within our power to develop a modern drama that shall have a permanent value and interest for future generations by reason of its faithful and scientific delineation of living character. I am aware that such a drama would not at first be popular amongst the masses of playgoers who seek only for excitement and laughter at the theatre, and do not care to inquire into the means by which they obtain it. The average British playgoer understands the playwright who says to him, " I've got a thrilling story of distressed virtue and superhuman heroism, with plenty of hair-breadth escapes from all sorts of bodily peril and pecuniary distress, and at last I'm going to reward my hero and heroine with a nice, snug fortune and a grand home, and let them live happily ever afterwards."

" All right," says the British playgoer, " go ahead."

The British playgoer also understands the playwright who says to him, " I've just put together the funniest set of situations, and tumbled into them the oddest lot of creatures, with the most side-splitting string of jokes you ever heard. There's just a little suspicion of something improper, nothing really wrong, you know——you can bring your mother and sister to see it."

" Go ahead," says the British playgoer again.

But if the playwright were to come to the average British playgoer and say to him, "My friend, the vast majority of our countrymen and countrywomen are not superhumanly virtuous or inhumanly bad. They do not pass the greater part of their time in getting into, and out of, extraordinary perils and unjust accusations. Also, the general run of Englishmen are not remarkably witty, and do not roll off funny theatrical speeches every time they open their mouths. But every one of them is a distinct human being, and has a nature and character of his own which is the exact result of the peculiar circumstances in which he and his ancestors have been placed, and of their lives and actions for countless generations past. See, here are a few specimens which I have tried to draw for you with what power and faithfulness there is in me." Then I think the average British playgoer would say, " No, thank you, I haven't got time and patience to go into the matter. When I go to the theatre I don't want to think ; I don't want to study a character ; I want to have a good laugh." And yet I fancy if once the British playgoer could be persuaded to give a little time and patience to go into the matter, he would soon find a real and lasting enjoyment in watching a drama from the standpoint I have indicated.

There is another saying which one frequently hears on the lips of constant playgoers : " When

I go to a theatre I want to be taken away from myself. Real life is dull enough and wretched enough, goodness knows—I go to a theatre to escape from it."

I do assure you with all the force of conviction there is in me that so far as you go to a theatre to be taken away from your real lives, so far your real lives are wrong and need to be altered. So far as you ask your playwright to take you away from real life, so far you ask him to carry you into regions of falsity, insincerity, absurdity, exaggeration, and unreality of all kinds.

What makes your lives so dull, you modern Englishmen, that you demand of that art whose one end is to faithfully reflect and picture them, that it shall take you away from them, and provide you with a means of escape from them ? What ails you, what makes you so dissatisfied with this real world, this England that you have made what it is to-day, that you should ask your dramatists to create a false world for you, until the very words "theatrical," "stagey" have come to mean all that is unreal, garish, pretentious, sham, and delusive ?

Again I assure you that the one thing our modern stage has got to set itself to do,—perhaps the only thing that it can do with any effect and thoroughness, —is to render a faithful account of the lives of the real men and women around us. I find that I have already overstepped the limits of my allotted time, and I am still standing on the threshold of my subject. I must leave the rest for you to think out for yourselves. Again I repeat I do not condemn any of the lighter forms of theatrical entertainment.

I am only asking that they shall be kept in their rightfully secondary place, and that many of them shall be perceived and acknowledged to have no connection at all with the drama as properly understood. Either the drama means what Shakespeare said it meant in Hamlet's advice to the players—either it exists to show " the very age and body of the time, its form, and pressure "—either it means this, or it means any haphazard medley of noise and nonsense, folly and inanity that will draw the shillings from the purses of an ignorant, half-educated public and leave their pockets and brains the emptier the next morning. You, as playgoers, have to decide which of these definitions shall describe the English drama of your day. We playwrights are in your hands. You are our masters; we obey your wishes : we slave to supply you with the entertainment that you demand. By your encouragement of this play and your rejection of that you decree what form English drama shall take in your generation. I have tried to indicate to you what seem to me the highest and most lasting sources of pleasure the theatre can afford you. The choice remains with you. You can guide us to fashion plays for you that will make audience and author alike the contempt of whatever calm artistic judgment shall in future time be brought to bear upon them, or you can urge us to the embodiment and portrayal of all that is of permanent and distinctive value in our national English life to-day, to the fashioning of living works of stage art that shall be held in loving remembrance when you and I have passed into silence.

Q

XIII

ON PLAYMAKING

(A Lecture delivered to the National Sunday League, at Newman Street Hall, on Sunday evening, 15th February 1891—Mr. William Archer in the chair.)

(Largely revised October 1894)

THERE are three leading aspects from which a play may be regarded. Firstly, as a piece of writing, a piece of literature. Secondly, as a representation of life, a picture of living men and women. Thirdly, as a story, a series of situations.

There are indeed a great many other ways of looking at a play, and it may be regarded from many other standpoints than the three I have named. For instance, when I go to the theatre and see an adaptation of a French farce whose scene is laid in a room with twelve or fourteen doors, I come to the conclusion that the British drama is the art of teaching people how to play hide-and-seek. When I go to another theatre and see the low comedian playing tricks with a bandbox, I come to the conclusion that the British drama is the art of squashing bandboxes by sitting on them. When I go to another theatre and see some of our latter-day burlesques, I come to the conclusion that the British drama is the art of playing the fool and debasing the English language. When I go to another theatre and see the peculiarly virtuous hero persecuted for five acts for no particular reason by a peculiarly vicious villain, I come to the conclusion that the British drama is the art of weaving a chain of circumstantial evidence around an innocent person ; and I come away with the uncomfortable notion that our convict establishments at Portland and Chatham are filled with poor prisoners who have been unjustly accused of murder and robbery.

Well, you may take your choice of all these ways of regarding the British drama. I just name them to you, and tell you that to-night I mean to ask you to look at it from the first three and primary aspects that I mentioned to you.

I'll repeat them to you. Firstly, a play may be regarded as a piece of literature. This is the art of the poet or man of letters. Secondly, as a representation of human life. This is the art of the dramatist. Thirdly, as a series of situations. This is the art of the theatrical playwright.

I shall touch on the first two aspects only in their relation to the third, and as soon as I have pointed out their connection with the third, I shall drop them and come to the main purpose of my lecture, which treats of the mechanical part of the work, the making of a play.

I deal with the literary aspect first because I consider it of the chief importance. It is often said in the theatre that the test of a play is, will it act ? This is merely a theatrical test, and can be refuted by all the heaps of forgotten theatrical rubbish that have been popular successes during the past two hundred years. Believe me, the true test of a play is, will it act and read? And it is because most of the pieces of Shakespeare and Sheridan stand this test that they still occupy the leading positions in our theatre and are still the most frequently acted plays. More money, I suppose, has been paid to witness *The School for Scandal* than any other comedy, and more money has been paid to witness *Hamlet* than any other serious play.

Next I come to the dramatic aspect—I mean that aspect which regards the play as a representation of human life and character. I am not certain whether I ought not to place the dramatic art before the literary art. The taste of life is after all the keenest pleasure that any work of art can give you. Mr. Matthew Arnold in a very-often-quoted sentence defined poetry to be a "criticism of life." But all art is a criticism of life. Dramatists, painters, sculptors, all criticise life. The statues of Phidias are a perpetual criticism of our modern city-bred population with their billycock hats. But as a matter of courtesy, at least, I have given the literary aspect of a play the first place, the dramatic the second. As a matter of fact it is often impossible to define the line which divides the two. Thus Shakespeare is at once our greatest poet and our greatest dramatist.

Now I'm not certain whether I ought not to make a still further division between the story-telling and the construction—the design that underlies it. But construction and story-telling are so very intimately connected with each other that it is impossible to entirely dissever them. Indeed, as I have just remarked, it is impossible to divide altogether the literary and dramatic qualities of a play, so it is also impossible to separate the constructive and story-telling qualities. I will therefore ask you to bear in mind that all these divisions of mine are very loose and undefined, and are only rough attempts at dividing things that are never found entirely apart. I will illustrate this for you by comparing the dramatist's art with the painter's. The picture that nature places before the painter's eye at any one given moment forms one perfect, indivisible consensus of form, colour, light, and shade. In a perfectly - painted picture all these attributes should be perfectly and indivisibly blended. But as a matter of fact, when an artist paints a picture, he either makes his feeling for colour his first object, and to that extent sinks his feeling for light and shade, or he renders his light and shade perfectly, and to that extent neglects his colour. So it is in writing plays. If the author puts literature first, he is compelled to some extent to do it at the expense of character and of situation. If he puts his story first and aims only at placing before you a series of exciting, breathless incidents, then to some extent he does it at the expense of literature and character. In a perfect play all these things, literature, character, and situation, should be only different aspects of one and the same thing. But as no perfect play ever was or ever will be written, as all plays partake of the weaknesses and the infirmities and the idiosyncrasies of the author, it is almost impossible to find a play where the three qualities of literature, character, and situation are mutually balanced and conjoined.

After this I am going to leave the literary standpoint altogether, and to say no more about it, as it requires dealing with on its own account. I will only just mention in passing that the highest literary judgment of the age declines to concern itself very much about the modern acted drama, and has, indeed, ruled it outside literature altogether. That is a very serious fact for authors, for actors, and for theatre-goers. But I am afraid that the substantial justice of that decision can scarcely be called very much in question. It is for us who are writing for the stage to-day to try to remove that reproach from our art.

I leave the literary standpoint, and I want to contrast what I have termed the dramatic and the theatrical standpoints.

When I was a boy of about twelve, I was very much attracted by a bookseller's window which used to display week after week an illustrated instalment of the adventures of Mr. Richard Turpin, and I frequently resisted the blandishments of the confectioner and the pastry-cook that I might become possessed of the enthralling incidents and episodes contained in the twelve pages. I am bound to say that the adventures of Mr. Richard Turpin did possess a very considerable attraction for me in those days; and while I was not quite blind to certain eccentricities regarding the eighth commandment in my hero's conduct, yet his life was so stirring, his bravery so distinguished, his prowess so redoubtable, that his character, so far as I studied it, appeared to me on the whole as sympathetic as his manner of life was exciting and enviable. I did not apply any very subtle analysis to the character of Mr. Richard Turpin. So far as I thought about his character at all, it was only in relation to his adventures. I did not ask myself, " Is this character consistent and credible and lifelike? Is it like what does or could possibly happen in the actual world around me?" I asked myself only whether on the whole Mr. Richard Turpin's career, previous to the unlucky accident that brought it to an untimely end, was not very much preferable to that of any schoolboy in the land? And I came to the conclusion that Blueskin, Jonathan Wild, and Starlight Bess were on the whole more entertaining companions than Euclid and Lindley Murray.

I suppose that the first demand of an average theatrical audience to its author will always be the same as the child's "Tell me a story." And I don't wish to decry or to belittle the very delightful art of telling a story without reference to any moral to be drawn from it, to character, to fact, to history, to instruction, or to any other end than entertainment. And when we go to a theatre, a good many of us like to be children, and to listen to a thoroughly good story, without any other consideration whatever. But I wish to suggest to you that this demand for a story, for a series of incidents, irrespective of truth, of character-drawing, of lifelikeness, is comparatively a childish demand, and it is only by becoming to some extent a child that one can accept, with any pleasure or satisfaction, a dramatic story in which the character-drawing is sunk and forgotten under the swift current of exciting and empty situations. I wish to bring out this contrast between character-drawing and story-telling in dramatic work very clearly and vividly, because it will guide the whole drift of my talk to you to-night. And I wish to submit to you this maxim founded on the contrast. Story and incident and situation in theatrical work are, unless related to character, comparatively childish and unintellectual. They should, indeed, be only another phase of the development of character. Thus all the tremendous and moving scenes of the murder in *Macbeth* are exactly correspondent with, and spring from, the characters of Macbeth and Lady Macbeth. Thus all the moving and dramatic scenes in *Lear* are exactly connected with the characters of the King and his daughters, Kent, Gloster, and Edgar. Again, in *Hamlet* you will find the same direct and intimate relation. Taking literature as the chief quality, we find that character-drawing is valuable and permanent only when it is embodied in language of lasting beauty, significance, or appropriateness. Thus our chief dramatic creations, the greatest characters of our drama and its greatest scenes, are married to its noblest verse. Shakespeare is, as I said, at one and the same moment supreme poet and supreme dramatist. A mere story, a mere succession of incidents, if these do not embody and display character and human nature, only give you something in raw melodrama pretty much equivalent to the adventures of our old hero Mr. Richard Turpin.

Very frequently the construction of a play is supposed to be bad simply because it is not theatrical. Very often the construction of a play is supposed to be good only in so far as it is related to the story

and to the action and to the series of incidents. But
we have already assumed that the story itself is inferior to the higher qualities of character-painting
and literature. If you are disposed to argue this
out with me at any time I shall be pleased to
go into the matter, but for the present you must
allow me to assume this. And I wish you to notice
that it is very often said that French audiences will
stand a lot of talk on the stage : English audiences
won't. And English play-construction is supposed
to be good merely in proportion to the quantity of
action, the quantity of incident it unfolds. And
this lands us in the dilemma that the French, who will
endure talk on the stage, and indeed like it, are the
possessors of a modern drama of world-wide reputation, whereas the English drama has been for some
generations quite inoperative in an intellectual sense.
In fact, the French have had a drama because they
will stand talk, which is at bottom only another way
of saying that French plays can be read, and English plays, having been composed chiefly of mere
theatrical tricks and carpenters' devices, cannot be
read. That is, the higher qualities of literature and
character-painting have been sunk in the English
drama, sacrificed to a construction whose only end
has been to exhibit a series of situations, irrespective
of character and literature.

Now I propose here this rule for you :—That
construction is perfect which exhibits all the qualities
of a play in harmonious conjunction, and that is
next best which errs on the side of exhibiting, so far
as is possible within the three-hours' traffic of the
stage, the greater quantity of the higher qualities of

character-drawing and literature. Please do not fall into the mistake of supposing I am condemning great and strong situations. The greatest but the most *melodramatic* situation in the whole range of the drama is the Play scene in *Hamlet*. The test of the permanent value of a great situation is, how far is it related to the development, the unfolding, the crisis, of a great character?

All round us to-night are thirty millions of our fellow-countrymen, each of them speaking the English language, not often, I am afraid, in a very literary style, but at any rate using the same words that you will find in all our best poets and men of letters. This is the raw material of the literature of our plays.

Further, each of these thirty million human beings has a distinct individual character of infinite complexity in ceaseless development. This is the raw material of the character and human nature of our plays.

Again, each of these thirty millions is living a life of constant and varied action and incident, at times and for certain moments placed in more or less dramatic situations. This is the raw material of the story and action of our plays.

Now the art of dramatic construction consists in so blending, so arranging, so condensing, so selecting from all these materials as to give you what the playwright considers to be the essence of it, the essence of the literature, the essence of the character, the essence of the action. And this has to be tightly packed into three or four acts of about half an hour each.

Now it is quite evident that these three or four acts cannot be exact copies, or even approximate copies, of the huge mass of English human life at this moment, or even of that part of it which the playwright sets out to represent. Don't believe that a play is a good one in the proportion that it exactly copies all the minute details of real life. Don't believe that a play is " true to life " in the proportion that it exactly copies these minute realistic details.

Of all the questions relating to the drama there is none so little comprehended, so much misunderstood, even amongst our most constant playgoers, even amongst our most cultivated critics, as this question of being " true to life " on the stage. The art of the drama is different from all the other arts in that its presentation employs living men and women. And this gives rise to the utterly false notion that a play should in all its details be an exact copy of life, and that it is a good play and " true to life " in so far as it does copy all the details of life, and in so far as its personages do everything exactly as they would do it in real life. I assure you that if you will carefully watch and analyse any play that was ever put on the stage, you will find that at the bottom it is no more " real life " than a landscape painted on canvas is mountain and water and woodland. To begin with, the playwright has an average of about twelve minutes for the presentation on the stage of any character. Nature has seventy years. That is, reckoning a day as twelve hours, the playwright can give you only the one-million-five-hundred-thousandth part of what nature gives.

And bearing in mind the immense complexity of every human personality, the infinitude of aspects in which it may be viewed and presented, it is just conceivable that there are in a life of the average seventy years' span, some hundreds of thousands of varying characters, according to the moments the playwright selects for presentation, and according to the aspect from which he surveys them. If the playwright is to make any attempt to portray the *whole* of the character, to make it complete and many-sided, so as to give the spectator the impression of having known the whole life-history of the man, his details and his methods of presentation must be widely different from nature's details and methods of presentation. A millionth part of a character cannot be like the whole character. Nor can a character that has to be presented in twelve minutes be *realistically* like a character that is presented in seventy years. There must be immense concessions, immense accommodations, immense disdain and rejection of realistic details. Nay, further, at times the playwright must lend himself to immense *falsification* of mere realistic details, if his characters are to be " true to life " in their essential, and vital, and innermost qualities.

Again, the same thing is exemplified in situation and incident. The method of presentation of every story on every stage is a pure convention, as unlike real life as the wildest fairy-tale. Does this mean that there is no such thing as the sincere, faithful representation of character and human history on the stage ; that the current word " theatrical," implying something radically false and unreal, must, by the

very law of the stage's being, sum up and circum-
scribe every representation thereon? Not at all.
Large events and large characters with high and far-
reaching significance can be rendered quite truthfully
on the stage. But never *realistically*. The irony of
art is that the greatest verities on their first appeal
to the common average mind appear to be the greatest insincerities. Thus, to use an illustration I am
never tired of using, the splendid masterpieces of
Turner in landscape are to this day a stumbling-
block and an offence to the average spectator in the
National Gallery. You will never see a crowd round
them as you will see round some cheap and easily-
recognisable transcript of some most ordinary scene.
The average spectator sees in Turner only extraordinary effects which are not those which he most
readily recognises. He knows nothing of the im-
mensity and complexity of this unfathomable
universe, or the mystery and subtlety of beauty
which the painter is trying to realise for him ; he
knows nothing about such effects except that they
are not of hourly occurrence in Clapham. And if
he dwells upon them at all, he comes away baffled,
and confused, and distressed, and with a feeling
that Turner is not "true to life."

So likewise the average playgoer constantly mistakes an *unusual* character for an *unreal* character,
an *unusual* situation for an *unreal* situation. It is
amusing and maddening to listen to the complacent
verdict of good folks from Clapham or Kensington
who find a play "unlifelike" because its characters
and situations are not such as they meet with every
day in Clapham and Kensington. They do not

know, and cannot be brought to see, that what happens in Clapham or Kensington is of no account whatever. For all this, every individual in Clapham or Kensington is of the utmost interest and importance to the dramatist. But if a play deals with unusual characters who do not hail from Clapham, and unusual occurrences which do not happen in every Clapham household, instantly the man from Clapham thinks it unreal. Now it is very necessary that the difference between an *uncommon* situation and an *unreal* situation should be understood. The Play scene in Hamlet is a most *unusual* situation, which is scarcely likely to happen more than once. Yet it is of transcendent significance, and is built into a scheme of wonderful grandeur and complexity. But it is not an *unreal* situation, such for instance, as is the constantly-occurring situation in modern plays where one character overhears long scenes between other characters in the same room.

Yet playgoers who continue to accept with rapture these stale, these impossible, old theatrical situations, will often cavil at some situation which is merely unusual on the stage and has not happened within the limits of their own experience at Clapham or Kensington.

Now as regards probability of situation, we find nature violating it every day and every moment. We can scarcely take up a newspaper without reading of some almost inconceivable incident or situation. And when we see an unusual situation on the stage we should not condemn it because it is foreign to our own immediate concern and experience. We

should only ask whether it is vividly imagined and
realised by the dramatist, whether it is well knit into
his scheme, and whether it is placed in definite and
consistent relation to the development of his characters and the progress of his story. And this
brings me back to remark again that as the
dramatist has to make immense concessions and
accommodations in the presentation of his characters,
so he has to make immense concessions and accommodations in the conduct of his story. Here again
there is no such thing as being " true to life " in the
sense of copying life. The stage is not real life.
Those who want " real life " can go into the streets
and get it, heaps of it.

I'll give you an illustration which will perhaps
help you to understand my meaning, and also help
you to understand what the art of dramatic design
is, and what relation the drama of a nation should
bear to the sum total of the national life. I want
you to picture one of the many Gothic churches that
were raised in our country from the twelfth to the
fifteenth centuries. I want you to picture the
surrounding country before the church was built,
the countless thousands of careless and varied and
indeterminate lines and curves which the surrounding
landscape then presented. Now comes the builder
and builds the church, and puts it on the top of the
hillside in the finest position that he can select.
Contrast that church with the landscape around it.
What has the builder done? What is the difference
between the lines of that church and the lines of the
landscape? The lines of the church, the lines of the
architecture, the lines of the building are straight,

determined, symmetrical. There is design and intention in every inch of it. The surrounding landscape is careless, undefined, confused, and unsymmetrical in its outlines. Now what the builder of that church has done for that country-side, the dramatist of a nation should do for his country's life and character. First of all there should be design in every portion of his work. If you look carefully into the Gothic work of the best period, you will find that there is design and meaning in every portion of it. All the windows are filled with varied and different tracery; all the niches are filled with different saints; all the mouldings are deeply and definitely cut, with beautiful effects of light and shade; all the ornaments are exactly copied from nature and present an infinite variety. There is no repetition. But it was all hewn from the surrounding hillside. The stone was quarried there. The delicate tracery and leaves were copied exactly and minutely with loving conscientiousness from the leaves of the surrounding native trees. *But the church isn't in the least like the landscape.*

To sum up, the total effect of the church is due to the fact that it was built upon a plan. The total effect of the landscape is due, on the other hand, to the fact that it was apparently thrown down without a plan. Nature's work is apparently full of carelessness and wilfulness — I say apparently, because at this moment it is inconvenient to go into the question of design in nature—nature's work apparently, I say, is full of carelessness and wilfulness and confusion. Man's work is full of purpose and decision and arrangement, not perfect, of course, but so far as there is any good and lasting result in it, always aiming at perfection.

Now this contrast is likewise perpetually present between a work of art and the raw materials of that art. Art, dramatic art, every art, is nothing at bottom but design, selection, arrangement, and ornament.

Here I would wish to make some distinction between the words "plot" and "design" in stage-work. The word "plot" has lately come to have some very bad associations. It is connected with all the mechanical and artificial tricks of situation and theatrical devices that have so long disfigured our English stage. One of our leading critics has recently expressed a wish to see a drama without any plot. I don't think he quite meant what he was saying. But in so far as the word "plot" has come to signify an artificial and mechanical and palpably unnatural and impossible series of theatrical accidents and coincidences, I cordially agree with him in his desire to see the modern English drama have as little to do with plot as is possible. I would like, then, to mark off the word "plot" as signifying something quite mechanical and artificial and unnatural. But the word "design" is a larger and better word, and may be taken to comprehend all the good and necessary significations which the word "plot" contains, while it also extends to something further, and includes that spirit of determination and selection, of straightness of outline and harmonious conjunction of parts which is typified in my simile of the church.

Now, reverting again to my contention that the English drama should be the art of representing English life, so far as is possible, in all its fulness and grandeur and many-sidedness, and construction being quite a secondary thing and only the hand-maid and minister—it follows that construction is good only so far as it allows a play to exhibit the largest quantities of the most permanent and vital qualities of English life. And you will find that this will not be the neatest construction.

I have often heard sneers at Shakespeare's construction by people who do not consider how widely different were the scenery and accessories of his time from ours, and who also do not consider what is far more important—the volume and quantity of human life and action and character which are contained in his plays.

You can make a great many mistakes, you can go wrong in a thousand different ways in building a cathedral, and when you have finished you will find it full of imperfections, and most likely some of the leading parts of your design will never be carried out. None of our great Gothic cathedrals was ever completed. But you can't make many mistakes in constructing a modern villa at £40 a year. You can have the neatest possible construction, and you can turn out thousands of them without any fear that you won't be able to carry out your design.

Now many of the plays of Shakespeare and of some of the other Elizabethan dramatists are like our great Gothic cathedrals in their dealing with great masses and volumes of human life and character and emotion. The mere quantity of material in a play of Shakespeare's is something almost incredible until one has watched scene after scene, grouping after grouping, character after character. To read Shakespeare through is almost like watching the great pageant of human life itself, so varied, so rich, so many-sided is the display.

But we cannot claim that Shakespeare's construction is neat, in the modern sense of the word. Sometimes an act extends over thirteen scenes and several years. But what I want to point out to you is that it is not on that account necessarily bad. It is only bad if, and in so far as, the representation and exhibition of human life and character contained in it could have been compressed into a less number of scenes, and into a shorter period.

Our modern rules of construction scarcely allow us (except in melodrama) more than one scene in an act ; and it is the playwright's business so to arrange and condense and mass his action that it can all take place in three or four acts of some half an hour to three-quarters of an hour each.

Three or four scenes in an act, and especially what are called "carpenters' scenes"—that is, front scenes which drop down from the skies at about three feet from the footlights while the carpenters are busy arranging another large set behind—this number of scenes in an act is apt to disturb the thread of the story, and to give us uncomfortable reminders that we are in a theatre. We have lately done away with a great many of the old absurdities in this way, and of recent years I do not remember seeing at any first-rate theatre what has been described, I think by Charles Lamb, as "two stage-carpenters rushing at one another, each with half a castle in his grasp." It is a very palpable gain that we should be able to sit through an act from the rising of the curtain to the fall without being disturbed by the shifting of the scenery three or four times, and by the ascent and descent of sections of blue firmament, and by catching glimpses of carpenters' legs. But we purchase this neatness of construction in the modern drama at the cost of still further emphasising the fact that all dramatic construction whatever, whether of one scene in an act or thirteen scenes in an act, is a matter of pure convention, absolutely unlike real life.

If you come to the question of absolute reality and fidelity to bare facts, Shakespeare's thirteen scenes in an act are quite as near to what could actually take place as the one scene in an act of our latter-day realists. As an exact and literal copy of real life, Zola's *Thérèse Raquin*, for example, is quite as false as Shakespeare's *Hamlet*.

Never in this world did the dramatic and characteristic incidents in the lives of any series of persons take place so that they could be put on the stage exactly as they did really occur. If you look into your own lives, you may have had dramatic moments, dramatic scenes of some few minutes' duration, and you all have characters and are living lives that are worth being studied by the dramatist, and are worth being put on the stage. But none of you has ever taken part in any scene that could be, exactly and in all its details, and in its precise duration in the matter of time, made into an act or even into a scene of a play.

But to say this——and it cannot be disputed——is at once to give the death-blow to realism on the stage. I repeat here what I have often said, that I cannot imagine why those who wish for sordid and mean and disgusting details of life to be shown upon the stage in their naked and ugly truth—I repeat that I cannot for the life of me imagine why they want a stage or a theatre at all, when already every detail is being acted in the outside world, and can be seen all around them without the payment of a single shilling.

But if it is urged that the realists are only clamouring for an approach to lifelikeness—for getting as near nature as possible—if this is all they want, then they yield their point, and it becomes at once a question of selection and degree. The fact is, every dramatist is a realist and an idealist in different proportions, and every play is a blend of realism and idealism. This being so, it becomes a question of arguing out what details shall be selected, and what left out, and what proportion the one shall bear to the other.

Lately a school has arisen amongst us which proclaims that the details of ugliness and disease are of the chief importance for us to study, and that curious and distorted forms of vice and selfishness and human degradation are the essential elements to be preserved and treasured in our plays. I protest against it with all my might. I say that all great art is instinctively healthy, instinctively rejects and hates and tramples upon all mere disease, ugliness, and vice, and uses them only by way of contrast, and to produce the impression of truthfulness. I think that in this respect art should strictly follow nature by preserving a balance, as nature always does—a balance of health, of beauty, and pleasure in life.

Now I come to another point of construction which I will just notice for a moment or so—I mean the use of the soliloquy on the stage. You know that dramatic action is made up chiefly of contrast and conflict. There is nothing so dramatic and nothing so effective on the stage as a conflict between two people — a conflict of wit, a conflict of swords, a conflict of fists, a conflict of passions. There is nothing so dramatic as a conflict between two people, except, what is frequently far more dramatic still, the conflict that takes place in the solitary human soul. Now the soliloquy, which is often the very essence of a play — witness the soliloquies of Hamlet and Iago—the soliloquy is of course a pure stage convention. It should be used very sparingly, and never when the same knowledge can be given to the audience and the same effect obtained without it. But, bearing in mind our leading rule to-night, that the aim of a play is to show the greatest quantity and highest quality of human life and character, it is very often impossible to avoid the soliloquy. The most tremendous battles, fraught with the most tremendous issues, take place in the solitary heart of man, and sometimes these cannot be rendered or even suggested by dialogue.

To lay down a broad general rule on the subject, we may say that it is never permissible to do by soliloquy what can be adequately done by dialogue. To put this rule in another form : the story of a play should always move hiddenly beneath the dialogue, like the works of a watch beneath the hands, itself unseen. Soliloquy should never be used to carry on the story ; it must sometimes be used to reveal character.

(In my two recent modern plays I have not employed the soliloquy, and I have been praised for its disuse. Now there is no doubt that soliloquies, and still more asides, are to some extent disturbing and destructive of *vraisemblance*. And also there is a pleasure in laying aside conventions and obtaining results by finer or by more natural methods. To conquer an unnecessary convention is one of the greatest delights of an art ; to loyally accept and work within a necessary convention is no less a delight. Now in many plays of modern life, character may be sufficiently, if not quite exhaustively, conveyed by dialogue ; and the soliloquy may be largely, and in some cases entirely, dispensed with. At times a great appearance of subtlety of character-drawing may be obtained by the absence of soliloquy. When there is no chance of the dramatist or his characters explaining what on earth they mean by a certain strange course of action, carried on by means of strange conversations amongst strange people, a tremendous reputation for subtlety may arise if the dramatist is only fortunate enough to find industrious and ingenious commentators, and is wise enough to hold his tongue. But in no case should subtlety be claimed or allowed for mere eccentricity or contradiction of character. And in all cases where the soliloquy is discarded we must feel sure that the dramatist thoroughly understands and sees into the hearts of his characters, and that he could instantly explain and justify and reconcile their actions and words and thoughts into perfect unity if he were challenged. With so much of explanation, it may be allowed that much of *vraisemblance* is gained by the disuse of the soliloquy in certain modern work where no great subtlety of character has to be unfolded. But mark the paradox. The moment any great and subtle character has to unfold itself on the stage the dramatist must frankly employ the most simple, the most childish means—he must make that character talk aloud to himself. There is no help for it. Don't tell me that there are all sorts of subtle things revolving in the mind of this or that commonplace modern personage, or in the mind of their creator as he surveys them. I don't believe it. I want the dramatist himself to show me what these subtleties are, and I want him to do it by the simple, old-fashioned way of letting his character talk aloud, so that I may judge for myself how far he has penetrated into the conscience and heart of that character, and so that I may get one of the highest delights the drama can give—the watching of the reflections and re-reflections to and fro the outer world and a man's soul. The rejection of the soliloquy by the modern realistic drama proclaims, more than any other of its rules and methods, the essential meanness of its aims, its self-condemnation and self-consecration to a parochial sphere, parochial interests, and parochial views of life, its determination to traffic only in smallwares and trumperies. So far from the rejection of the soliloquy giving power and subtlety to the dramatist, I am persuaded that it terribly limits and weakens his opportunities of subtle character-portraiture. There is no possibility of any great, subtle dramatic creation without soliloquy, or without certain stealthy, significant actions and sinister, glancing by-words, which sometimes do its office. The drama could not make a greater mistake than to abdicate the soliloquy. We all live to ourselves. In a loneliness more remote from human touch and sight than the central waste of an African desert, in a solitude profounder than any Arctic night, much of every life is passed. Every soul is a world ; it has its busy cities and thronging highways, but these are mere dots on its surface. Its great land and sea marks are its vast wildernesses, its unlighted forest deeps, its unpathed waters. Why should the dramatist throw away this most powerful instrument, this piercing spy-glass, the soliloquy : his only means for showing to his audience those shadowy recesses, those entrancing twilight realms, those starry altitudes and hellish abysses where every man walks alone with his God ?—VENICE, 21*st October* 1894.)

To return. As I have said before, all rules of construction are merely conventional, and the intent of a play is not to give you a neat and perfect bit of stage workmanship, but to give you a knowledge of human life and character, and to tell you a story, not as it exactly happened, but so that it may leave an impression upon you akin to that which would have been left upon you if you had been able to give the days or months or years to watch it, and if you had known intimately all the actors and all their thoughts and passions ; so that at the end of the play the impression remaining upon you should be much the same as would remain in your memory years after you had witnessed the scenes in real life.

If you had been concerned in any great course of dramatic action, after a time you would lose the memory of all the unimportant incidents and accidents, and only the most vivid and important details would remain with you.

Again, you see, construction is nothing but condensation and selection. Very often neatnesses and niceties of construction have to be sacrificed to the necessity of giving broad and vital truths of character.

Here I come back to that opposition between situation and construction on the one hand, and life and character on the other, with which I started. It has, indeed, been one of the main objects of my lecture to thrust this contrast upon you. Where construction is made of the first importance, where neatness and perfection of construction are obtained, it is generally at the cost of truthfulness and force and subtlety of character. Where naturalness of action and character are aimed at, it is generally at some sacrifice of niceness and perfection of construction.

In many of the writers of the French school—in Sardou and Scribe, for instance—perfection of construction has been carried to such a point that the human passions and the human characters that are dealt with seem to be absolutely of no importance to themselves and to the great mass of human life. The one object of their existence seems to be to show the ingenuity of the playwright.

The moment the construction of a play becomes so ingenious as to be noticeable, at that moment it passes its limits, and convicts the playwright of an attempt, not to paint human nature, but to show his own cleverness.

That construction, then, is the best which sinks itself and is entirely unobtrusive, and moves quite silently and unnoticed under the story and under the truths of character and life which the dramatist has to present.

I touched a little while ago on Shakespeare's construction, and claimed that it was admirably suited to the drama of his time. We have passed into a different world, and different modes of construction must necessarily be in vogue in our drama to-day. But Shakespeare still remains a master of stage-craft ; his broad, loose, natural construction is still a model in many respects to modern playwrights. I don't mean that we are to put thirteen scenes into an act and to have one act extending over several years ; but I mean that his large methods of handling human nature, his splendid and vivid contrasts, his carelessness of mere neatness and dexterity, of mere *vraisemblance*, when some great character or scene has to be expressed — I say these are all admirable qualities of construction, whose study and example should inform our modern work with a larger relation than it now possesses to our national life and to human life as a whole.

I wish to show you some of the difficulties under which a playwright labours in making a play for a modern audience. First of all he has to obtain a story which shall be of the widest possible interest to all classes. Next he must imagine from his memory and observation original characters to carry it on. Then, having thought out the main incidents of his story, and having thoroughly realised his characters in his mind, he has to chop up his story into three or four acts, each of them containing a tolerably equal portion of the action of the play. This in itself is oftentimes very difficult. But difficulties are further increased when, having mainly divided his incidents and action into separate acts, he has to devise the sequence of the scenes in each act.

Before coming here I analysed an act of a modern play. In the French drama the word "scene" in an act is used to signify, not a change of locality, but a change of characters. Thus, if one character were alone at the beginning of the act, the first scene in that act would be his soliloquy. If another person were to enter and have a conversation with him, that would be scene two. If, again, two more people were to come on, that would be scene three, and so on.

In the act that I analysed there were twenty-one different scenes carried on by different numbers of personages, from one person alone on the stage to a crowd of some fifty or sixty. Each of these twenty-one scenes was necessary to the play, and each had to be arranged in such an order that it could carry on the action of the story in the most natural way, and without bringing the characters on too often, and so as to give them all a natural reason for their exits and entrances.

Now these twenty-one scenes could have been arranged in some thousands of different ways, and that may give you some idea of the thought and study that generally has to be expended in getting the sequence right and natural.

Further, every scene in every act of a play has to
be so thought out that its various elements may give
the best possible effect. Thus in a quarrel scene there
are perhaps a dozen or twenty speeches and actions
to be so blended as to bring a proper climax. In a
quarrel that takes place in real life you will find a
great many undramatic repetitions and anti-climaxes,
and sometimes a vast amount of unnecessary language. On the stage all this has to be avoided.

Once more, not only has each act to be so subdivided, and each scene in the act so subdivided and
arranged, but also every sentence in every scene should
have these four qualities :—Firstly, it should carry on
the story. Secondly, it should illumine and develop
the character who speaks it. Thirdly, it must be colloquial—that is, it must be such as might be spoken
in ordinary English everyday conversation. Fourthly,
it should not be merely colloquial ; it must not descend to bathos or commonplace ; there must be
some feeling after literary style and expression in
it. And it should do all this quite unconsciously
and implicitly, and as if the actor and author were
quite unaware of it.

That perhaps will give you some idea of the
great complexity of the dramatist's art, and it will
explain how it is that so few have the patience to
learn it. It will also explain how it is that a play,
which after all is the length of only ten or a dozen
newspaper articles, may possibly contain quite a
year's hard work.

I had many other secrets of play-writing that I
wished to tell you, but perhaps I have said enough
for the present. And so I will very swiftly

summarise the two or three things that I wish you to carry away with you.

I wish you to remember that plot and story and construction should be inferior to the truthful exhibition of life and character. I wish you to be discontented with all merely ingenious construction, all that savours of artifice and trick. If I were asked to name the one quality that all great art has, I should say it has no trick. You can see it again and again without finding it out. When you suspect that we are tricking you with ingenious situations and devices, ask yourself, "What should I think of this if I had to see it a dozen times over?"

Then I wish you to distrust all judgment of a play that views it as a mere copy of real life, and to remember that neither in the drama nor in any other art can any great thing be painted in mere imitation of nature.

Next I would like you to remember, what perhaps scarcely came into the scope of my lecture to say— and yet I could not help saying it,—that no great school of art can ever be founded upon the study of vice and ugliness and disease.

Finally, I hope you will grow to dislike merely neat, ingenious, theatrical construction. I remember, when I was a child, passing by the garden of a farmhouse where the box hedges and trees were clipped into the likenesses, one of a bird, one of a bee-hive, and another into the exact form of the trees that are sometimes put into a child's Noah's Ark. You can train and clip your national drama, prune it with a set of small, hard, artificial rules, choke it with Puritan prejudices, rob it of all its healthy natural growth, make it formal, conventional, childish, petty, pretty, geometrical, logical, trim, neat, anything but like a living tree.

Contrast that clipped and unnatural tree with the Scotch fir, that will not be trimmed into any kind of neatness or artificiality, but stands in its rugged vigour, defiant of formula, its roots clasping and shattering the granite, its red trunk flaming and beaconing to the sun, its dark, thick foliage lifted in amazing masses of wild, irregular beauty against the eternal heavens.

Let this be the type of our national drama.

OUR MODERN DRAMA—IS IT AN ART OR AN AMUSEMENT?

(A Lecture delivered to the Playgoers' Club 5th November 1892)

SOME years ago I entered the pit of a provincial theatre in the middle of the evening. It was about half full, and in one of the middle rows, just in the shade of the dress-circle, was a group of young fellows belonging to the town. The play was not to their liking, for instead of listening to it they were gathered round one of their number, who was entertaining them with some witticisms of his own upon the play, upon the performance, and upon the actors. This critic of the drama was a young man, apparently of the lower middle class; his hands were in his trousers pockets, and he sat balanced upon the back rail of the pit seat; he was dressed in a rather large check tweed suit and a billycock hat, which was pushed far back on his head. As the play progressed his remarks became more and more facetious; and his companions evidently found his entertainment far more lively than the entertainment on the stage, and his dialogue far superior to the dialogue of the play. The play was *Hamlet.*

That billycock hat has haunted me ever since, until it has become to me the symbol of all pert, foolish, uneducated, unthinking dramatic criticism— the criticism which sees in the drama nothing but a childish pastime whereby empty minds may while away an empty hour. I call such criticism "billy-cock-hat" criticism. And it exists among all classes ; it is found equally in the dress-circle and stalls as in the pit.

I am afraid by telling you this story first I have anticipated the answer to the question contained in the title of my lecture. At least you are thinking that your lecturer has made up his mind that our drama is, or should be, anything but an amusement, is in fact a very formidable affair. But, if you please, we will consider the question still open.

Perhaps I had better explain here that throughout this lecture I shall restrict the words "amuse" and "amusement" to a somewhat narrow and specialised meaning—I shall employ them to signify mere care-less, irresponsible, unthinking, unintellectual enjoy-ment as opposed to thoughtful and cultivated delight in works of art. In a former lecture that I gave you I used the words "amuse" and "amusement" in a much wider sense, so as to include all the varied sources of pleasure. In that lecture I spoke of being rightly amused and wrongly amused, and of there being nine Muses, one of whom was Melpomene. My broad division-line between art and amusement is to some extent the same division-line that I drew in that lecture between right amusement and wrong amusement. Our language does not afford words whose definition is strictly limited to the states of

S

feeling I wished to describe, and therefore I am obliged to define my terms at starting. In one sense the pleasure in a work of art may itself be called amusement; but I shall not allow that wider meaning to the words "amuse" and "amusement" to-night.

We will, if you please, consider our gathering here as a conference between playwright and playgoers to discuss the status and aims of modern English playwriting and playgoing. Only, as you cannot all talk at once, you must allow me to state your part of the case for you, and I'll try and do this fairly and fully. And I introduced our friend in the billycock hat merely because I wanted an extreme type of playgoer — a playgoer who regards the drama very decidedly as an amusement. Now I want you to picture him very clearly to yourselves, bodily, mentally, and spiritually. There he sits on the rail of the pit, his hands in his pockets, his legs sprawling out, and that billycock hat pushed back so as to give full play to his foolish grin and chuckle. He has perhaps been at work all day, and he has called at two public-houses on his way. He has come to the theatre to be amused. His natural tastes and sympathies are not in the direction of philosophical speculation, of profound and subtle characterisation, of beauty and loftiness of language; while his course of education has not taught him to conceal his intellectual deficiencies or to be ashamed of them. He has come to the theatre as he would go to a boxing-match, to a circus, to an exhibition of a two-headed calf, or to a nigger minstrel troupe. He lumps them all together, and judges them favourably or unfavourably according as they have amused him—that is, according to the degree in which they have assisted him to pass his evening without any necessity for intellectual exertion. He is totally without any measure for gauging the play of *Hamlet;* he does not even try to understand it ; he simply finds it dull, and votes it a bad play. To-morrow night he will be at a music-hall, and will hail with rapture the latest medley of nonsense and slang, and will bawl himself crazy with ecstasy over some entirely foolish cockney song. And he will vote the latter entertainment a good one because it was entirely relative to his tastes and habits, because it never demanded one moment's thought, because it " amused " him. Deep calleth unto deep : the depth of folly in his mind responded to the depth of folly and imbecility in the song. Now that is one type of playgoer. I have purposely chosen him as an extreme type because I wished to get what those who study microbes call a " pure cultivation " of the germ. When the microbe-hunter wishes to thoroughly understand the nature and habits of a certain microbe, he separates it from all the other microbes and breeds it apart, so that he may watch its development in the simplest conditions. And I wanted to get what I call a pure cultivation of the amusement-seeker—the playgoer who not merely does not question whether the drama is an art or an amusement, but who has no idea of there being any such question, and who, so far as he thinks about it at all, is quite sure that it is an amusement pure and simple of the waxwork and circus order. Therefore I have not credited him with any emotion in witnessing *Hamlet ;* I have cut him off even from that source of entertainment which is one of the causes of the play's popularity to-day. Those who do not enter into its obstinate questionings and philosophical scepticism can yet dwell upon the largeness and fulness of its action and its domestic pathos and suffering. But I have shown you a playgoer to whom none of these things appealed.

Now I want you to examine another type of playgoer. And again, because I wish to get a pure cultivation of the artistic spirit as opposed to the amusement-seeking spirit, I will take an extreme type. I will take the great Goethe in the presence of this same play of *Hamlet.* You will find his criticism of *Hamlet* in the earlier part of *Wilhelm Meister ;* it is a criticism that has largely shaped the nineteenth-century view of *Hamlet.*

Now I wish you to contrast this attitude of the poet Goethe towards the play of *Hamlet* with the attitude of the young man in the billycock hat. There is perhaps the greatest, the sanest, and most universal intellect of these two centuries taking the keenest pleasure in the play : here is the typical young man of our present day finding it dull and empty.

And I claim for the poet's pleasure in the play that it is not merely greater in volume and force, but I claim that it is altogether different, altogether distinct in kind from the young man's pleasure in his music-hall entertainment. Let us try to enter into the states of mind of the two so far as we can. It is perhaps rather rash of me to assume that we can fully enter into the state of mind of the poet Goethe.

> It is not possible for thought
> A greater than itself to know,

sings the mystic poet William Blake. But if we cannot comprehend Goethe's delight, we can apprehend it.

I think we can all get some notion of the state of feeling of the young man in the billycock hat. We may perhaps summarise it pretty much as follows : " I've been working all day—what do I want with blessed Hamlick a-spouting of his blank-verse rot ?   Give me somethink I can understand—somethink lively—a daunce or a song as I can join in the chorus—I've paid my bob, ain't I ?   I come to a theatre to be amused—s'elp me, I didn't come here to be lured to a blessed funeral."

And if you read to that young man Goethe's criticism of *Hamlet*, you would merely bewilder him. If you said the drama is the art of portraying human life, and here is, on the whole, the greatest picture of human life that human imagination has ever conceived, he would only reply that it did not amuse him. He has no conception of the artistic pleasure to be derived from watching the secret and subtle workings of the human heart from such a standpoint ; you cannot explain it to him ; it is wholly hidden from him.

Now if you turn from him to the poet, and try to fathom his pleasure during an adequate representation of the play, you at once allow that his is the more enviable state of mind. Whatever may be our own feelings of delight when we hear

" Ta-ra-ra-boom-de-ay" and our feelings of boredom when we witness *Hamlet*, I don't think there is one of us who will not own that the man whom *Hamlet* delights and whom the music-hall song displeases has the purest, highest, most rational, and most lasting pleasure. Further, although it is quite impossible for the billycock-hat young man to understand the artistic pleasure to be derived from seeing a play as a study of human life, it is quite easy for the poet to thoroughly understand, though he does not share, the feelings of the young man to whom a play is mere foolish amusement. We can all take a certain kind of delight in the vocal talent which sings a foolish song well, in the strength that lifts and holds a great weight in a difficult position, in the dexterity that keeps a dozen balls flying in the air. And though I hope it is quite impossible that any of us could take any kind of pleasure in, or could ever witness without expressing our disapprobation, any contortion or distortion of the human frame, or any exhibition of dangerous and useless flying feats, yet we may be quite sure that there is no unfathomable pleasure to be derived from the contemplation of these things, and that those who do find a delight in them are not to be envied, but to be pitied and censured. If we don't enjoy these things, we may at least flatter ourselves that it is not owing to any alarming deficiency in the construction of our brains.

Therefore there is no question that the man who goes to the theatre merely to be amused, and regards a play as a pastime for an idle hour, gets not merely less pleasure from the theatre, but gets from it a pleasure of a distinctly inferior and sometimes of a degrading kind. Let me quote to you here the opinion of the greatest art critic the world has ever seen, John Ruskin—

" The end of art is not to amuse. All art which proposes amusement as its end, or which is sought for that end, must be of an inferior, and is probably of a harmful, class."

I want to insist very strongly that these two kinds of pleasures are totally different in their essence. That will be the first thing that I shall try to prove to you.

My second proposition will be that the art-pleasure is greater and higher than the amusement-pleasure.

And then further, I shall ask you to agree with me that it is desirable there should be a wide public knowledge and recognition of these differences, and of the nature and scope of the dramatic art proper.

If you regard a play as an alternative for any other mere pastime ; if you go to it to pass away the evening, as the phrase is, you may indeed pass away your evening, and it is gone, but you have cheated yourself of the highest pleasure. I maintain that the point of view which regards a play as a representation and study of human life is wholly distinct from the point of view which regards it as an after-dinner amusement whose highest function is to please the greatest number of the emptiest minds and the fullest stomachs. The one stand-point classes the drama as a competitor of circuses, waxworks, music-halls, strong men, fat women, two-headed calves. The other standpoint classes it as an art with its sister arts, painting, poetry, sculpture, music.

You do not judge any of these other arts by their ability to delight the young man in the billy-cock hat. A painting by Sir Edward Burne-Jones or Sir Frederick Leighton is not accounted successful according to its power of sending the first beholder into fits of laughter. If a spectator objected that a painting in the National Gallery did not amuse him, you would say, "No; it was not the artist's intention to amuse you; the artist meant to inter-pret this phase of human life to you, or to show you the beauties of that landscape; if you insist on his playing the buffoon, you will degrade him, and defraud yourself of the highest pleasure that his art could afford you for the sake of a momentary laugh."

There are, as you know, various opinions as to the value of the annual exhibition of the Royal Academy. But whatever may be the just appraise-ment of that exhibition, whether you rate it highly or whether you condemn it, there can be no doubt that it would be thoroughly lowered and degraded if every picture were judged according to its power of making the first spectator laugh. You recognise this art - pleasure in the case of the picture; you see at once that it is something alto-gether different from and higher than the enjoyment of a jest.

Now I maintain that there is the same kind of pleasure to be obtained from a play, and that when once the playgoer has tasted this higher pleasure, the lower pleasure, the mere amusement, will seem insipid and contemptible.

But perhaps you will reply, "You are taking a great deal of trouble to tell us what we already know, and to convince us of what we never disputed. We are all persuaded that the right attitude towards such a play as *Hamlet* is the attitude of Goethe, and not the attitude of the man in the billycock hat. There is no question between us; we answer your question in the affirmative—the drama is an art. Our minds as playgoers are made up, and you will find that the great body of playgoers throughout the country is agreed with us." Am I rightly expressing the opinion of those playgoers who are listening to me? I will take it for granted that I am. If there are any of my listeners who think that there is a great deal to be said for the amusement-seekers, I will consider their objections presently ; but for the moment I will assume that you agree with me that the English drama is the art of representing English life, and not the art of amusing young men with vacant minds. And you further agree with me that the art - pleasure is higher in kind, and greater in quantity, and keener in taste, and more enduring than the amusement-pleasure.

Our minds, then, are made up. Yes, but our minds are also made up about the Ten Commandments and the Sermon on the Mount : we consider them to embody on the whole an excellent theory of human life—not very workable perhaps when it comes to practice, but an excellent theory nevertheless. And I wish to call your attention to the fact that the question at the head of my lecture is not what our modern drama *ought* to be, but what it *is*. And whatever it ought to be in theory, I am afraid there is not much doubt that in practice our present modern English acted drama has very little aim except that of satisfying a crowd of amusement-seekers on the level of our billycock-hat friend. At the best it is a compromise, a hybrid—so much so that the playwright in sitting down to write a play does not know whether he will be praised in some quarters for having written a successful play, and blamed in others for not having produced a work of literature and art; or whether he will be blamed in some quarters for having descended to the tastes of the mob, and applauded in others for having had the courage to produce a play that ran only three nights, ruined the manager, and shut up the theatre.

Now I want to convince you first that this higher pleasure, this art-pleasure, is a reality. I have tried to do so by showing you how the play of *Hamlet* affected one of the master-minds of these two centuries; I have compared dramatic art with pictorial art, and showed you how you would degrade your school of national English painting if you insisted that pictures should be judged by the same test that you apply to plays, the test of providing mere amusement. Still one is constantly meeting with explicit or implicit denials that the drama has any other business than that of enabling people to pass away their time without thinking, or that there is any other kind of pleasure to be obtained from it than may be obtained from music-hall songs or nigger minstrels. When one endeavours to indicate the way to this pleasure, one is accused of spelling art with a large A, and is supposed to have discovered some new way of boring people. Now I don't deny that *Hamlet* did bore the man in the billycock hat, and that the most senseless music-hall song pleased him. But *Hamlet* did not bore Goethe ; and since the highest and most cultivated Europeans of the last few centuries have found pleasure in *Hamlet*, I prefer to ascribe the deficiency to the man in the billycock hat, and not to the greatest minds of our nation. And surely if any man has leisure and brains, and will take the pains to understand this question, he will own that perhaps the greatest intellectual pleasure our civilisation affords is to be derived from this study of the human heart and mind and spirit in the form of a stage-play.

Nothing concerns us so much as our own lives, and there is no art so searching, so sympathetic, so consoling, so universal, so instant in its appeal, so flexible in its aims, so gorgeous in its setting, so far-reaching and so helpful in its ministry to the human spirit, so various in its sources of pleasure, so gigantic in its possibilities, as this art of Shakespeare, this art compact of literature, of poetry, of music, of painting, and of sculpture.   For whereas all these other arts exist by and for themselves, the drama combines them all, and there is no pleasure that any of them gives that the drama cannot also give in its degree.

So I hope you will allow me to affirm that this art-pleasure which the drama can give is a very real one and a very high one, and when you hear a play criticised from the point of view of amusing the young man in the billycock hat—the young man who doesn't know and doesn't care about this pleasure, and who doesn't take the trouble to understand it—I hope you will call such criticism " billycock-hat criticism," and let it weigh with you for what it is worth.

Of course this pleasure in a play as a representation of life does need some cultivation. But you can't get much enjoyment out of football or cricket without pains, without training for the game. It is astonishing how infinitely less trouble our patrons of the drama take to qualify themselves to enjoy a play than they would take to qualify themselves to enjoy a game at billiards. I believe it costs some years of leisure, a great deal of practice, and a hundred pounds or so to learn to play an average game of billiards. At the end of that time you know the game, you have learned its technique, you can appreciate its subtleties, its master-strokes, you can understand its difficulties. But this great game of life which the dramatist has to represent to you on the boards of a theatre is, believe me, altogether more subtle than an average game of billiards ; you are far more concerned to know its technique, and the pleasure of watching it and understanding it is, I assure you, transcendently greater than the pleasure of watching any game of skill.

But granted there is this art - pleasure to be derived from watching and understanding this great game of life, is it worth learning personally, and is it worth making some collective or national effort to establish this art on a firm basis, with a definite standard of laws and rules ? Is it worth the trouble to learn the game ? Well, the man in the billy-cock hat would say " No." But take my advice and try it. You see I am calling it a game, I am putting

it on the level of a mere amusement, so that the
two things may be compared merely in the amount
of pleasure gained. And as you begin to go to the
play with this determination, to watch it as a picture
of human life, a study of character, a piece of literature, and not as a childish, funny entertainment, you
will gradually find a new source of pleasure opening
out to you ; you will see possibilities in the stage
that you never dreamed of. You will take a constant interest in comparing its scenes and characters
with the real world around you ; you will be moved
by a thousand touches, suggestions, hints that escaped
you before ; you will judge a dramatist, not by the
number of times he has made you giggle, but by
the harvest of human experience he has gleaned for
you ; you will discover what are the necessary limitations and conventions of the art, where an author
ought to exactly copy real life, and where he ought
to depart from it—that is, where he can exactly
copy the literal fact, and show you the essential
truth of the scene with the added literal fact ; and
where the pursuit of the essential truth obliges him
to discard the literal fact and trample upon it. You
can closely follow the words of the play, and watch
how he handles this majestic and beautiful instrument, our English tongue, this organ of Milton's,
this lyre of Shelley's, this clarion of Byron's, this
trumpet of Swinburne's, this Pan's-pipes of Keats',
this human and divine voice of Shakespeare's. I do
not say that the modern English drama in its
present state will afford you all these high and
varied pleasures, but I do say that it should afford
them to its student, that there is nothing in the

nature of things to hinder such a development of our art—nothing in the nature of things except the general sluggishness and indifference of the English public, its failure to understand that the theatre can be anything but a rather shady kind of amusement, where nonsense and folly have their fling. But in a degree you can already taste all of these pleasures in our present theatre. And the cost in money and leisure will be—well, considerably less than you would pay to learn to play an average game of billiards. I leave it to you whether it isn't worth your while to try to earn this pleasure.

I pass on to consider the desirability and possibility of some collective or national effort to establish a school of English drama — some public recognition that it is an art, and not a means of digesting dinner or escaping from thought. It is constantly urged that, granted that the drama may be a serious art for a few, it will never be anything but an amusement for the multitude—they will never take it seriously. But do the multitude really care for any of the other arts? A little perhaps for music; but for poetry, for painting, for sculpture? Is there any widely-spread knowledge or judgment or care for these things among the English nation at large? I don't think that there is. I don't think our friend in the billycock hat cares as much for poetry as he does for the drama, and certainly he is no better judge of the one than the other; nor does he care for painting or sculpture; while his opinion and criticism of all of them is worth—just nothing at all. But the difference between these arts and the drama is that he does not affect to judge or criticise, while in the drama he is often supreme umpire. That is, painting and poetry and sculpture are fairly established as arts, and not as amusements, and they are out of the reach of his meddling. Now it is objected that the drama is after all only a very small thing in the sum total of the national life, and that things are very well as they are, and that the matter is not worth troubling about. And so we go on, not knowing whether we are artists or buffoons, or what standards we are to be judged by; confused in our aims, unsettled in our methods, bewildered by criticism, puzzled by our rewards. No other art is subject to this uncertainty of status. The fact that the multitude do not care for painting or poetry does not count against a national recognition of these arts. Painting is subsidised by the Government, and rewarded with very great social honours and distinctions. Music is also very substantially rewarded and honoured. And in consequence we have a school of English painting and a school of English music, and these arts are not at the mercy of the mob. Why should there not be some recognition that the English drama is an art? Will it be argued that he who has portrayed our national life in a play has done a less arduous, a less honourable, a less intellectual, a less artistic, a less dignified thing than he who has portrayed it on canvas? I am not now pitting any individual dramatist against any individual artist, one personality against another: I am pitting the art of the dramatist against the art of the painter, and I wish to know why the one is held in so little esteem as compared with the other.

I am not saying that we have as many competent playwrights as competent artists—we have not had a national dramatic academy for a hundred years —I am only affirming the intrinsic importance and value and dignity of the dramatist's art. And I shall be glad to know why, if there is to be any public recognition of art in England, if the wealth and intellect and judgment of this nation take a pride in collecting and preserving and honouring the achievements of those who on canvas, or in marble, or in song have adorned our England of to-day—I shall be glad to know why the art of the dramatist is not to be thus honoured and recognised. If it is said that its present professors are not worthy of such recognition, then I can only reply, " No, you have trained us to amuse that young man in the billycock hat ; you have rewarded us for tricking you with all sorts of folly and sensation and theatrical devices ; you have said, ' We have dined too well— help us to digest our dinner ; we have made our lives terribly dismal—help us to escape from them. Amuse us anyhow, by any means, amuse us.' "

I think a present-day playwright would be justified in making such a reply to those who spoke slightingly of our modern playwrights as a body. But our present deficiencies should not be accounted a reason for refusing recognition to our art. Rather they should be a reason for inquiry. And, I repeat, if England has any love for art, if she has any public care for anything beyond shopkeeping, and horse-racing, and the Stock Exchange, and those curious religious dry-bones that her two hundred sects squabble about—if England has any desire for

beauty and decoration in her national life, I cannot
conceive why any intelligent man should deny that
it is desirable to foster a school of English drama.
And I shall by and by submit to you that it is desirable there should be this fuller public recognition of
the nature and standing of the drama.   Surely the
crowning glory of our nation is our Shakespeare,
and remember he was one of a great school.

Now before I could come to the gist and scope
of my lecture, before I could unfold the full bearings
of my subject to you, it was necessary for me to
establish three things.   I will reiterate them here,
because they are important in themselves, and because
I shall take them for granted and build upon them
in the remainder of my lecture.

1st. That view of a play which regards it as entertainment is distinct from and opposed to that view
of a play which regards it as a work of art ; and that
pleasure which is derived from a play as entertainment is distinct from and opposed to that pleasure
which is derived from it as a work of art.

I do not say that some plays, or portions of plays,
may not be regarded from both these points of view,
and may not minister to both these pleasures.   In
point of fact most modern plays are a curious compound of both these kinds of pleasures in varying
proportions.   But your mental attitude towards a
play, or towards that particular scene of it which is
engaging your attention for the moment, is quite
different and opposed according as you are regarding
it from one standpoint or the other.   Take the
amusement-pleasure in one of its simplest, most un-
sophisticated forms, the drama of Punch and Judy.

The child gets a vast amount of pleasure from it, and you, for the moment becoming a child, can also obtain pleasure from its performance. But how do you obtain the pleasure? By becoming a child, by the absence of all thought and inquiry, the absence of all intelligent effort, the severance of the performance from all relation to the realities of life, the acknowledgment of its utter preposterousness and absurdity, the instant dismissal of it from your mind the moment it is done, its entire failure to influence you in any way afterwards. That is the secret of your pleasure. Is not that also the secret of the success of many entertainments at some of our so-called theatres? Compare that kind of pleasure with the pleasure derived from witnessing a play as a picture of life. Here you obtain your pleasure by exactly the opposite means. In so far as it is a work of serious intellectual effort, you brace yourself to understand it; you think and inquire; you watch the language; you are alert to catch the subtlest points of character and shades of meaning; you instantly bring the mimic stage into comparison with that vast outside stage, the world; your pleasure is great according as the play is related to the greatest realities of life, to those wide-reaching truths that include and transcend all individual experience; you acknowledge the essential truth and reality of the thing, and you are delighted in proportion as you perceive this; instead of dismissing it from your mind, you dwell upon it and recur to it again and again; and according to its power and truthfulness, your views of life, your ways of thinking, your modes of expression, and perhaps your courses of action, are modified and influenced and dominated by it.

Therefore I affirm that this art-pleasure is utterly opposed in every way to the mere amusement-pleasure, inasmuch as it is secured by definite and somewhat complex mental operations, by constant reference to real life, or to the realities of life ; it is intellectually remunerative, fruitful, and enduring. On the other hand the amusement - pleasure is obtained by the absence of thought, its want of relation to real life or to the realities of life ; it is connected with poverty and vacancy of mind ; it is at best harmless, and is quite transitory and barren. On all these counts it is opposed to the art-pleasure, and it is no answer to my argument to say that certain plays may be so constructed as to administer to both these kinds of pleasures accordingly as they are viewed in different scenes, by different minds, from different points of view.

These kinds of pleasure are, I affirm, distinct and contrary, and vary in inverse proportion, the one being greater as the other is less or non-existent.

2nd. The art-pleasure is greater and higher than the amusement - pleasure. This follows from the analysis I have already given of their natures ; and I think you will readily concede that the pleasure Goethe obtained from *Hamlet* was both greater in quantity and altogether higher in kind than the pleasure the young man in the billycock hat obtained from his music-hall chorus.

I am obliged to make a separate point of this, because those of us who are engaged in trying to bring home to the English people what a national drama really means, are constantly accused of wishing to establish some kind of worship of dulness in the theatre. I want to call your attention to the argument by which those who have secured a comfortable freehold in the ignorance, and carelessness, and bad taste of the English playgoing public, support their assertion that a higher drama means a duller drama. Before using the word "amusement" to-night, I was obliged to define in what sense I should use it, so that you might follow my argument and see that I was not juggling with words. Now the word "amusement" is very loosely and vaguely used. Its scope may best be judged by pointing out to you that it is used in antithesis to "boredom," and also in antithesis to "intellectual enjoyment." These two meanings are utterly distinct. To-night at starting I told you I should use the word in antithesis to intellectual enjoyment, and I have kept strictly to that use of it. But see how widely different these two meanings are, and what utterly different states of mind they connote.

"You went to the play last night—were you amused?" "No, I was bored to death." That's one negative answer you can make.

"You went to the play last night—were you amused?" "Well, not exactly amused, but interested, excited, entranced, enthralled; all the strongest feelings of my nature were aroused; all my best emotions, all my keenest intellectual powers were called into play. Amused? No, I had a far higher pleasure than mere amusement." That's another negative answer you can make to the same question.

Now I wish to point out to you that those

who are concerned to keep the English drama in
its present condition continually juggle with these
two meanings of the word " amusement," and, by
a species of verbal thimblerig, substitute the one
meaning for the other, and persuade, or try to
persuade, theatre-goers that the word " amusement "
has only one antithesis, that of " boredom." I wish
to come to very close quarters with this argument.
I wish to press it home. We constantly meet, in the
public press and in public discussions, with advice to
playgoers to be amused. If I know anything about
playgoers, the one thing on which it is quite superfluous to offer them any advice is about being bored.
The general run of theatre-goers have quite made up
their mind on this point. Every manager and every
author very quickly discovers that the public needs no
advice on this matter. Now in any future discussion
on this subject, I wish to call on every one who
enters upon it to define his use of the word " amusement." Does he use it in antithesis to " weariness
and boredom," or does he use it in antithesis to
" intellectual enjoyment " ? If he uses it interchange-
ably in these two senses, according as it suits his
purpose, and in order to persuade the playgoing
public that the drama has no higher and better
pleasure to offer them than empty, unthinking
entertainment, then whether or no he is deceiving
himself, he is certainly deceiving the public, and is
juggling with words. I ask those who constantly
advise theatre-goers to take care they are amused,
to define their terms.

Why all this eagerness to insist that the public
must be amused ? When you advise the public to

be amused, do you caution them against being bored? It is, believe me, quite unnecessary. The public will take care of that. Or do you caution them against a higher and greater intellectual enjoyment? And for what reason? Why should playgoers be advised against the intellectual development of the drama, except that this would be a severe condemnation of some forms of entertainment. Once more I say that this argument is founded on a confusion of the two senses in which the word "amusement" is used. Amongst the unthinking the argument is accepted, because the populace can always be deceived with words, and no refutation is possible without some such thorough examination of the whole subject as I have here made. But if I have convinced you, I am sure you cannot be doing a greater service to the drama than by disputing the assertion, wherever you hear it made, that those who wish to raise the drama intellectually wish to make the theatre dull.

Say rather that those who wish to keep the drama on its present level wish to keep the theatre dull. If you care for the theatre, if you have any interest in the drama—and your coming here shows that you are not indifferent—lend a hand to throttle this cowardly, this insidious, this contemptible falsehood. Will you challenge those who make it? Will you ask them to establish their position that a higher drama means a duller drama? Will you ask them how it is possible that any fuller play of intelligence exercised by the theatre-goer upon any form of the drama can fail to brighten and gladden him? One constantly meets this assertion, until one is prompted to ask why the theatre of all places should be the only one (except perhaps the church) where it is considered shameful and ridiculous to exercise one's brains.

3rd. My third proposition is, that it is desirable there should be a fuller public recognition of the nature and responsibilities of the dramatist's art ; that the English drama should be allowed to be on the level of its sister arts, and should be as far as possible disentangled and severed from mere popular funny entertainment.

These are the three things which I have repeated constantly all through my lecture, because I wished you to carry them away with you as the basis of your thinking and your arguments on the subject whenever it should come up before you for discussion.

We have arrived at a very critical period in the history of our English drama. Some twenty years ago when I began to study and to write for the English theatre, our modern drama was very generally regarded as an entertainment pure and simple. There was no question of this difference between art and amusement. In the comedies of the English school there was a considerable sprinkling of puns, and a good many rather feeble jests which were generally led up to in a very laborious manner ; there were usually two pairs of very innocent lovers, one comic and the other sentimental; all the serious affairs of life were carefully avoided ; there was not even any attempt to render faithfully the *manners* of the personages, let alone their *passions* and the subtler aspects of their characters. All was carefully adapted to minister to the amusement of the average philistine of that period, to whom even that moderate indulgence in the theatre was a desperate and dangerous experiment. There were many adaptations from the French, but these were always desexualised, and the general heat and vitality and lifelikeness of the characters were about those of a china shepherdess. That school passed away ; it was quite inoperative except for providing entertainment ; it has left no mark upon the general literature and art of its time ; it had no vitality; it provided entertainment for certain people in 1870, but it did not leave a lasting picture of English life in 1870, much less a picture of the human life and the human heart in all time such as Shakespeare left. That school was succeeded by a few years of stormy melodrama, which, again, seems to have spent its force and lost its influence, except such influence as the *Family Herald* and a police-court report may have. These two schools have virtually perished, the first because it lacked insight, life, force, reality, because the amusement-seekers who supported it tired of its trivialities and feeblenesses. The second school is perishing from extravagance, theatricality, improbability, and sensationalism, because the amusement-seekers who support it are tired of its violence and fustian and outrageous coincidence.

Now mark, the two leading dramatic movements of our time have perished because they have supplied the entertainment-pleasure, and because they have denied the artistic satisfaction. I am here speaking of the modern English drama, and not of our classic masterpieces. It is highly gratifying to notice that during the last few years our great Shakespearean drama has gained in force and influence and authority, while the amusement drama has lost. But I am not here concerned with the classic drama, and you will forgive me for thinking that, without a living, creative force of to-day, our interest in the drama of the past will be mainly antiquarian, perfunctory, and scholastic. A lively interest in our own age and generation, in the art of to-day, is the best safeguard for our reverence towards the art of antiquity. It was the Puritans, who had no art, who to this day in their blind and bitter ignorance and superstition cannot understand the meaning of the word — it was they who destroyed our Gothic cathedrals.

Besides, our past art treasures remain our possession : they are already ours, and it is the accumulation of new art wealth that chiefly concerns us.

I have shown you why our two recent schools, if schools they could be called, that had so little to teach and so much to unlearn—I have shown why our two recent schools of the drama have perished without influence and renown. They did not minister in any large degree to this intellectual pleasure, to this artistic satisfaction.

Gradually our audiences during the last few years have been undergoing, what I hope I may call without being misunderstood, a process of education in the drama. Theatres have been multiplied ; different theatres have pursued different policies and have given different entertainments. And this has afforded some opportunity of comparison. If I were to say there has been any very great improvement of public taste, I should be puzzled to prove it or to show where it was manifested. But I think there has been considerable advancement all round; many playgoers are educated at least up to this point: they can detect the theatricality and insincerity of many of our plays. But they have become infected with the idea that an intellectual play means a dull play, and they will not give the time and the patience to understand the matter.

All through my lecture you will observe that I have implicitly answered my question, "Is our modern drama an art or an amusement?" somewhat in this fashion: "It ought to be an art, but as a matter of fact it is a curious mixture of the two. And dramatic art, the art of portraying life, exists only on sufferance and by making large concessions to the demand for popular entertainment."

Now if we ask in what direction future progress must lie, it will, I think, be clear to you that the only hope of our establishing a national drama is in cultivating and encouraging that view of the drama which recognises it as an art with clear and definite aims beyond that of merely helping the young man in the billycock hat to pass away his time. We must as far as possible separate it from popular amusement.

But, it may be urged, there are thousands and even millions of amusement-seekers in our large cities who seek light and thoughtless entertainment after the work of the day. Why should they not be considered? To that I reply, "There is no doubt they will be considered — popular amusement will take care of itself; it stands in no danger of suffocation from competition with dramatic art. I wish to God it did. It stands in no danger of inanition through neglect. You may be quite sure that the young man in the billycock hat will amuse himself one way or the other." You will notice that I do not propose extreme measures with those who want mere amusement. I do not propose to send them to gaol, or to subject them to a course of lectures, or to any other penal treatment or process of torture. I propose only to leave them to their own devices.

And I may remark here that I have consistently advocated free-trade in the drama. If the music-halls wish to perform stage-plays, I think they should be allowed to do so. As a matter of fact there is no line of division at present between theatres and music-halls ; the entertainment given at some theatres is just as witless and frivolous and puerile, and has as little connection with dramatic art as the entertainment given at the music-halls. There is a certain indefinite line of division between three or four of our leading London theatres and all the rest of the theatres and music-halls. It is this line which I would like to make definite and permanent and to emphasise, not by legislative enactment, not by prohibiting the music-halls from giving entertainments with some feeling after artistic form and spirit, but by constant endeavour on the part of manager and author and actor to show the public how high a pleasure the study of life gives in comparison with the search for mere amusement, and by constant response of the educated public to higher and yet higher efforts. Therefore I say I have no quarrel with the amusement-seekers—they will take care of themselves ; their pastimes are in no danger.

But a very real danger does threaten dramatic art at this juncture. This partnership of art and amusement which has obtained for some years at our theatres, even at the best, shows some signs of dissolution. And the danger is that the amusement-seekers may get it all their own way, simply because their way is the easiest and shortest. I don't deny that the young man in the billycock hat obtains his pleasure or amusement, or whatever he calls it, at infinitely less intellectual exertion, on infinitely cheaper intellectual terms than does Goethe. And there are so many young men in billycock hats, and so few Goethes. And if it comes to a matter of voting, the poet is sure to get worsted. Now this is the danger, that dramatic art may get altogether swamped in the rush for mere amusement. This is a constant danger ; we need to be always on the alert, always on the defensive. No other art is placed in such a perilous position ; no other art is so much at the mercy of the crowd. And a great force of criticism adapts itself to the crowd, describes a play from its standpoint, confirms it in its notion that when it has snatched an hour's thoughtless pastime from a play it need concern itself no further. And while this confusion exists between dramatic art and amusement no right judgment of a play or of the merits of a play can be widely formed and widely known. What is a successful play ? Will you tell me ? A successful play, according to the standard of popular amusement, is one that runs three or four hundred nights. It has performed what it was intended to do. But what is a successful play according to the standard of dramatic art? It is one that has painted life and the great realities of life, and if it has done that it is a successful play, though it should run only three nights. You see this opposition between the two standards runs through and influences all dramatic opinion and all ways of regarding a play.

My third point, if you remember, was that it is desirable that the drama should take its place as a national art, and should be so judged and recognised. I do not suppose there is the chance of getting any such recognition by Government as is accorded to painting, though I should be glad to know why the theatre is not equally deserving. But putting that aside as hopeless for the present, what sort of further recognition and support can we get from the more cultivated and intelligent body of playgoers? How many entertainment-seekers can we persuade to be lovers of the drama? I drew two types of playgoers for you in the early part of my lecture, the young man in the billycock hat and the great Goethe. Between these two extremes there is the great body of playgoers in all their different grades of intelligence and in all their different stages of dramatic education. Our great hope lies in capturing some considerable number of them, in persuading them of the importance and dignity of our art, and in making them active on behalf of the cause I have advocated to-night. Have I made any converts amongst you? Have I persuaded any of you of the truth of those things I have repeated so constantly till I am sure you are tired of hearing of them—

First, art and mere entertainment are two utterly different things.

Second, art - pleasure is altogether higher and greater than amusement-pleasure.

Third, it is worth while to establish our modern drama on an art basis.

If I have persuaded you of the truth of these things, will you try and make them generally known? Great questions are awaking around us; great social forces are stirring; new beliefs and hopes are spreading. In that new world which is shaping round us will the drama sink to the level of a childish pastime, effete, inane, inoperative, contemptible, the mere toy of the unthinking crowd, or will it take its place as a recognised and honoured art, with boundaries as wide, and significance as profound and immeasurable, as human life itself?

THE RELATIONS OF THE DRAMA
TO EDUCATION

(An Inaugural Address delivered at the reopening of the City of London
College, Michaelmas term, 12th October 1893—Reverend Preben-
dary Whittington in the chair.)

HAS the drama any relations to education? I have
looked carefully through the prospectus of your
studies for the coming season, and with the exception
of a class for elocution, I do not find any evidence of
the existence of such relations. Surely if there were
any very direct and vital relations between the
drama and education, it would be at once apparent
in the programme of an institution like the City of
London College. I stand appalled at the range and
depth of your studies. You oppress me with your
encyclopædic knowledge. I am embarrassed in
assuming anything that approaches to the attitude
or manner of a teacher in such an assembly as this.
I cannot help being abashed by the thought that I
can presume to lecture people who know all the
intricacies of the Incorporated Law Society's Inter-
mediate examination, and others who can heckle
me on obscure points of Portuguese syntax, or
expose my dramatic fallacies in the glibbest and

choicest colloquial Hindustani. Therefore I propose to talk over with you this matter of the relations of the drama to education in a questioning, open-minded spirit; and I begin by asking you if there are any such relations. The fact that in such a comprehensive prospectus as this of yours, where there are set down all possible subjects for study, there is no mention of or allusion to our national drama, is almost enough to answer my question in the negative. The City of London College prospectus tacitly affirms there are no relations between the drama and education. Unless indeed your elocution class may be held as an indication of some such relations,—but here again I am afraid a visit to many of our West-End theatres would convince you that our modern drama has no necessary concern with elocution.

If, on the other hand, I turn to the theatre and ask what business it has with education, I am met with a storm of derision and disapprobation—from all whose interest it is to keep the theatre on the intellectual level of a penny peep-show. Nothing is more interesting to notice than the anxiety of those who are providing popular amusement on the lower levels of the drama to assure the English people that there are no higher levels. There are no men so convinced that the English drama ought to mean nothing and teach nothing as the men whose reputation and occupation would be gone if it did. To sum up the general opinion of the theatrical world on this question of the relation of the drama to education, taking the whole body of playgoers, managers, actors, critics, and authors, we may say that the vast majority would scout and laugh at the idea that the drama could or ought to teach or educate anything or anybody, that a great number would be undecided and indifferent, and that a small minority would assert the right of the national drama to-day to take a very high and a very definite position as a national teacher.

And this minority would contain all that is operative and progressive, all that is intellectually penetrative, all that is alive, all that can hope to have any lasting power and influence in the drama of to-day. If I may venture, then, to make myself the spokesman of this small minority, I claim that there should be very strong relations between the drama and education. And seeing that we are not discussing a matter of politics, we may perhaps venture to show some respect for the opinion of the minority. We will therefore, if you please, at once sweep aside as of no possible account the opinion of the vast majority, and go on to ask what it is that the drama can or should teach, and in what way, and by what methods it can or should teach.

What is the object of education? We hear a great deal about technical education, that special training which is to fit a man for some special place he is to occupy in life. I notice that many of your classes supply a special kind of knowledge not likely to be very valuable or useful except to those whose business or hobby it is to acquire it. I have lately read of a naturalist who spent all his life in acquiring an exhaustive knowledge of the forehead of a carp. At the end of his days he knew almost all that could be known of his subject.

U

Then there are other studies in your list that are of slightly more general interest, more likely to be of use or interest to a greater number of persons. Passing by these, we come to the fine arts, some practice or knowledge of which is considered a necessary part of every liberal education. We may not all be able to understand or practise music, painting, or sculpture, but we all show a great respect for those who do practise and understand them, and we should all like to practise and understand some or one of them if we had the time and the talent. Now I am not here to claim a place for the drama as an art. I am not come to speak to you about that aspect of the drama. I leave it entirely on one side for the present. But I suppose we should all allow that the arts are of considerable general interest to the community, and that they are of considerable educational value. Passing the fine arts, we come to studies that are of still more general interest, still more necessary to every one of us. An appreciation of Wagner is not perhaps necessary or possible to all of us, but a firm hold of the truth that two and two do always make exactly four, and never a fraction more or less—a firm hold of this truth is desirable for every man and woman born, because for want of a comprehension of this truth in all its bearings people go and waste their time and money in backing horses, in rotten companies, and in all sorts of follies, bringing ruin and misery on their families. But passing beyond even such elementary sciences as reading, writing, and arithmetic, what yet more elementary, more necessary science is there than all of them? Tell me, what science is of the utmost importance to every one of us, irrespective of occupation, position, age, or sex, and for lack of whose knowledge men and women are destroyed ? The science of life, the science of living.

How to live wisely is a far more necessary study for a man than anything that is taught in board-schools or in universities. And apart from mere technical knowledge and skill, apart from mere bread-and-cheese considerations, all education is only of value as a means to this end, as a help to the art or science of living.

Some of us can perhaps remember old men and women of the days before school-boards and board-schools, men and women who could not write their names, or do an addition sum, or read a word, yet who did possess a natural wisdom and shrewdness and insight, a natural health and integrity of character, a perception of the cardinal facts and duties of life that certainly made them better-educated people than the average scholar that the board-school is turning out to-day. That is, they understood and practised the art or science of living. This last generation has seen a wonderful increase in the means and appliances of education ; the State gives a wider and, on the whole, a better education to every child of England than two generations back was in the reach of any except a few of the privileged classes. That education has been beneficial only if and so far as it has taught its recipients, not how to scramble for material advantages and to outwit each other in the race for money, but if and so far as it has taught them what is the lasting and final end of all education—the science of living.

The man who in the midst of all the tangled

threads and rank growths of our latter-day com-
mercialism knows, and knows surely, that honesty
is the best policy ; the woman who knows, and knows
surely, that her virtue means health and strength to
the next generation—this man and this woman are
in possession of the profoundest truths, the deepest
secrets of national prosperity and well-being, compared with which all other education is secondary,
auxiliary, and illustrative.

Now mark that all great dramas, however complex and intricate the trend and compass of
their story may be, do yet mainly illustrate the
greatest, and simplest, and tritest, and most universal
of these great truths of life. *Hamlet, Macbeth,
Faust*, the *Agamemnon* do teach, and teach most
impressively, these great central truths. And because they do teach, and because they purpose to
teach, they are greater than dramas which do not
concern themselves with these great central truths,
and have no message for mankind, either about the
mysteries of the Unseen, or the conduct of human
affairs here. That is, the greatest dramas teach, and
concern themselves about, the greatest and tritest
and most central truths. But beyond this purpose
to teach which marks the greatest dramas of all, there
is in the drama an immense power of inculcating a
wide knowledge of life. It is of course very difficult
to divide this knowledge of life from the great
central purport in the plays I have just spoken
about, seeing that the two are more or less mixed
and blended in any play, and in the greatest of plays
are almost completely fused. The knowledge of life
and mankind teaches, is in itself an education.

Now this wide knowledge of life and mankind is what the drama can give in a transcendent measure. No book, no other art, no mere spoken address, no system of education can so instantly and vividly burn and brand the memory with the realities of life, and leave them for ever stamped and pictured in the chambers of imagery as can the acted play.

Those of us who are engaged in writing and producing plays are constantly startled to find how magnifying and concentrating is the power of the theatre, how it isolates, how it vivifies, how it enlarges, how it inflames! The outside world is for the time annihilated, it does not exist. There on the stage in front of you is the whole drama of humanity being played out ; no other men and women are alive ; there is the very sum and substance and essence of human life. Now in this great power of presenting life and the realities of life in such a way as to give the spectator the same knowledge of them as he would possess after years of observation and experience, the stage is supreme.

But is this wide knowledge of life desirable ? How far does it tend to perfect the science of wise living, which is the ultimate end of all education ? I say the two are inseparable. Though in individual cases there is or seems to be no necessary connection between full knowing and wise doing, though there is an eternal warfare between man's passions and man's peace, between what men preach and what they practise, between aspiration and accomplishment, yet, taking a wide survey, there is a constant ratio between what a nation or a race *knows* and what it *does*, between what it holds as the highest truths and the smallest daily actions of its people. Intellectual advance means sooner or later moral advance, and intellectual advance always comes first.

I say then that this wide knowledge of life, of good and evil, is a good in itself. And further, we live in an age when there is a loud and general demand to know the truth about life. It is an age of upheavals, of inquiry, of searching. Smug half-truths and wandering benighted prejudices are everywhere being challenged and stripped. " Come out into the daylight " is the cry of this age to national beliefs and institutions. " Unmuffle ! let us see whether you are an eternal truth or only a notion."

You cannot quench this demand for knowledge of what life is and what life means. It is not only on the stage that this demand is made ; it meets you everywhere—in the reviews, in the latest novel, in drawing-rooms, in the talk of the street, in the pulpit itself. And unless I much mistake the drift of modern thought, it will not be easily quieted and answered.

Now the questions of how far it is lawful or expedient to represent on the stage the darker realities of life, and what aspect of them is to be represented, and the mode of representation—these questions, with all their implications, scarcely come within the direct scope of my address. Yet they are allied to the present part of my subject. And I will therefore say briefly that the mere representation of physical diseases and horrors and brutalities and sordidness on the stage is to be unreservedly condemned. The present epidemic of physical horror

and disease which has very slightly attacked the
English stage is a town-bred mental disease arising,
I believe, from the nausea of town-life, an insanity
that to escape from its own self-weariness and self-
disgust plunges its nose more deeply into the fumes
and the mire of its own creating.

I would admit, then, on the stage no physical
horrors or disease for their own sake. As a matter
of art they are outside our own present discussion ;
as a matter of education or knowledge these subjects, so far as they are necessary to be known, can
be better treated in pamphlets.

Taking into consideration the vivifying power of
the stage, I say that all representation thereon of
mere physical horror and disease and suffering is to
be condemned on the educational side because the
evil morbid effect produced on the mind is greater
than the good of the knowledge gained. We should
all desire, I hope, to avoid watching the death, say
from cancer, of some one unknown to us, and to whom
we could not render the least aid.   We should shun
it. Why then should we wish to watch purely
physical struggles and evils on the stage ? But
though no physical suffering or horror or disease is
to be shown for its own sake, I say on the other
hand show as much as you please, cut to the bone,
pierce to the quick, uncover the very heartstrings
till we see their every pulse and quiver—if—if what ?
—if you can show a higher spiritual beauty beyond.

Whose are the greatest physical sufferings in all
literature ? The sufferings of Prometheus with the
vulture tearing out his heart. But what a spiritual
significance they have. Where do we find the

baldest, the strongest, the most terrible naturalism in all literature? In Zola? No; in Dante. Zola is not nearly as grim, as direct, as poignant as Dante. But in Dante we are everywhere sheltered from the mere frightful physical reality of the suffering by its spiritual significance, and by the beauty and loftiness of the language.

I have touched briefly upon this subject, and I have indicated what are the relations of the drama to all physical disease, horror, and suffering. While no abyss of evil in the human heart should be left unsounded, while there is no physical distress that may not be transfigured into spiritual beauty, I affirm and reaffirm, with all the force of conviction that is in me, the uselessness, the mischief, the folly, the barrenness, the deathfulness of all representations of disease and horror that are not related to spiritual issues, to issues of fortitude and wisdom and peace. Of course the advocates of physical horror and disease on our stage may always proclaim that they derive a spiritual comfort from the unalloyed exhibition of dirty misdeeds, that they see a profound spiritual significance in the sordid, commonplace talk of sordid, commonplace people, and that to them a carbuncle glows with a diviner beauty than the rose of Sharon, and erysipelas burns with a brighter radiance than any sunset ever painted by Turner. There is no disputing about taste. We'll leave them to their carbuncles and erysipelas, shall we?

To return to the point at which I broke off. With this reservation only, that no horror or disease or ugliness or evil shall be represented for its own sake, I say the wider, the deeper, the fuller knowledge

of life that the stage can display, the more it should
be welcomed and received and acknowledged as a
national teacher. We have within the last ten years
witnessed not only a great addition to and enlarge-
ment of the subjects dealt with on the English
stage, but these subjects are being handled in a freer
and bolder manner and with more directness and
plain-speaking. I think that is an unqualified good.
Why is it that the Bible and Shakespeare are everywhere allowed to be the two sovereign teachers of
the English nation? Because life and the great
realities of life, the whole heart and nature, the whole
body and soul of man are therein dealt with in the
freest and plainest and simplest way. How is it
that the man who knows well his Bible and Shakespeare is a well-educated man? Because of their
wide and searching knowledge of life, of their free
handling of character and conduct, of their plain
dealing with all that relates to a man's ordering of
his steps in this dim world.

Condemn your theatre to a narrow and childish
view of life; shut out from your dramatists the discussion and representation of all subjects that relate
to the great realities of life; say to them, "A man's
character is profoundly influenced by his religious
beliefs and his views of the unknown world. But you
mustn't indicate this in your plays: your characters
must have no religion. Again, the institutions of
the country and their influence upon its citizens are
matters of great moment. But you mustn't indicate
this in your plays: your characters must have no
politics. Further, the relations of man to woman are
the most important of all the relations of life; the

whole health and happiness and vitality of the nation depend upon the adjustment of these relations. But you mustn't indicate this in your plays: your characters must have no sex." Say this to your dramatists; enforce the narrow prejudices that governed the theatre until a few years ago; and you may have spread all over the country a series of large puppet-shows, with living marionettes, but you will have no national drama. Now this matter of the relations of man to woman is obviously one that requires the greatest care and delicacy in handling, not only on the stage but also in a lecture. But as it is precisely the question which is always to the fore on the stage, which confronts us more than any other, it is one that ought not to be shirked. If this were a perfect world, and we were all perfect men and women, there would be no drama and no religion. But as the world is not perfect, it is in this strife of good and evil, of right and wrong, that religion and the drama find their element to work in. Now upon this matter of the relations of man to woman we have a great ferment in the outside world, and we are likely to get some considerable discussion of it on the stage. The old ideal of woman's ignorance and innocence is being roughly handled, and is faring badly. Now whatever is the truth about these matters, I say it is best that it should be known.

Please mark me here. I do not say that it is best that we should know the facts. I deprecate any exposure of the facts. The facts of any case are only valuable in so far as they indicate the essential truth that underlies them. If you reply, "But you can't have the truth unless you have the facts," I say, "Very well, give us as little of the facts as you possibly can, only as much as is necessary for us to know the truth—as little of the facts and as much of the truth." I think this will indicate the spirit in which the drama should approach what is called the "eternal woman question." This part of my subject touches very closely on the preceding one, the exhibition of physical horrors and distresses on the stage. It is, indeed, only another aspect of the same question which is at its root, nothing but the old, everlasting quarrel between materialism and spiritualism.

I have said enough, I hope, to convince you that, while the drama claims a right to deal fearlessly with the whole nature of man, to blink nothing, to shirk nothing, to extenuate nothing, but to proclaim the whole truth about him, yet if this is done in a reverent and faithful way, I hope I have said enough to convince you that you need not hesitate to entrust your dramatists with the plenary powers that this implies, and you need not fear that anything but good can come in the long-run if the widest and most searching knowledge of the heart of man is shown you and taught you by means of the stage.

But the stage is not merely the most vivid and forcible teacher of the truths and wisdom of life. It is also the most flexible, the most humane, the most tolerant teacher. Schools and creeds, by their very nature, tend to become rigid and inadaptive to the ever-changing necessities of their supporters. The drama, by its nature, is the most flexible, the most adaptive, the most humane and large-hearted teacher. Consider the magnificent humanity and tolerance and wide sympathy of the drama! With how large and kindly an eye it can afford to look on human littleness and human transgression! It is not constrained to damn anybody. It has no party to conciliate or to support; the very cliques and feuds among its own votaries are a part of its own subject-matter; the quarrels of this school or that school, even the disagreements of critics, if I dare whisper it, are all a part of that delightful imbroglio, that great, perpetual tragi-comedy, human life.

But beyond giving a deep and searching knowledge of the heart of man and the great truths of life, the stage has a lighter and pleasanter task in teaching good manners and the delicacies and amenities of social intercourse. Our old comedies are, I fear, to be commended rather as teachers of manners than as teachers of morals. Their good manners are widely different from the good manners of to-day, but they have a charm and distinction of their own, which when they are well rendered on our modern stage (alas, how rarely they are well rendered!) contain a much-needed lesson in deportment to a democratic age.

Again, the pleasant, frank, natural manners and easy, unstudied grace that characterise our better classes of to-day, when portrayed in our modern stage drawing-rooms, as they frequently are, by actors and actresses who belong to the life they are representing, may gently hint to Brixton that it would be well to remit at times a little of the unloveliness of middle-class virtue, and may persuade our sturdy lower classes that a monopoly of honesty and morality is not necessarily a monopoly of sweet

behaviour.   And   perhaps   Brixton   and   our   lower
classes stand in need of these lessons.

But I claim further not only that the drama may
and does teach—I claim that to an observant mind
it must teach.   Even the silliest farce, or the most
outrageous melodrama, can scarcely be seen without
calling forth some criticism of life, and raising some
question of moment about high matters of human
conduct and duty, and grave and sacred relation-
ships.

I hope, then, I have convinced you that the drama
has very strong claims to be considered as a teacher,
that it has very real and permanent relations with
education.   Taking the word " education " in its wide
derivative sense as that which " leads, draws forth,
trains, and exercises the powers of the mind, the
passions, affections, dispositions, habits, and manners,"
there is no instrument so powerful, so instant, so
effective as the drama.

I have perhaps persuaded you that the drama has
so much to teach that it is a very serious, nay a very
dull affair indeed; in fact, that it is, or ought to be, a
good deal like a sermon.   Not a bit of it.   I hasten
to reassure you on this point.   If you remember, we
not only set out to discover if the drama did teach
and what it teaches, but we also proposed to ask
how and by what methods it teaches.   I hope our
chairman will not take it unkindly if I dare to suggest that the stage has an advantage over the pulpit
not only in the matter but also in the methods of its
teaching.   The pulpit is a direct, an absolute teacher.
So are all your other teachers who come here to instruct you.   The drama is not.   I am going to give

you a paradox, yet a profound truth. The drama does teach, must teach, is a potent influence and also a great art in direct proportion as it does teach; yet *the moment it sets out to teach, the moment it takes the professorial chair, the moment it assumes the professorial robes, it stultifies itself, it usurps a function and an authority that it has no right to or business with, and it becomes a meddler and a bungler. The drama cannot directly and explicitly affirm or teach or solve or prove anything.*

Those dramatists who set out to teach or prove anything are called doctrinaire dramatists. Shakespeare was not a doctrinaire dramatist; Molière was not a doctrinaire dramatist. We will suppose a doctrinaire dramatist who sets out to treat, say, of the equality of the sexes. He is in this dilemma. He must either solve his problem, or leave it unsolved. If he solves it according to his gallantry or prepossessions in favour of women, he has only to devise a story in which the women are palpably the intellectual and moral superiors of the men, and the thing is proved. But at once you say to him, " Of course, my dear fellow, when you choose your own characters and your own story, and follow them through developments that you arrange to your own end, you can prove anything you please. You have provided a solution to your problem, but it is utterly worthless, because you have arranged the world and your characters to your own liking." But, on the other hand, suppose the doctrinaire dramatist does *not* solve his problem, then instantly you have him on the other hip and say, "You elected to treat this burning question, but you

have left it where it was ; you haven't proved anything." Of course he can reply, " I didn't try to
prove anything : I set myself to paint the thing as I
saw it, without any prepossession or favour for one
side or the other, and without a care or wish to prove
or teach anything." But if he says this, he owns
at once that the drama has no business to pose as a
direct teacher with a mission to prove this, that, or
the other.[1]

You will tell me I am contradicting all the
earlier part of my lecture. No, I am not. I am
giving you the two sides of the same truth. The
paradox I am putting before you is the paradox of
all art, nay, the paradox of life itself. What does
life teach ? Can you tell me ? Does life teach you
that honesty is the best policy ? Are all the honest
men you know in the best positions of their class ?
If life teaches anything directly about honesty at
all, I think it rather inclines to that fine bit of
worldly wisdom and Bible teaching which you will
find in Ecclesiastes : " *Be not righteous over much :
why shouldest thou destroy thyself ?* " Again, does
life teach that lying does not prosper, that virtue
leads to happiness ? You know it does not teach
these things directly, for every case that goes to
prove these maxims could be matched with one
that contradicts them. No, life does not teach
directly. It is profounder than any copy-book. But
does life teach nothing ? Yes, it teaches us these
great truths in a large, indirect way. We all read our
own interpretation into life's experience. It teaches

---

[1] I think this ought to "solve" all the childish nonsense that has
recently been written about so-called " problem " plays.

us all just what we find in its book. And sooner or later we all find these great central truths written there.

Again, what is the end or meaning of life? It always escapes you; you never pluck the heart out of its mystery. So with the great masterpieces of the drama. You can read into them any meaning or any teaching that you please; their secret will always escape you. What does *Hamlet* prove? Nothing, no more than life itself. What does it teach? Just whatever you please; just whatever you like to read into it.

The most obvious lesson of all the greatest tragedies at the first glance, and to the ordinary man, tends rather to teach the futility of virtue, the uselessness of high endeavour. Look at Othello, the great, valorous, high-minded captain, given over to the wiles of Iago and perishing from the noble simplicity and ingenuousness of his character. What a fool was Othello! How clever Iago!

This is the paradox of life, and it is equally the paradox of art—that though it must have a meaning and an end, they always elude you when you search for them. Therefore I say that the drama is following life, is following nature, when it teaches in the same way, not directly, not absolutely, not for an immediate result, but hiddenly, silently, implicitly, and with results and consequences that are removed and far-reaching, and not obvious at the first glance to the average man.

To sum up then on both points. The drama should teach; if it does not it is meaningless, empty, puerile, trivial. It should never teach directly and with a set purpose; if it does, it is meddlesome, one-sided, intolerant, irritating, and tiresome. Briefly we may say, it should teach, but it should never preach.

If you ask me how far the modern English drama takes the position in our national life that I have claimed for it, I can give no certain answer. We are in a state of transition. Those of you who have been playgoers for ten or fifteen years cannot have failed to notice that there has been a considerable change both in the tastes of playgoers and in the character of the entertainments provided for them. The history of the English drama in those ten or fifteen years may be summed up in one sentence : " There has been a tendency to separate dramatic art from mere popular entertainment, and to establish a school of English drama whose aim is to interest the public in the study and interpretation of life rather than in saying and doing funny or sensational theatrical things."

I am often misrepresented as being an enemy of popular amusement. Nothing is farther from the truth. I have the greatest sympathy with all forms of entertainment that have for their object the lightening of the burdens and the easing of the hearts of our overworked city populations. And I have been constantly in favour of removing all restrictions from those who provide entertainment for the people, whether in theatres or music-halls. But I cannot help recognising that we shall never have an English drama worthy of a great nation while the mere entertainment of the masses is the only object of our plays. The pursuit of mere amusement defeats its own end. The more you pander to the lower tastes of the public, the more

you have to pander to them, the less and less
satisfaction you give it, until at the last if it does
not turn and rend you, it despises and forgets
you.

On the whole, the outlook for the English drama
is brighter and healthier than it has been for some
generations. One can discern the gradual formation
of a sound taste and a sound body of public opinion.
Whether the progress that has certainly been made
will be continued, depends upon how far the drama
as the portrayer and interpreter of life can be still
further separated from mere funny theatrical entertainments. Again and again I say that I am not condemning these entertainments or those who patronise
them. They have their own spheres, their own duties
to the public, and their own rewards. But I do most
earnestly and passionately deprecate the counter-
opinion which is so largely held and so brazenly
proclaimed, that when the drama has satisfied the
immediate clamour of the mob to be amused in the
emptiest way, it has done all it can or ought to do.
No English drama is possible while that opinion
prevails and is acted upon.

When I commented upon the absence in your
programme of any class that could be directly
associated with the drama, I did not intend any
reproach to you. As you will see from the latter
part of my address, I do not hold that the drama has
any direct concern with the business of teaching.
But I often wish, for the sake of the dramatist, that
some scheme of dramatic education could be made
general. One of the strangest fallacies of popular
dramatic criticism is that which credits the author

with the words, and opinions, and nature, and tendencies of his characters.   This is an everlasting
source of wonder and irritation to the playwright,
who finds himself quite unable to explain to the
auditor that, like Nature herself, he must, by virtue
of his office, hold a perfect balance and allow fair-
play to all opinions, to all tendencies, to all characters,
and must fashion his Iagos and his Othellos, his
Richards and his Hamlets with equal affection and
sympathy.   Another popular fallacy of the ordinary
playgoer is that all plays dealing with questions of
immorality are immoral in themselves.   If this be
true, the Bible and Shakespeare are the most immoral books.   The morality or immorality of a play
is its most subtle, its most intrinsic quality.   It
depends not in the least upon the author's theme or
subject : the same theme may be treated in all kinds
of ways, moral or immoral.   Nor does the morality
of a play depend upon the author's intentions : we
all have the best intentions.   It depends upon the
author's heart and nature, and inevitably and irresistibly springs from them, by virtue of the law
which decrees that men never gather grapes from
thorns or figs from thistles.

But this is only another way of saying what I
have said before——that the drama does not teach or
educate by direct means or direct intention.   Yet I
hope I shall carry you all with me if I again affirm
what the title of my lecture implies, and what your
kind invitation to me to address you also implies——
that there are lasting relations between the drama
and the wider education of men ; that it is and
should be a guide and teacher ; and that it is not a

matter of indifference or unconcern to our land whether the art that portrays and interprets its national life is palsied, supine, effete, diseased, and imbecile, or whether it is living, active, healthy, clear-eyed, clear-brained, clear-souled, and clear - tongued, always conveying, indirectly, implicitly, at least this one message—

> That life is not as idle ore,
>
> But iron dug from central gloom,
> > And heated hot with burning fears,
> > And dipt in baths of hissing tears,
> And batter'd with the shocks of doom.

PREFACE TO *SAINTS AND SINNERS*

I

THE passing of the American Copyright Bill is a fact of the highest import to English playwrights and the future of the English drama,—that is, if the English drama has a future. It will, indeed, afford an accurate gauge of any individual playwright's pretensions, and of the general health and condition of the national drama. Hitherto the publication of an English play would have incurred the forfeiture of the American stage-rights, in many cases a very serious pecuniary loss. It would also have been attended with a very grave artistic risk. The best American managers—those who are capable of doing justice to the author in the production of a play—would naturally have refused to touch it unless their stage-rights were protected. It would have been presented, if at all, under the worst auspices, and with the worst and most haphazard stage management and surroundings.

Under these circumstances it is a question whether the placing of a play in the hands of the reading public would have compensated for its loss of influence in its legitimate sphere on the stage, and for the discredit brought on the author by inadequate and irresponsible production and performance.

Further, in the present uncertain relations of English literature and the modern drama, an author may be excused for having some doubts as to whether the interests of either are to be served by the publication of plays whose perusal may only serve to show how sharp is the division between them. The American Copyright Bill removes these disabilities, and makes it inexcusable to yield to these doubts. If, from this time forward, a playwright does not publish within a reasonable time after the theatrical production of his piece, it will be an open confession that his work was a thing of the theatre merely, needing its garish artificial light and surroundings, and not daring to face the calm air and cold daylight of print. And further, if a custom does not now arise in England, such as prevails in France, of publishing successful plays, and if a general reading public is not gradually drawn round the drama, then it will be a sign that our stage remains in the same state of intellectual paralysis that has afflicted it all the century. Our drama will continue to be a " Slough of Despond " in the wide, well-tilled field of English literature, an irreclaimable bog wherein, as in John Bunyan's, " twenty thousand cartloads of wholesome instructions " have been thrown without improving the way.

But it will be urged that many successful plays will not " read " at all, while in many others the passages that charm us most in the study are those that bore

us most on the stage, and the passages that do not
strike us at all in reading sometimes come out in
letters of fire at the theatre.   This brings me to
remark what it is one of the chief objects of this
preface to enforce and illustrate, namely, that there is
a certain very strong antagonism between the literary
and theatrical elements of a play.   Very often this
antagonism is more apparent than real, very often it
is the just rebellion of the theatrical ass (I am speaking quite figuratively) against carrying a load of
literary luggage that does not belong to him ; very
often it is his native friskiness refusing to carry any
literary luggage at all,—that is, to drop metaphor, it
is the mere impatience of intellectual exertion in a
theatre on the part of both entertained and enter-
tainers.   But whatever the cause of the quarrel, and
whatever the various and debatable circumstances
that may place the blame on the one side or the
other, there does exist this very palpable antagonism,
and jealousy, and desire of mastery between the two
elements, theatrical and literary, that make up a
play.   So much so that on seeing some popular
plays one is tempted to exclaim, " The worst and
deadliest enemy of the English drama is — the
English theatre."

It is not my province here to deal at length
with the relation between English literature and the
modern English drama, or rather with the want of
relation between them.   I am only concerned to
establish the general rule, that the intellectual and
art values of any drama, its permanent influence and
renown, are in exact proportion to its literary qualities.
Shakespeare and Sheridan are popular playwrights

to-day strictly on account of the enduring literary qualities of their work. They have admirable stage-craft as well, but this alone would not have rescued them from oblivion. The French drama has been operative intellectually, and has commanded the respect of the civilised world because its authors have been men of letters, and because their works have always been available and recognisable as pieces of literature. There has been a definite literary standard below which it was impossible for any French dramatist of standing to sink. In England there has been no literary standard, and no ready means of marking the literary and intellectual position of the modern drama. The most amazing master-pieces of artificiality, extravagance, and theatricality have been rapturously received by the great British multitude without ever being examined as works of literature or studies of life. Every great literary critic of the age has spoken contemptuously of the modern drama, or has more contemptuously ignored it. If any little flame of authentic literary fire has arisen, it has quickly flickered out in the inane air. Perhaps the most accurate idea of the literary status of the modern drama can be gained from the style and form of pre-sentation of those plays which for necessary business theatrical purposes it is considered advisable to print. Nothing could better express the frank contempt of the English theatre for English literature.

Perhaps some of my remarks would be more ap-plicable to the theatre of ten or twenty years ago. In quite recent days it may be gratefully acknowledged that in London at least a new spirit is kindling our audiences, and a new strong desire is openly expressed that the modern drama should take its rightful position as a national art in definite relation with literature and the other arts, with an acknowledged intellectual status and declared intellectual and artistic aims. The piercing light of science has been sprung upon us behind the scenes, and our old worn-out apparatus of theatrical effect and situation looks half ghastly, half trumpery in that cold, cruel beam. Ancient and well-established purveyors of the old regulation theatrical fare are pathetically declaiming against the fickleness of the public taste. Strange that this poor, docile, good-natured public, which has always been so comfortably conservative, should at last get a glimmering in its head that the English drama is, or should be, mainly and chiefly the art of representing English life, and not the art of sensational and spectacular illusion, nor the art of building up an ingenious Chinese puzzle of comic or thrilling situations! Strange! What will become of the British drama if this new idea should take root and grow?

To return to the examination of the opposing literary and theatrical elements in a play. The comparative intellectual and literary degradation of the modern drama for two or three generations past is due to the fact that plays have been considered and exploited chiefly from their purely theatrical side, and as a vehicle for exhibiting the powers and peculiarities of an actor or a company. Now it is quite natural and just that an actor should have the highest opinion of his art, and that he should wish to subordinate the purely literary element in a play. I do not mean that he will wish to cut any literary speech that occurs in his part, or that he will not like to win the praise that is bestowed upon a literary production. But naturally and of necessity under our present system those plays, and those parts of a play, will be exploited which give the actor an immediate chance of dazzling the public. And the play will be considered with this chief end in view, of ministering to the popularity of the actor, rather than with any idea of presenting a perfect piece of literature and of restoring play-writing to its lost dignity of a national literary art. It will of course be said that this is the dramatist's concern and not the actor's. Quite so, but it cannot be anybody's concern while the playwright is the actor's servant. The present system in England of manufacturing plays to order and to exploit some leading performer is quite sufficient to account for the literary degradation of the modern drama and for the just contempt with which it has been viewed by the intellect of the nation during the last twenty-five years. How is it possible that a writer can put his best work into what does not spring spontaneously from his heart and convictions? And a comparison of the stages of England and France for the past generation gives an exact answer to the questions "What is the result of putting the theatrical elements of a play in the first place?" and "What is the result of putting the literary elements in the first place?" While it is highly significant that the recent adoption by a leading French playwright of the English practice of writing plays to order for a star performer has marked a notable decline in the quality of his work. And the effect on the audiences is also correspondent and answerable. For the public is pliable and teachable within very considerable limits, and by a natural law it grows tolerant of and responsive to the conditions imposed upon it. And further, it is impossible for an actor who sees nightly audiences deeply impressed and stirred by theatrical devices not to suppose that these are the very essence of the dramatic art. Finally, so many and so binding and so perplexing are the necessary conventions and limitations of play-writing, that the author, watching his public closely and for dear life's sake being obliged to keep in touch with it, becomes also confused, and is often led astray to mistake some stale trick of the stage for a fundamental law of its being.

Now the custom of publishing our plays at least offers a chance of escape from some of these difficulties and absurdities, if it does not open up a larger and higher sphere for the dramatist. In dealing with this question on a former occasion I omitted to distinguish between the two kinds of success that a play should strive to win. There is the immediate theatrical success, which is largely due to acting, stage arrangement and management; and there is the more permanent and worthy renown, which is literary and intellectual rather than theatrical. Thus, while in the case of *The School for Scandal* this higher renown belongs to Sheridan, the theatrical success of any revival depends upon the cast and stage management and other details entirely belonging to the theatre. Now my contention is that our present system tends to deny this higher and permanent renown to the dramatist, tends to keep his eyes off his great task and his great reward, tends to docket him as a journeyman-assistant in the cheaper and temporary theatrical success. When one glances at our great Victorian literature, at its conspicuous achievements in poetry, in fiction, in history, in biography, in science, in criticism, it is impossible to doubt that it might have been equally triumphant in the domain of the English drama had some stream of its great flood been by chance diverted across that arid common. Perhaps if one searches a little into causes, the intellectual poverty of the drama of this century may be chiefly ascribed to the Puritan dread of the theatre, and to those other reasons which have kept the English from being a playgoing nation as a whole, and have also kept any considerable portion of cultivated playgoers from forming a body of sound dramatic opinion amongst themselves.

But the prejudices that have kept the English from being a playgoing nation are rapidly breaking up, and more encouraging still, a body of carefully discussed and examined dramatic opinion is being gradually formed amongst the more advanced section of playgoers. The intellectual ferment of the age has reached the theatre, and has begun to leaven it. I have tried to indicate what appears to me one of the great hindrances to our advance to a higher level. While audiences are trained to regard the theatrical elements of a play as the essence of the matter, plays will succeed or fail mainly on their theatrical merits, and at best we shall remain in our present position. No very high literary or intellectual average will be maintained, because the prizes are to be looked for in another direction and for other qualities.

Nothing that I have said must be held to imply contempt of theatrical success, or disrespect of those whose devotion to their own art naturally inclines them to rank it in the highest place. And I am very glad to acknowledge here my immense debt to those who have been associated with me in the representation of my plays. It would be impossible for me to appraise my indebtedness to them too highly, or to give them too much credit for their share in the measure of theatrical success that I have obtained.

But I hope I shall not be misjudged or censured if I continue to insist upon the comparative worthlessness of all mere theatrical success. The passing of the American Copyright Bill will prove the mettle of English playwrights. It will show whether we are capable of seizing and holding our great legacy as the inheritors of our Elizabethan forefathers, or whether we are only fit to be the lackeys and underlings of French *farceurs*, supine, effete, disabled, and foolishly dallying with the great issues of human life as with a child's box of wooden toy men.

The English drama has a great chance to-day. There is but one way of advancing or even of holding our own, and that is by making the theatre a national art with a definite literary and intellectual basis, disdainful of all theatrical effect that will not submit to take an auxiliary place. There are a dozen, a hundred different ways of tumbling back into folly and insincerity and theatricality.

II

I leave the general question of the advisability and importance to the English stage of establishing a custom of printing successful plays, and come to the smaller matter of the individual play here given to the public in its printed form for the first time.

After I had obtained a great financial success in melodrama, and was temporarily in a position to write a play to please myself rather than the exigencies of a theatrical manager, I gave many months to the writing of *Saints and Sinners*. I was not then very well acquainted with all the many necessities of theatrical production, and the niceties and peculiarities of audiences at particular theatres, and I confidently reckoned upon as great a success in my new venture as I had just obtained in what I knew to be the cheaper and coarser art of melodrama. But at the outset the piece was very dubiously received, and the general impression obtained in theatrical circles that I had only proved my incompetence to write plays away from the theatrical leading-strings which had hitherto guided me. And before I knew that the piece had settled into an assured success, I had weakly sold myself to what the *Saturday Review* justly calls "the dull devil of spectacular melodrama." And I remained a bond-slave for many years.

I am conscious of very many defects in the play. I wish I could ascribe them to the bad school in which any English playwright who began to learn his art in 1870 was necessarily nurtured. And I wish I had the time and will to remedy them. But having once left a play I find it very difficult to re-enter into its spirit, and it is almost impossible for me to give additional vitality to characters that I have once parted company with. And with more important tasks pressing me, I do not think it would be profitable for me to do more than I have done during the last few days, namely, remove a few extravagances and touch up the dialogue where I could do so easily, and without disturbing the general tenor and necessary succession of the scenes. But, though I may not lay the flattering unction to my soul that the artificial conditions of the English drama at the time of my learning stagecraft were responsible for all the failings of *Saints and Sinners*, I think I may honestly plead them as an extenuation of some of its worst defects.

Nothing could give a better idea of the stand-point of the average British playgoer, of his utter incapacity to view a play as a study and representation of life, or to look upon it as anything but a comic entertainment designed to make him laugh by any possible means, than the first criticism I over-heard upon *Saints and Sinners*. The play was produced for the purpose of getting the players easy in their parts before facing a London audience, at the Theatre-Royal, Margate, in the presence of a holiday audience. A very uproarious farce had previously been running at the London theatre where *Saints and Sinners* was announced for pro-duction on the following Thursday. The Margate audience assembled in the expectation of a repeti-tion of the broad nonsense which such an association promised. They showed a certain amount of interest, but their chief feeling was one of puzzled and somewhat shocked uneasiness and discomfort. I went into a hotel to call for a friend, and heard a group at the bar discussing the play. One sentence fell upon my ear, uttered in a puzzled, distressed, dissatisfied tone, "A lot of folks going into a little chapel!" That an English playwright should select for representation on the English stage a scene in which a great body of his countrymen constantly figure one day in seven, and which is of the utmost significance in the general sum of English life, seemed to this honest Margate playgoer so outrageous a violation of all the known canons of play-writing that I have never to this day been able to rid myself of the sense of having done him a deep personal injury. While the same failure to understand the elementary axiom of dramatic composition was exemplified by an otherwise intelligent free-thinker, who was observed to show great resentment and contempt whenever the minister gave utterance to any sentence implying a religious belief.

Half the audience thought I was canting, and the other half thought I was blaspheming. The play ran almost two hundred nights at the Vaudeville Theatre, much of its success being undoubtedly due to the discussion it raised as to the playwright's right to portray contemporary religious life. The article I wrote in defence of my position in the *Nineteenth Century Review* is here reproduced.[1] It was never answered, and not one of its conten-

[1] See *ante*, p. 26.

tions was combated. The liberty there demanded for the dramatist has been since most freely accorded on all sides, and the boundaries there marked out indicate the present recognised domain of the stage. Perhaps other stage reforms which are resisted to-day will be also accepted as matters of course when as many years shall have passed from the statement of their claims upon the goodwill of the public.

Though the first general reception of the play was chilly and carping, I received very warm recognition of its aims from one or two quarters. Especially the sketches of the smaller characters and the deacons were much praised, and also in certain quarters much blamed. The character of Hoggard was censured as impossibly vile. But allowing for the necessary sharpness and swiftness of stage portraiture, and the impossibility of exhausting or even suggesting all the minute motives and aspects of character in a theatre, I think Hoggard may be claimed as a not unfair representative of a very widely-spread class in narrow English religious communities. There is of course a very strong connection between the general character and conduct of a nation and its creed, but every day gives us instances of a ludicrous want of harmony, or apparently of even the most distant relation of any sort between a man's religious professions and his actions. And this at-first-sight astounding discordancy of belief and practice is much more frequent in the narrower and smaller and less intellectual sects, and is partly the correlative of a low degree of intelligence. Any one who has carefully studied the curious and grotesque inconsistencies of religious profession and conduct in England will, I think, readily concede that a bitter and stubborn and blind disregard of the primary duties to one's neighbour is not at all an uncommon characteristic of religious professors in the class from which Hoggard is taken. At the same time I think it would have been better to have shown in some way that this is not necessarily the accompaniment of the deacon's office. A well-known Nonconformist minister, while cordially recognising the faithfulness of the types of deacon in Hoggard and Prabble, and declaring that he knew them personally, suggested that I should also have made George Kingsmill a deacon, and thus removed all suspicion of bias. I found that scarcely possible, and I thought that in the person of Jacob Fletcher I had rendered a full acknowledgment of the sterling qualities to be found in English Dissenting life.

Upon the occasion of its first performance the piece was played, apart from a few quite unimportant alterations, as it is here published. But the death-scene proving too sad for the genial associations of the theatre where it was to be performed, I changed the last scene into a happy union between Letty and George.

In restoring the original ending, I may mention that I am acting not only in harmony with my own feelings, but also with the judgment of Mr. Matthew Arnold. In appending a letter he wrote me after seeing the piece, I am pleased to acknowledge his constant courtesy and encouragement, and to remember that I was instrumental in bringing him to

the modern theatre after a great many years of
absence. His letter runs as follows :—

"I went to see *Saints and Sinners*, and my interest
was kept up throughout as I expected. You have
remarkably the art—so valuable in drama—of exciting interest and sustaining it. The piece is full of
good and telling things, and one cannot watch the
audience without seeing that by strokes of this kind
faith in the middle-class fetich is weakened, however
slowly, as it could be in no other way.

"I must add that I dislike seduction-dramas (even
in *Faust* the feeling tells with me), and that the
marriage of the heroine with her farmer does not
please me as a *dénouement*.

"Your representative middle-class man (Hoggard)
was well drawn and excellently acted."

So wrote to me the sweet singer who lies silent
to-day by the banks of his beloved Thames. No, not
silent ! For another saying of his comes aptly to my
memory and has a bearing upon the present attempt
to bring together English literature and the English
stage—"The theatre is irresistible ! Organise the
theatre !"

If I have earned his commendation and "weakened
the faith in the middle-class fetich," much battered
in other quarters of recent years, I have fulfilled my
main design in presenting this play. For I do not
claim any merit for *Saints and Sinners* apart from
that of representing with some degree of faithfulness, and with due regard to the requirements of
the modern stage, some very widely-spread types of
modern middle-class Englishmen. If it be objected
that they are rather commonplace and uninteresting,

I can only urge in self-defence that it is impossible to suppose that the original creation of four-fifths of the present inhabitants of the British Isles can have been an exploit of a highly imaginative order, or one whose execution brought unmingled pride and self-congratulation to the Creator, while it is also impossible to contemplate the Divine Image in the person of the average British tradesman without an uneasy suspicion that the mould is getting a little out of shape.

LONDON, 14*th April* 1891.

DEDICATORY PREFACE TO
THE CASE OF REBELLIOUS SUSAN

An Original Comedy produced at the Criterion Theatre
on 3rd October 1894

To Mrs. GRUNDY

DEAR AND HONOURED MADAM

In dedicating this little comedy to you I
have no other object in view than that of bribing and
blinding your well-known susceptibilities, and of en-
deavouring to win over and conciliate that large body
of English playgoers who take their opinions and
morals ready-made from you, the august and austere
effigy of our national taste and respectability.

The truth is, my dear lady, I am a little fearful
that, without some such shelter as your powerful
protection, many excellent persons may be in doubt
as to the exact moral which this comedy sets forth,
or indeed may go farther and doubt whether there
is a moral in it at all, or, dreadest and cruellest
alternative, may actually proclaim that it is *im*moral.
The mere possibility of this latter alternative is so

painful to me, that I am obliged to recall a conversation which I recently overheard in a railway-carriage.

"Ah, who wrote that play?" I heard one passenger inquire of another.

"That man Henry Arthur Jones," replied his neighbour.

"I hate that fellow," said the other. "He's always educating the people."

Now though I cannot honestly credit myself with any such unselfish motive in writing plays as my fellow-passenger ascribed to me, I could not help feeling a glow of virtuous pride when I found that my natural ingrained tendencies were so salutary and so patriotic. And if I have in any way contributed to the State Education Grant, or even abated the School Board rate in any single parish, I hope I shall not be deprived of the glory that attaches to such public benefactions merely because they have been quite involuntary and unsuspected on my part.

Now, my dear Mrs. Grundy, I will not go so far as to say that I know with any degree of certainty what the moral of this comedy is. I prefer to leave that for you and the public to discover. And I am very hopeful in this respect when I remember that one of our keenest and most analytical critics, in interpreting for us a recent masterpiece of the lob-worm-symbolic school, declared that though he could not be quite sure what the play did mean, yet he was quite sure that it meant a heap of unutterable things. And so, my dear ma'am, I will not pin myself down to any one definite, precise, hard-and-fast, cut-and-dried moral in this comedy. Why should I ? Why should I needlessly limit the possible scope of its beneficent operation, or curb my boundless desire that all sorts of unexpected collateral good may haphazardly visit those who witness its representation ?

I know of no task wherein the critical playgoer may be more profitably employed than in finding a profound significance in passages where the author himself would never have detected it, and in dragging to light profound moral truths from hiding-places where the author himself would never have imagined them to be lurking. Therefore, my dear Mrs. Grundy, if you will be pleased to wink at any little outside indiscretion, and if the public will set its wits to work, I have no doubt a very serviceable moral is to be extracted from this comedy.

Look at life itself, my dear lady. The moral of it is not very obvious at first sight, but there must be a tremendous moral hidden somewhere in it. Nay, there must be hundreds of morals in it, and I am not without a suspicion that in claiming only one moral for this comedy I have done myself a very grave injustice. For all I know it may be teeming with morals.

But perhaps you will say that my comedy is quite unlike life. I am aware that I have no warrant in the actual facts of the world around me for placing on the English stage an instance of English conjugal infidelity. There is, I believe, madam, a great deal of this kind of immorality in France, but you will rejoice to hear that a very careful and searching inquiry has not resulted in establishing any well-authenticated case in English life. And even had the inquiry revealed a quite opposite state of things, I am sure you will agree with me that it would be much better to make up our minds once for all that the facts are wrong and stick to that, rather than allow the possibility of anything hurtful to our continued self-esteem and self-righteousness. I am too sensible, madam, of the honour of belonging to the same nation as your own revered self to do anything to impair its holy self-respect and worship of its own conviction that it is the most moral, most religious, most heaven-favoured nation under the sun.

Happily, as I say, there is not the slightest necessity for disturbing our cherished national belief that immorality is confined to the Continent, and especially to France. Let us therefore again thank Heaven that we are not as other nations are, and let us avoid seeing or hearing anything that might disturb our belief in our own moral superiority.

So, my dear madam, I have to own frankly that I have not the slightest justification in fact for laying the scene of my comedy in England, and I am again justly open to the charge, so often made against me, of being quite false to life as my countrymen see it.

And now, my dear lady, having endeavoured to win your approbation by every means in my power, let me again say that my only anxiety is that you should not too hastily condemn the piece because its morality is intrinsic and not extrinsic. For I do stoutly affirm, adorable arbitress of British morals, that there is a profound moral somewhere in this piece. Only, if I dare hint so much to you, dear

lady, it is well at times not to be too ferociously
moral.   There is a time to be ferociously moral, and
a time to refrain.   The present, my dear Mrs.
Grundy, is an eminently suitable time to refrain.
Let us not be always worrying books and plays for
their morals.   Let us not worry even life itself for
too plain or too severe a moral.   Let us look with
a wise, sane, wide-open eye upon all these things,
and if a moral starts up naturally from them, let us
cheerfully accept it, however shocking it may be ;
if not, let us not distress ourselves.

If, my dear ma'am, you cannot see any moral in
this little comedy, take it for granted there is one,
and—go and see the play again.   Go and see it,
my dear Mrs. Grundy, until you do find a moral
in it.   And remember that it is not only trifles
like this that are naturally repugnant to you.
Remember how hateful to you are all the great
eternal things in literature and art.   So much so,
that if our grand English Bible itself were to be
now first presented to the British public, you would
certainly start a prosecution against it for its in-
decency and its terrible polygamistic tendencies.

Refrain, my dear lady, refrain ! refrain !   And
if you must have a moral in my comedy, suppose it
to be this—" That as women cannot retaliate openly,
they *may* retaliate secretly—and *lie !* "

And a very shocking moral it is, now we have got
it.   But oh, my dear Mrs. Grundy, Nature's morality
is not your morality, nor mine.   Nature has ten
thousand various morals, all of them as shocking as
truth itself.   The very least of them would fright
our isle from its propriety if it were once guessed at.

Refrain, my dear madam, refrain! And—
excuse me—isn't that foot of yours rather too near
that tender growing flower—I mean the English
drama? And your foot is so heavy! Don't stamp
out the little growing burst of life. Refrain, my
dear lady, refrain! Adieu!

> Yours, with the deepest reverence for all
> things worthy of reverence,

HENRY ARTHUR JONES.

DIEPPE, 28*th August* 1894.

P.S.—My comedy isn't a comedy at all. It's a
tragedy dressed up as a comedy. But it is so far
like life—you can shut your eyes, tuck your tongue
in your cheek, and declare it is a comedy—or even
a farce.

XVIII

FRAGMENTS AND EXTRACTS

PERHAPS you think there isn't much need for me to insist that when you go to a play it should gladden you and make you happy. You'll take good care you don't go to a theatre to be made miserable and dull! I have no doubt you will. Authors and managers have found out that to be unsuccessful a play can only have one fault—it must be dull. So we are quite agreed upon this first point. I want you to be happy at the theatre, and you'll take good care you don't go unless you are. And if you are gladdened and delighted you'll go often and naturally enough, and to all my coaxing to get you there, you'll reply to me as Dan'l Peggotty did to Mrs. Gummidge when she said she was sorry she was driving him to the public-house, " Lor' bless you, I don't want no driving!" We are both determined, then, that you shall enjoy yourself at the theatre, and you shan't go unless you do. So the thing is settled.

No! I'm going to have a little talk with you about the sort of things that gladden you at the theatre. What jokes do you laugh at? What persons amuse you? What actions and words do you think funny? I was at a pantomime some time ago with a party of children, and a man came on the stage dressed as a woman, with a nose painted red, and wearing dirty petticoats which he took a delight in kicking about so as to show his stockings, while he continually gave vent to a senseless cockney catchword. A little girl who was with me, and who has a very keen sense of humour, looked at me and said, "Why has he made his nose red?" and when he tumbled about the stage showing the dirty stockings and petticoats, she asked blankly, "Why does he do that?"

The child saw nothing funny in a man painting his nose red and performing foolish and rather indecent antics. Do you? Are these the things that gladden your heart at a theatre? Do you think it witty, clever, brilliant, for a man to sprawl about the stage showing a dirty pair of stockings, imitating a gin-sodden voice, and labelling his nose "drunkard." Don't you think it rather dull and depressing? And yet the majority of the audience seemed to consider it funny. I have no doubt that some—I trust a large part—of the mirth of the audience was due to mere carelessness, ignorance, and the high spirits attendant upon a holiday. People have surely never asked themselves why they laugh at such things; a moment's reflection would surely be fatal to merriment derived from such a source. So far as their enjoyment was deliberate and self-conscious, so far it was besotted and diseased.

I daresay some of you will remember a very powerful and truthful scene in Robertson's play of *Caste;* I mean the scene in which the drunken old

Eccles raves and drivels over the cradle of his baby
grandson, and arraigns society and government
because the infant possesses a coral necklace, while
he, the poor old grandfather, has not the wherewithal
to buy himself a quartern of "cool refreshing gin."
Cool refreshing gin! Imagine what that man's
palate was like! Think of the state of his tongue,
his stomach, his liver! Ah, but you can get your
intellectual palate into as bad a condition as old
Eccles's drinking apparatus, till it kicks at all
wholesome nourishment and thirsts for vitriol to
refresh it! There is a strange law by which our
bodies grow tolerant of poison when taken in
gradually increasing doses, so that the few drops
of certain drugs which would be enough to kill a
healthy man may be taken scores of times over
without immediate harm by the poor victim who
has accustomed his system to them. One of our
greatest literary geniuses at the beginning of this
century used to take his tumbler of laudanum
negus at a sitting. And when once such a habit
has fastened upon a man, his system craves for the
wonted solace until it may positively be an immediate injury to his health to refuse him his daily
dose of poison. So that lately, I have read, a
physician, in counselling us how to ensure long life,
said : "Beware of giving up old habits—even bad
ones." Well, I want to impress this fact upon you,
that by constantly indulging your leisure with
foolish and imbecile forms of humour you may rob
yourself of the power of enjoying or even understanding what healthy wit and humour are. I
cannot help saying that many of the forms of public

amusement which delight the inhabitants of our large cities seem to me nothing but the symptoms and expressions of social suffocation, stupefaction, and disease.

* * * * *

I suppose while this nation holds together there will always be one or two popular actors playing or trying to play Shakespeare. And so far as fashion or their own genius is powerful there will always be crowds round them. That is a permanent fact in English stage history. It does not mean that the great theatre-going public has any deep love for, or comprehension of, Shakespeare, that it would naturally choose either his stage-craft, his language, or his exposition of human life, if left to its own judgment. The continual popularity of Shakespeare on the English stage, where it is not a matter of scenic effect, means simply that the judgments of great literary minds, the criticisms of those half a dozen men who do know and who do care, gradually penetrate the indifference and ignorance of the millions who don't know and don't care ; the few who have the means and power of judgment in literary and artistic matters do in the long-run get an authority over the many who have no means and no power of judging, and whose natural tastes are very often the worst possible guides for them. So that thousands now nightly go to see Shakespeare not because their natural tastes lead them to him, but because there is an accumulated weight of authority in his name ; they vaguely feel that it is the right thing to do.

* * * * *

I want to dwell for a moment on the kind of enjoyment and delight that can be obtained from the graver and more serious forms of dramatic art. The Greeks, with all their love of joyous sensuous life, took the greatest delight in tragedy. Rightly understood, tragedy should not make you dull or unhappy. Especially in our Shakespearean and Elizabethan drama, the majestic blank-verse line at once informs you that you are not to take it for real life—you are not to be affected by these griefs as if they were real. You are first of all to be pleased by the splendour and power of the language, by the force and vividness of its images, by the wisdom and truth of its teaching, by the felicitous word-choosing, by the cadence, by the style. There is no great tragedy without great treatment ; the difference between *Macbeth* and the police report of a murder lies merely in the treatment. Then next, in certain modern tragedies where great poetic treatment is impossible, or unattainable, your feeling in seeing them is still to be one of pleasure so far as the author affords you opportunities of witnessing the great passions in full play, so far as he shows you the dignity, the grandeur, the power of endurance and self-sacrifice of which human nature is capable, so far as he shows you beautiful natures proved and sweetened and strengthened by suffering, and triumphant over all the snares of fortune and evil. And even the final overthrow of virtue, the deaths of Hamlet and Cordelia, the success of Iago's devilish scheme, are not to cast you down or sadden you ; because these are related and set forth in such a way as to show the transcendent fearlessness of virtue, her entire absence of self-seeking, her carelessness of reward, her contempt of death.

You know the greatest tragedy of antiquity is the *Prometheus* of Æschylus, where the god is chained to a rock in the Caucasus because he has dared to befriend the race of men against the anger of Jupiter. Now we have a very vivid picture of his sufferings which you can read in our own Shelley—his heart eaten out by vultures, his flesh and bones rotting and cankered with the rust of his chains, sleep forbidden him, exposed to all the extremes of heat and cold, afflicted with all the tortures his omnipotent enemy can devise; and yet we take the keenest delight in reading of his sufferings, because they are not so horrible as his patience and strength and defiance of the tyrant are beautiful; the very cruelty and malignancy of his torments become the measure of our admiration and the levers of our praise. Our shudder of revolt at his sufferings is not so great as our wonder at his dauntless endurance; the physical horror is nothing compared with the spiritual beauty.

*   *   *   *   *

I daresay you have often looked up at the blue summer sky and tried to pierce it with your eyesight. You never got very far, did you? But the farther you seemed to see, the deeper and deeper grew the folds of that veil. One of the latest speculations about the blue of the firmament is that in reality it is but the absence of light; the all-surrounding darkness takes that colour in every part of the heaven except the small place where the sun is. Almost the greatest quality a work of art can have is mystery. I do not mean that cheap manufactured mystery which tricks you into thinking it profound because it is merely unintelligible. Never think anything clever or fine simply because you cannot understand it. Great artists nearly always try to be plain ; they study simplicity and intelligibility. I mean that other mystery which comes from depth, not from obscurity of meaning : the mystery of Faust, of Hamlet, for instance, which men were trying to fathom a hundred years ago, and are trying to fathom to-day, and will be trying to fathom in a hundred years' time.—*From a lecture delivered to working men in Manchester, Sunday afternoon, 24th February* 1889.

* * * * *

What are the best interests of the drama ? If we could all sink our own personal vanities, what should we all agree to be the best things we could desire for it at the present moment? On what side, in what qualities is it weak and deficient?

To bring the modern drama into relation with our literature, to make it strike its roots into every corner and cranny of our national life, to make it representative of our age, illustrative of our national tendencies and currents of thought,—these seem to be the first things we ought all to bend our shoulders to, because they are of the highest importance in themselves, and because in these respects our drama is lamentably weak and deficient.—*From an article in the " Fortnightly Review," July* 1890.

* * * * *

The foulest images of evil play in happiest concord in and round our most beauteous churches.

Z

Beasts and Spirits, Brutes and Gods are we. One-eyed, palsied, and for ever barren as the east wind are all religion, philosophy, literature, and art that do not make their peace with both these never-dying enemies within us, that do not equally accept and love them both. Let us make haste to adore the God and propitiate the Brute within us, else we are surely damned like an ill-roasted egg, all on one side.

*　　　*　　　*　　　*　　　*

No amount of explanation suffices to make even critical playgoers understand that in modern prose drama the sovereign merit of dialogue is not that it shall be witty, brilliant, terse, strong, poetic, or even grammatical. The first, last, and only necessary quality of good dialogue is that it shall be exactly illustrative of the character in the exact position in which he is placed.

*　　　*　　　*　　　*　　　*

It is not judicious to interpret Providential decrees and dealings too definitely and explicitly. But I am sure I have fathomed the Divine purpose in the creation of Venice and her centuries of splendour, and beauty, and magnificence. It was to provide Mr. Kiralfy with the means of amusing Londoners, and paying a huge percentage to his shareholders at the end of the nineteenth century. And the absence of all splendour, beauty, and magnificence in the daily lives of the London populace was clearly designed by Providence for the same beneficent end. — VENICE, 21*st October* 1894.

*　　　*　　　*　　　*　　　*

"The end of tragedy," says Aristotle in his often-quoted definition, "is to purge the mind by moving in us pity and terror." "That is," according to Milton, "to temper and reduce these and such like passions to just measure and a kind of *delight*." I went to see a modern realistic tragedy. "No," said I at the end of it, as I tried to rally my stunned senses, and dragged myself home to continue the nightmare in my sleep. "No! You are wrong, Aristotle. The end of tragedy is to knock us down with a dirty bludgeon."

    *   *   *   *   *

So Exeter Hall and Leicester Square are at war, and you ask me which side I take? Neither. For many years I have tasted the sweetest philosophical delight in the contemplation of these two converse British institutions. No thought brings home to me a more vivid reminder of my blessings and privileges than the constantly recurring one that I belong to a nation whose vital and active religion is symbolised in the one, and whose vital and active amusements are symbolised in the other. And were it not profane, one might dare to imagine how dear a morsel of satisfaction in His handiwork must be afforded to the Spirit of the Universe when a sweeping eye-glance from above the pinnacles of Charing Cross Station brings in His review the portico of Exeter Hall and the façades of Leicester Square.

Never have the splendid humours of our national morality imbroglio made so irresistible an appeal to me as on this morning, when from fog-bitten, cant-bitten London its murmurs reach me here amidst these gaudy palaces and shining waters. Come to Venice, my dear W——, if you would get a just perspective of the strange pranks of our countrymen.

You ask me if I have no pity for all that human wreckage daily and nightly surging, and stewing, and putrefying in our West End. Oh, the deepest pity, believe me. But join me, my dear fellow, in as deep a pity for these other wasted lives, for these poor self-defeated castaways of Puritanism, jaundiced with superstition, green-sick with unholy self-denial, cancered with self-righteousness—is not this human wreckage too? Is not Exeter Hall as far astray from sane humanity as Leicester Square? If Leicester Square blasphemes one side of our nature, does not Exeter Hall starve the other?

Why should you and I take sides? No, let Exeter Hall and Leicester Square hurl their war-cries at each other. At this distance they fall upon the ear only as mellowed strophe and antistrophe in the great human tragi-comedy. Shriek, Exeter Hall! Rouge and leer, Leicester Square! Rave, Exeter Hall! Reel and hiccup, Leicester Square! Pray, Exeter Hall! Dance, Leicester Square! Preach, Exeter Hall! Practise, Leicester Square!

Strophe and antistrophe! Will ye never learn wisdom? Again! Again! Ebb and flow, systole and diastole, ye twain are in perfect unison, though ye know it not. — *From a letter to London dated Venice, 22nd October* 1894.

*   *   *   *   *

A strong dirty man has written plays, and now every feeble dirty person thinks himself a dramatist.

Dear me, what a lot of feeble dirty persons there are in the world !

    *   *   *   *   *

For the elect, for the wise, for the sane, for the strong there is but one rule of conduct—that supreme commandment, blithe and life-giving, laid down by Rabelais and prophetically backed by St. Paul.

> " Do what thou wilt," says Rabelais.
> " All things are lawful," says St. Paul.

The wisdom of that is for the wise, the strength of it for the strong. But poor timorous humanity cripples itself with a thousand superfluous precepts, breaks its shins against the Decalogue, rubs its shoulders raw under the yokes of priesthood, fetters itself in the stocks of prohibition, lines its daily paths with the barbed wire of self-denial, sticks up " Thou shalt not " over the gates of every pleasant vineyard, warns itself off this pleasure, whips itself off that, and yet . . . can never go straight.

> " Do what thou wilt," says Rabelais.
> " All things are lawful," says St. Paul.

This is the broad, easy way that leads to life. Few there be that find it.

    *   *   *   *   *

I had taken the newly - opened railway one Sunday in spring along the valley of the Var through the pass of La Mescla to the ancient and hidden towns of Touët de Beuil and Puget Théniers. A party of Nice townsfolk had also taken the Sunday excursion to these unexplored regions. I stood dwarfed and oppressed with admiration beneath a mountain that rose, brown and sullen and sublime, five thousand feet above me and a hundred thousand years my senior. A little Nice tradesman, a creature of the utmost insignificance, whom Nature and a cheap French tailor had bantered with the silly jests of a ridiculous figure and ridiculous garments to cover it, came and stood beside me and looked up at the mountain.

"*Pas grande chose*," said the little Nice tradesman.

I agreed with him.

I had been watching the play of *Hamlet* at a provincial theatre, and badly though it had been played, and slovenly though the mounting had been, I had yet most comfortably deluded myself with an impression of grandeur and mystery in the central character. At the end I went round to shake hands with the leading performer, a provincial tragedian of the old school.

"After all," said the provincial tragedian, "Hamlet's philosophy is precious shallow, you know. He says nothing above the level of any schoolboy."

I agreed with him.

*　　　*　　　*　　　*　　　*

The English drama will ultimately be priced at whatever value its votaries and professors like to set upon it. But human life is subject to a like valuation. Human life—your own life—is at your own valuation, every moment a jewel of inestimable price, or mere dust on the whirlwind, just as you please. And human love is also at a like valuation—something that can be bought for a song at any street corner, or something that inspires and hallows Dante, touches his lips with fire, and sets a crown of deathless praise upon his head. It's at your own valuation. It's worth just whatever you think it is.